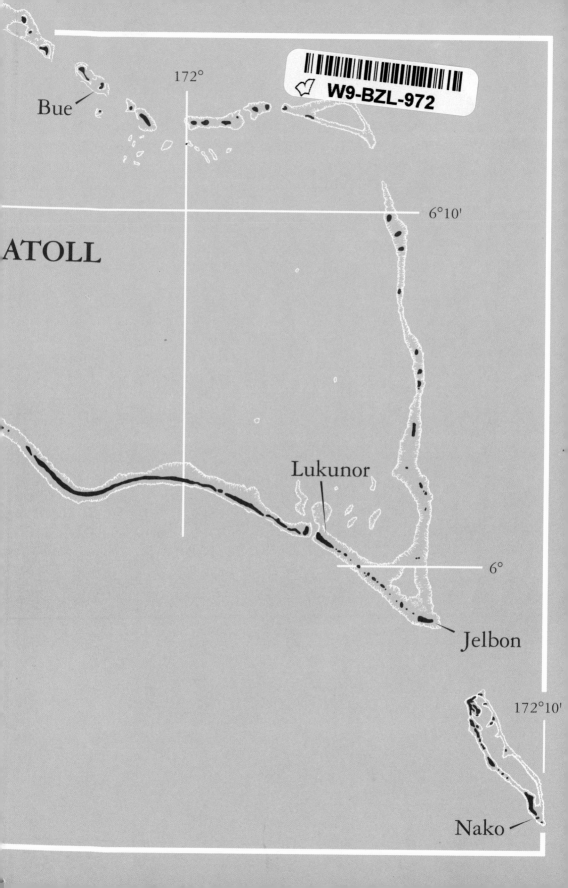

ATOLL

Bue

172°

6°10'

Lukunor

Jelbon

6°

172°10'

Nako

MUTINY ON THE GLOBE

ALSO BY THOMAS FAREL HEFFERNAN

Stove by a Whale: Owen Chase and the Essex

Wood Quay: The Clash over Dublin's Viking Past

MUTINY ON THE *GLOBE*

THE FATAL VOYAGE OF SAMUEL COMSTOCK

THOMAS FAREL HEFFERNAN

W. W. NORTON & COMPANY
NEW YORK LONDON

George Comstock's "Narrative of the Mutiny, Capture, and Transactions on Board of the Ship Globe of Nantucket after Sailing from Edgartown" and Henry Glover's "The Young Mutineer" are printed courtesy of the Nantucket Historical Association.

John Lumbert's letter is printed courtesy of the Martha's Vineyard Historical Society.

Excerpts from the journals of Elisha Loomis and Levi Chamberlain are quoted courtesy of the Hawaiian Mission Children's Society Library.

Isaac Hull's letter to Cyrus Hussey is printed courtesy of the New York Historical Society.

The manifest of the *Globe* is printed courtesy of Renny Stackpole.

For information about permission to reproduce selections from this book, write to Permissions, W. W. Norton & Company, Inc., 500 Fifth Avenue, New York, NY 10110

The text of this book is composed in Adobe Garamond
with the display set in Bodoni
Manufacturing by the Haddon Craftsmen, Inc.
Book design by Chris Welch
Composition by Julia Druskin
Production manager: Amanda Morrison

ISBN 0-393-04163-8

W. W. Norton & Company, Inc.
500 Fifth Avenue, New York, N.Y. 10110
www.wwnorton.com

W. W. Norton & Company Ltd.
Castle House, 75/76 Wells Street, London W1T 3QT

1 2 3 4 5 6 7 8 9 0

For Frank and Win Gallagher

CONTENTS

LIST OF ILLUSTRATIONS

ACKNOWLEDGMENTS

My gratitude for the help and the friendship of "Bata Rich" McAuliff, S.J.; Chugi, Beverly, Ben, and Emi Chutaro; Alfred Capelle, Republic of the Marshall Islands ambassador to the United Nations; and Fran Hezel, S.J., head of the Micronesian Seminar, is immense. Knowing them is my main unanticipated reward for undertaking the writing of the book. Other *ri-Majel* who put me in their debt are Dadashi Lometo, senator from Mili Atoll; Ramsey Reimers; Jessica Reimers; Peter Fuchs; Alson Kelen, authority on Marshallese outrigger canoes; Erwin Bollong, *iroojlaplap* of Mili Atoll; and Kuniga Lometo Bollong, for her hospitality on Mili.

In Hawaii I enjoyed the help of Robert Kiste, Byron Bender, Jack Tobin, and Leonard Mason and of some of the University of Hawaii's classically generous librarians: Karen Peacock, Nancy Morris, Lynette Furuhashi, and Ross Togashi. I am particularly grateful to Marilyn Reppun of that researcher's gem, the Hawaiian Mission Children's Society Library. And my thanks go to Charlene Avallone and Chip Hughes and to the staffs of the State Archives of Hawaii and the Bishop Museum.

For help on Nantucket I am especially grateful to Elizabeth Oldham and Betsy Lowenstein and to Nathaniel Philbrick, who gave me, at the Egan Institute, a first opportunity to discuss the *Globe* publicly and has been supportive in many ways. My thanks go to

Frank Milligan, Niles Parker, and Ralph Marie Henke, all of the Nantucket Historical Association, and to Dwight and Mimi Beman, Helen Winslow Chase, and Robert Leach. At the Martha's Vineyard Historical Society I thank Matthew Stackpole, Jill Bouck, Catherine Mayhew, and Peter Van Tassel, and in Maine, Renny Stackpole, of the Penobscot Marine Museum.

The authoritative advice of Milton Viederman, M.D., Douglas Price, M.D., Scott Norton, M.D., and Marjorie Scandizzo, M.D., was of great value to the treatment of medical and psychological questions. The close and solid study of Samuel Comstock's character that Dr. Viederman shared with me defined perceptively the limits of what is psychologically knowable about the mutineer.

At the National Archives, Washington and Waltham, I thank Jack Saunders, Rebecca Livingston, John Vandereedt, and Stanley Tozeski.

Many others to whom I am greatly indebted are, in alphabetical order: Janet Baldwin, Explorers' Club; Lester Baltimore; Robert R. Craven; Lee Descoteaux; Mary K. Bercaw Edwards; James H. Ellis; Christopher Ferguson; Tina Furtado, New Bedford Free Public Library; Rebecca Garnett; Jill Gidmark; Kate Giordano, Portsmouth, N.H., Public Library; Linda Guerreiro; Martin Haas; Warwick Hirst, Curator of Manuscripts, State Library of New South Wales; Alice Hudson, New York Public Library Map Division; Dean King; Kate Lennon, USS *Constitution* Museum; Robert Madison; Linda Maloney; Neil Miller; Gale Munro, Naval Historical Center; Trudi Neubauer and the staff of Adelphi University Library's Inter-library Loan Division; Patricia O'Donnell, Swarthmore Friends Historical Library; Jean Powers, Massachusetts Historical Society; Laura Reitano; Gloria Roberson; Robert Scheina, Industrial College of the Armed Forces; Sandy Shryock, Maine Historical Society; Brian Sieling, Smithsonian Institution; Darlene Waller, University of Connecticut Library.

I am very grateful to Alfred Capelle, Fran Hezel, S.J., Nathaniel

Philbrick, Sebastian Junger, Lester Baltimore, Martin Haas, and Milton Viederman, M.D., who read the mansucript.

Three people could not have done more than they did to help my idea of the *Globe* turn into a book about the *Globe*: my agent, Chris Calhoun; my editor, Starling Lawrence; and his assistant, Morgen Van Vorst. I am deeply grateful to them and am grateful as well to Bill Swainson and Pascal Cariss of Bloomsbury Publishing for their attention to and advice on the book's British edition.

And unique thanks to two golden links in the chain from which this book hangs, Elizabeth Fitton and Mary Beth Keane.

GHOSTS OF NAKO

In two long back-slashes the Ralik and Ratak chains of the Marshall Islands slope across the Pacific halfway between Hawaii and Papua New Guinea, directly north of New Zealand. At the top of the western or Ralik chain stands Bikini Atoll, where the sky once sprouted atomic mushrooms from nuclear tests and where today divers on pricey excursions swim like tropical fish around the sunken hulks of the test targets, the aircraft carrier *Saratoga* and the battleship *Arkansas*. Here, in the 1970s, the natives, evacuated by the government since the days of the testing, were officially reassured that their homes were safe and were allowed to return and to eat food grown in the cesium-laden soil, only to be evacuated once again.

Diagonally across the Marshalls from Bikini, at the bottom of the Ratak chain, lies Mili Atoll, whose eight hundred people live mainly on the harvest of copra, dried coconut meat. Air Marshall Islands flies in and out of the atoll, landing on a hillside lawn cut through a grove of coconut trees. The islands of Mili Atoll are in the running for recognition as the site of Amelia Earhart's forced landing.

On February 10, 1824, a Nantucket whaleship sailed northwest from the Gilbert Islands toward Mili and came even with the atoll's little southeastern spur known as Knox Island, at the tip of which lies the island of Nako. Nako is, in Marshallese lore, the place where all the dead of the world either reside or ascend to the next life. It was fortunate for the more superstitious members of the ship's crew that they did not know that, for they would have feared coming close enough to the eerie island to meet the bloody wraiths of their captain and their first, second, and third mates—and the reunion would not have been a happy one.

The ship was the *Globe*, a whaler of some distinction. On one previous voyage it became the first whaleship to return more than two thousand barrels of oil, and on another it discovered the celebrated "Off-Shore Ground" west of northern Peru, one of the richest whaling grounds in the world. But two weeks before it sailed toward Mili, it had achieved its crowning distinction: it was the stage of the bloodiest mutiny in the history of American whaling. And not merely bloody, but strange. The murder of all the officers of the ship was the stark and ghastly fact and was all done in a matter of minutes. But why was it done? Not for any reasons that would have made sense in the whale fishery up until the *Globe's* fatal day. What went before the mutiny and what came after it make a tale of violence, mad caprice, survival, and wild chance.

Nantucketers, from the time when whaling began on their island in the seventeenth century, watched their fisheries expand as if whaling grounds were liquids poured out and spreading over a map of the world. Whaling voyages lengthened to more than three years as the tonnage of the ships increased. The crew lists from captain to cooper contained names that had been whaling names for generations— names like Starbuck and Howland and Gardner that are still to be found next to small islands on maps of the Pacific. Pushed to the kind of risk and toil that war requires, the Nantucket whaleman was exactly what *Moby-Dick* makes him out to be: he was Bulkington, who needed the fatal sea more than he needed the safe land; he was Starbuck, the devout Quaker; and Flask, drunk on adrenaline. And was there an Ahab among the Nantucket whalemen—someone who went to sea out of impulses so at odds with the spoken and unspoken morality of his little island that no one there would have conceived of such a soul?

The following is a story of one man so led by fantastic impulses as to be creatively vicious and so immune to the promptings of conscience as to need a universe of which he would be the sole occupant. It is also the story of a cowed and confused crew, marooned seamen turned native and surviving by wits and luck, naval heroes, prostitution riots and offended Hawaiian missionaries, and six men making a nearly impossible crossing of the Pacific in a disabled ship.

It is, as well, the story of three brothers caught up in a bloody mutiny: Samuel Comstock, the chief perpetrator; George Comstock, the horrified observer; and William Comstock, the later chronicler. George, who lived through the mutiny, wrote "Narrative of the Mutiny capture and transactions on board of the Ship Globe of Nantucket after Sailing from Edgartown"; it is the authoritative first-hand account on which subsequent tellings of the *Globe* story rest. Brother William, who became a popular writer after some whaling experience, recorded—if that is the verb—the years of Samuel Comstock's life before the mutiny in *The Life of Samuel Comstock, the Terrible Whaleman.* William is almost as interesting a figure as his terrible brother, not least of all when he binges with his muse and leaves the sober reader clearing his throat, raising his hand, and ahem-ing to get the author's attention. For material on Samuel Comstock's early years, William is, for better and worse, the only game in town; nonetheless he did capture his brother's mind and life.

In the end the psychopathology of Samuel Comstock overshadows everything else in the *Globe* story. The mutiny on the *Globe* is starkly tragic, but it is a designed tragedy behind which we glimpse a mind and an imagination as daunting and terrifying today as they were over a century and a half ago.

Samuel Comstock was a river running underground. Up above in cities and towns were everyday scenes where characters moved about with comprehensible motives and assumed that everyone else's motives—which could be admirable, ugly, or mixed—were as comprehensible as their own. But then in the middle of the landscape erupts the incomprehensible. It is behavior that does not fit within familiar limits—it is not anywhere between *a* and *z* but written in a new alphabet. And the onlookers cannot read that. When Samuel Comstock's river surfaced, it was a river of blood. It had been flowing underneath appearances.

In time his family sensed that there was something wrong with Samuel. If others did, they have left no records of their impressions. Maybe young John Cotton and John Lincoln, Samuel's companions on the *Foster*, thought he went beyond the limits when he asked them to join him in flogging a mate. Up to the last month of his life, every quirk and idiosyncrasy of Samuel's could be reduced—in the eyes of most who knew him—to something explicable. Was he a risk taker? Was he passionately adventurous? Well, if that was all, . . . But that was not all. The moment came when the common conversational hyperbole, kill, lost every meaning but the most literal in Samuel's mind.

The most chilling thing about Samuel's deeds of blood was his equanimity throughout them. His attack on the *Globe*'s officers left the cabin so covered with gore that it could hardly be scrubbed clean, yet he would order a memorial service for his victims as if they had simply died of a plague. When he brought the *Globe* to its anchorage off Mili Atoll, where he planned to murder everyone else on the ship, he went ashore to lay out his fantasy city, setting aside a prominent place for a church. Those killings, which he was never able to carry out, were planned with the same everyday-ness as the unloading of supplies from the ship. It was just part of the necessary work, after which all would be well.

The pranks and violent play of his childhood, recounted by his brother William, never turned homicidal, but the inhibitions were growing thinner with every passing year. The river was still underground. His childhood companions played around him, his teachers lectured to him, his shipmates on the *Edward* took him for an ordinary greenhand, the residents of Talcahuano passed him in the street, and his pretty cousins on Nantucket welcomed him back from his first whaling voyage. And none of them knew what a dark force was in their midst. *Probably* none of them knew—probably.

MUTINY
ON THE
GLOBE

CHAPTER ONE

BROTHERS

The children had to leave Nantucket. Samuel Comstock was eight, William was seven, George was three, and that bustling island port marinating in the smell of whale oil had been their playground. But there was nothing for it; their father, Nathan Comstock, had given up his job as a Nantucket schoolteacher and bank cashier to become a merchant of whaling products in the big world of New York commerce, and the whole family, which also included five-year-old Lucy and the baby Thomas, had to make the move. Samuel, William, and George were to become part of the legend of the island they were leaving behind, even though the Comstocks were not, by island standards, a Nantucket family. Their roots were on the "continent," as Nantucketers referred to the main-land, and their time on the island of whales, between Nathan Comstock's arrival and his family's departure, amounted to about a dozen years.

The three brothers were a remarkable conjunction: Samuel was violent, William was creative, and George was innocent and clear-eyed. The younger two were not exactly satellites of the oldest, but they were fascinated by him and watched him grow into an icon of strangeness; when the time came to say what they saw, William said it with flair, and George said it with horrified precision. All three brothers had a role in making the legend of the mutineer.

Even though Samuel, William, and George had only a brief child-hood exposure to the island, it was a formative one, and they were to turn to Nantucket when the time came to sign up on whaling ships. For the boys, while they were still island children, the goings-on in the port were dazzling to watch. The wharves were anthills of activ-ity; ships were unloading or preparing to sail, their awesome captains ("keppins") supervising the work, hordes of craftsmen and laborers installing and stowing, and the mates ("mets"), boatsteerers, and crew coming aboard as sailing time drew near. Along the wharves were stacked gear and provisions—sometimes new sails or spars; always oil casks and iron hoops, nails, boards, copper sheathing, tar, ropes, and casks of water, beef, pork, flour, and coffee—and other victuals too, depending on the whim of the shipowners, a class not fabled for munificence.

Nantucket was originally agricultural—there was still considerable farming, especially sheep raising, when the Comstock boys were on the island. It became a whaling port in 1668 the day that some of the islanders trapped a whale in the harbor and killed it. Four years later the town may—or may not—have brought a professional, James Loper, over from Cape Cod as official whale hunter, but for sure it did bring Ichabod Paddack to the island to teach whaling in 1690.

At first whaling was confined to drift whales; the next stage was spotting whales by lookouts ashore and launching small boats to hunt them and tow them to land. Soon the whale hunters sent out boats to cruise for whales; the next step was the use of ships of increasing tonnage, capacity, and range. The whales hunted were right whales, until in 1712 Christopher Hussey, blown off course by a northerly wind, encountered the first sperm whale and killed it. The Pacific became part of the whaling scene in 1793, the year the *Beaver*, Captain Paul Worth, returned from the first voyage by an American whaler around Cape Horn. It was a milestone of great importance, for it opened the riches of the Pacific to New England, and it opened Polynesia, Micronesia, and Melanesia to a multitude of abrupt penetrations by the culture of the Caucasian world. In 1802, the year Samuel Comstock was born, twenty-two whaleships sailed from Nantucket; in 1822, the year he sailed on the *Globe*, forty whaleships left the port. It was a heady time to be in whaling.

People on the wharves, even the three Comstock boys, knew that most of the ships' officers belonged to one of the island's aristocracies—the Coffins, Folgers, Starbucks, Gardners, Husseys, Swains, Chases, or other whaling families, a good two dozen of them. By and large the captains earned their eminence in town, for they brought home impressive returns: in 1805, when Samuel was three, Captain William Easton on the *Atlas* brought back eighteen hundred barrels of oil, probably a record in its day. A few ships, it is true, came back "clean," and some did not come back at all: As early as 1724 a Nantucket whaleship was recorded as lost. The *Commerce*, Captain Jesse Bunker, which sailed in 1805, was reported "last seen near the line, homeward bound, with a cargo of oil" and was not reported again. In 1807 one Nantucket ship, the *Union*, Captain Edmund Gardner, was only a couple of weeks out when it ran into a whale and sank, leaving the crew to sail in open boats six hundred miles to the Azores. That was a freakish occurrence by all whaling standards, but it did not match what was to happen thirteen years later to the *Essex*, an old workhorse of a whaler out on its ninth voyage that did not accidentally bump into a whale but was rammed and sunk by one; the episode gave Herman Melville the ending of *Moby-Dick*.

The boys grew up familiar with ships and their fates. And they were familiar with the reports that those great explorers, the whalemen, brought home. The real adventures and exotic encounters they told of were more engrossing than any fiction of the time—or most sea fiction since. To the non-whaleman every single cruise and every single lowering for whales were good adventures in themselves, but to the whaleman they were too commonplace to make a story unless something exceptional happened: a boat was stove, or line on an attached whale had run out to full length and the whaleboat was dragged along on a "Nantucket sleighride," or a ship had to stand off when hostile native canoes surrounded it, or there was a terrifying storm and the ship was "boarded by a waterspout." Or the ever-dreaded and all too familiar meeting of the men in the boats with violent death, the specter of which hung permanently over the ships and the town.

Some tales from the sea were not somber. "If ye touch at the islands, Mr. Flask, beware of fornication," says Captain Bildad in chapter 22 of *Moby-Dick* to a mate of the departing *Pequod*. Certain islands, like the Marquesas, were renowned for the native girls—to call them vivacious would be a euphemism—who swam out to meet the ships. "They never left land without at least so much clothing as a large green leaf, yet this light covering was generally lost by swimming any length of the way. By a few only were the leafy aprons preserved, and luckily for them we had no sheep or goats on board," wrote Georg H. von Langsdorff in 1813. (He was not joking: the missionary ship *Duff* did have some "knavish" goats on board that quickly ate the wardrobe and left the girls visiting the ship "entirely in their native beauty.") The frolicsome days on deck and lascivious nights in steerage and forecastle were not supposed to be talked about in the presence of the younger children, but the younger children knew. In time Samuel Comstock became fixated on the idea of Pacific islands, not mainly because of the island nymphs, but they were part of the picture.

For Samuel and William, and maybe a bit for George, it was interesting to hear what the younger returning seamen said; they were the cabin boys, who were back from the Pacific at age sixteen. The brothers knew who many of them were, and that made shipboard life seem almost within reach. To Samuel it meant that he had just a few years to wait before he would be able to swagger along Straight Wharf and down Main Street telling stories as good as the ones he had been listening to. The adventure in those stories appealed to him, but even the work of whaling seemed not all that bad, at least if it meant lowering for whales or working in the rigging (working at the try-pots where the blubber was boiled down was another story). As it turned out, in spite of the family's move to New York, Samuel would serve on three Nantucket whalers.

Since Samuel Comstock did not have the distinction of coming from one of the old island families, he could have been just one more child of the town. But he wasn't. To stand out against a plain background is easy, but to stand out against the mottled background of Nantucket, where everyone in the street was a character suitable for sketching or casting, took idiosyncracy, and in that Samuel abounded. At age three Samuel insisted that he be allowed to go alone to the butcher shop to buy beefsteak. The butcher shop was a mile from home. And he had to—*had* to—do it alone. Well, all right, he could go; God knows what would come of it. But the errand worked, and the odd little shopper carried the bundle home.

He was heedless of risks; still three years old he plunged without warning into the treacherous ocean breakers on the south shore of the island and was barely saved. And he was eerily insensitive to pain;

a claw hammer, over which he was struggling with his brother William, flew up when William let go, and hit him in the face, splitting his lip. A doctor was needed to stitch the cut up; during the operation not a muscle moved in Samuel's face. A few years later when Samuel was fifteen, William came upon him in their father's store robbing a wine cask; he had filled one large bottle through the bung hole and was trying to move the huge cask. Hold the lamp, he asked his brother. As William watched, the cask rolled and trapped one of Samuel's hands. Blood spurted out; William's horrified first thought was that the hand had been severed. He called for help from some young men in the front of the store. When Samuel saw the help coming, he grasped the large wine bottle he had filled and gulped down the contents, saying that no one was going to take advantage of the situation to keep him from enjoying his drink.

Samuel was a liar; his improvisational and outlandish fibs were works of art in the eyes of brother William. So were his caprices. When he was about five, he went into a store that was being minded by a girl of fourteen. Picking up a piece of colored paper from the floor, he stood turning it over and studying it. You can have that if you want it, the young clerk told him. He walked over to the counter, put down the paper, and solemnly said that he would indeed be very happy to have the paper, but he did not think it right for little girls to give away things that did not belong to them. Betty the clerk was speechless.

William was a shadow to Samuel in the manner of most little brothers. And Samuel, in the manner of most older brothers, was half-tolerant of the tot who always wanted to tag along. William especially wanted to follow Samuel on the excursions that the older brother would set out on after breakfast and not return from until dinnertime; these were mysterious to the younger boy—were they in town or out in the country, and did he get on board ships? Samuel would never say where he had been. One day William became more insistent—why couldn't he come? Because you can't, but to soften the refusal Samuel told William that when he came back he would bring him forty little kegs of molasses "all bound with bright golden hoops."

William, even in his earliest years, was struck by the romance in Samuel's behavior. When he became Samuel's biographer he titled his book *The Life of Samuel Comstock, the Terrible Whaleman*, but "Terrible" is not that terrible; it is of a piece with the term that William uses all through the book for Samuel, "our hero." Both terms have the pinch of drollery that fits a consistently detached and sometimes even bemused treatment of horrendous events. At one point, when the mutineers shoot a defenseless native of the Gilbert Islands, William denounces the killing bitterly, but that moment is exceptional. The mutineer's deeds were bloody and brutal, but there was something in them to wonder at, something mysterious, and that was, in William's eyes, romantic.

A time would come, in the last eight months before Samuel went to sea on the *Globe*, when William would observe a sinister metamorphosis in his brother, but no loss of imagination and no loss of that magnetism of the overreacher that had always been part of Samuel's character. For William, Samuel remained, in spite of his emerging dark side, or maybe because of it, every bit as engaging as he had been through all their years together. William never romanticized Samuel, but he was delighted to make use of him, for William loved wit, originality, surprises, paradox, the exploitation of circumstances, and anything irreducible to the commonplace; his brother's life gave him all of those. It is probably a safe guess that if there had been no mutiny, William would still have wanted to explain on paper what he had discovered in his almost unexplainable brother.

William enjoys the early anecdotes that he passes on about Samuel. But was Samuel the performer amused by his stunts and lies and quips? Strangely it seems not. There is a strong suggestion that the same lack of feeling that Samuel showed when suffering pain characterized other facets of his behavior. And here contradiction rules the day: Samuel was grateful for kindness; William affirms that. And Samuel carried around, like uncoiled rope, a strange tangle of religious feelings, some of which came out in the very midst of the mutiny. But he was by and large a whirlwind of *doing*; he did not seem to understand the logic of feeling, the recognition that a range of emotion was part of communication with others as surely as words were. His responses were triggered as easily as an animal's, but the responses were always action, often diffuse and gratuitous. He desired things—things sexual quite notably—and came to fixate intensely on them, but he rarely reposed in them. If wit could be autistic, Samuel would be a model of it.

William the chronicler supplies us with most of what we know about Samuel before he sailed on the *Globe*. The reader has to enter, sooner or later, into a contract with William that establishes the grounds for doing business with him: deliveries have to be opened and inspected before being accepted, rebuilt items have to be identified as such, and the reader will not agree to pay an exorbitant price—in credulity. Nonetheless, the trade is too good to break off; the goods are usually high quality, and they are not available elsewhere.

William, talking about his brother, is a blunt reporter when he chooses to be, but sometimes he handles his material the way a medieval manuscript illuminator would: the color and design are as important as the text, and at times, they may seem more important. He likes to clinch a vivid image, he likes drollery, he likes to be selectively venomous, he is drawn toward prophetic signs and sayings, he is incisively witty, and he has grievances to settle. Imprecisions there are in his account of his brother's life, for example about family genealogy, and there are details that could have, and maybe should have, been fitted not into Samuel's biography, but into William's novel, *A Voyage to the Pacific*, published two years before *The Terrible Whaleman*, or even into his satire of Artemus Ward, *Betsey Jane Ward . . . Hur Book of Goaks*.

Sometimes William is like Hippoclides in Herodotus's *History*, who, entering a competition to win the hand of a girl, dances exuberantly but cannot stop dancing even when he has been told that he has overdone his performance and lost her. William tingles with his story and, telling it as he has to, presents the most intimately aware and, in the long run, reliable picture of the mind behind the mutiny that anyone could have created. Some caricatures are truer than photographs.

The Comstock boys came from rugged stock. They were in the eighth generation of a family brought to America in the seventeenth century from Wales or Devonshire—reports vary—by patriarch Samuel Comstock, whose first name was popular through generations of the family. The first Comstock settlement was near Watertown, Massachusetts; subsequent locations were in Wethersfield and New London, Connecticut, and finally in Burrillville, Rhode Island. The family was to typify, generation by generation, the classic American progress from primitive colonial settlement to prosperous urban capitalism, the stage reached by the father of the mutineer.

Tales descended in the family about the early Comstocks being Indian fighters, and the stories are plausible enough considering that the family arrived in the colony shortly before King Philip's War. By the eighteenth century the Comstocks were clearing land and farming. One of them, if William's account is to be credited, was another Samuel, the grandfather of the mutineer, who had the makings of a character from a James Fenimore Cooper novel. Family legend describes him walking through the new fallen snow near his farm in Burrillville to check fox traps. A little way into the woods his dog began to whine and hover over something it had found in the snow, a huge print of a bare human foot. Dog and master followed the tracks until they led into a very dense part of the woods; at that point the dog became anxious to drop the hunt and stopped, howling and moaning. Samuel cut a staff, though, and plunged ahead, the timid dog following behind. Focusing closely on the now harder to follow tracks, Samuel did not look up until they came to a stump. There he raised his eyes and saw a towering figure with a hatchet in his right hand and a knife in his left. An immediate first impression would have been that this was a runaway slave, but the strangeness of the nearly naked figure—he wore only a bloody sheepskin loincloth— standing like a statue on a pedestal in the midst of the snowy landscape defied all logical guesses. When the giant threw the hatchet, Samuel sprang out of the way and swung his staff at his attacker's head, knocking him down. He leapt on the fallen figure, wrenched the knife away from him, and tossed it out of reach. Quickly overcome, the eerie attacker begged for his life; he was assured that he would not be killed. In time Samuel's calls summoned a hunter, whose shots had been heard nearby, and the two tied up the black man and took him to the home of a nearby slaveholder. Some time later Samuel found out that his attacker had tried to burn down the house in which he was being kept and at that point was shipped to a southern owner.

This Samuel's son Nathan came to Nantucket late in the 1790s and was hired as a teacher in the Quaker Monthly Meeting school. The school, which had been established in 1784, got off to a halting start but quickly stabilized. When Nathan Comstock was hired in 1800, the Meeting paid him two hundred dollars for the six-month term beginning July of that year. His contract was renewed up to 1803. The evident respect in which he was held in the circle of Friends guaranteed a comparable respect in the larger Nantucket community; he was also a cashier in a local bank.

One might think from the portraits of Captain Bildad and Captain Peleg in *Moby-Dick*, and from the great bulk of popular writing about the island, that God created Nantucket Quaker and that it stayed permanently, invincibly Quaker. In fact, throughout the island's seventeenth-century history (which began with settlement in 1659), Nantucketers were a religious miscellany, the Quakers among them being not much more notable than the Baptists. But in 1702 Mary Coffin Starbuck, who was the island's leading merchant and source of credit—a powerful woman indeed, who has come down in island history as "Great Mary"—invited John Richardson, a Quaker minister, to preach to an assembly at her house. The effect was like a bolt of lightning, instantly producing the "convincement" of the listeners and, most important, Mary herself. Quaker Nantucket was born. (Fortunately Great Mary had no way of knowing that one of her great-great-great-great-grandsons would be Samuel Comstock, the mutineer.)

Robert Leach, the historian of Nantucket Quakerism, writes, "In the entire world there was no community like Nantucket, where Friends dominated all affairs and where non-Quakers fell into Quaker ways just in order to survive." An indication of the Quaker control is the formation in 1780 of a Friends committee to remedy the problem of "children collecting together in the Evening in the streets" by walking "out in the streets . . . at proper Times to Endeavor to Discover who such children are, and to give advice both to parents and children as They shall judge Necessary or useful." There is no evidence that policing the curfew was called for because of any disorderly behavior on the part of the young people; they were simply out in the evening. That was enough. This vigilance was exercised over boys who were considered ready to go to sea at age fourteen and had probably heard a good deal about what they could find by "collecting in the Evening in the streets" of certain Pacific port cities.

One of the members of the vigilance committee was Edward T. Emmett, a prominent and idiosyncratic figure on the island. A watchmaker, teacher, and lover of long brisk walks by the seashore, he was withdrawn and solitary, one of those respected and irreducible figures who in some communities are private and public presences at the same time. When Nathan Comstock, about twenty years old, came to Nantucket, he and the elderly Emmett became close friends. It says something about Nathan that almost at once he was admitted into an intimacy that not many on the island shared. Emmett would have had no shortage of society if he had chosen to be gregarious, for he had the requisite ties to the sea: his father was an Irish sea captain who had disappeared with his ship at sea, and Emmett had married into the prominent shipowning Mitchell family—every whaler that Nathan Comstock's son Samuel would sail on was owned by one of the Mitchells.

Under the Emmett roof lived a son and two daughters, one of whom, black-eyed Elizabeth, was to be her father's legacy to Nathan; in 1801, three years after her father's death, Elizabeth and Nathan married.

There was a story in circulation in the Emmett family that Nathan would have heard early on: Captain Emmett, Elizabeth's grandfather, who disappeared on what he intended to be his last voyage, did not go down with his ship in a classic sea disaster; instead he was killed when his crew mutinied in order to make off with the large consignment of money the ship was carrying. It was a vivid tale and one of those family properties that there was nothing to gain by trying to verify. It made a good yarn but could hardly have been told with the thought that the lightning of mutiny would strike twice in the family.

Sooner rather than later Nathan Comstock became a wealthy man. When he left Nantucket to go into business as a merchant of whale products in New York, he was probably doing so on the strength of capital in hand as well as credit. On a schoolteacher's and bank cashier's salaries that would not be easy, but money grew in a lot of ways in Nantucket. How well off Nathan was after a dozen or so years in New York may be gathered from his offer to Samuel in 1822 when the young man was preparing to sign on his third whaler, the *Globe*: if Samuel sailed to the Pacific and conducted himself well (a marvelous condition to impose on Samuel), Nathan would buy a ship and give him command of it.

An even better index to Nathan's prosperity is the report that Nathan lost $75,000, a phenomenal sum for the day, in dealings with the financier Jacob Barker. Barker, a distant cousin of Nathan's wife, was a manipulator and dealer of prodigious proportions, a figure who anticipated by two generations the kind of fantastic financial operators that Mark Twain collected in *The Gilded Age*. Born in Maine, Barker came to New York, took a job with a commercial agent, and by 1800, at the age of twenty-one, possessed five ships and was an operator of an extensive credit. He lost his fortune at the age of twenty-two but recovered quickly. He raised a five-million-dollar loan for the government during the War of 1812, became a state senator, founded a newspaper, established a bank on Wall Street, and speculated in stocks. His bank failed in 1819, but his financial adventurism continued, and he was able to build up another fortune, most of which was lost in the wake of the Civil War. At what point in these projects Nathan was involved with Barker is unclear—it may have been in the course of some of Barker's oil deals—but his brush with lofty and dangerous finance was evidently survivable.

The timing of Nathan Comstock's move to New York suggests that he had been watching for commercial opportunities carefully and recognized that business prospects in the city were rapidly brightening as New York snapped out of one of the worst financial crises it had ever experienced. In December 1807 Thomas Jefferson had signed into law the Embargo Act, plunging the city into economic stagnation, unemployment, and social panic. Jefferson was responding to the threats to American shipping resulting from England's and France's mutual blockade of each other's coasts, which

would allow either country to seize and condemn any American ship
found entering the blockaded enemy's ports. Jefferson's solution was
simply to ban all sailing from American ports; his faith in the power
of American commerce was so great that he thought that denying
England and France American exports would be a severe blow to
them. In fact, it was a much more severe blow to the United States.
When John Lambert, an English traveler, visited New York in 1807
weeks before the Embargo Act went into effect, he was struck by the
energy, bustle, and spirit of the city's commerce; returning a few
months later, he found gloom and hopelessness. "Not a box, bale,
cask, barrel, or package, was to be seen upon the wharfs," he wrote,
and grass had begun to grow in their place. Only one American ship
managed to slip out of port: by a stupendous ruse John Jacob Astor
had gained permission for his ship, the *Beaver*, to sail for Canton carrying an "esteemed citizen" of China home for compassionate reasons. Esteemed citizen was a phony, Jefferson had been duped, the
ship was carrying furs for trade, and Astor was $200,000 wealthier.
On a subsequent voyage of the *Beaver*, in 1817, Astor was again going
to lie about the ship's cargo, contraband arms. This time the ship did
not have an esteemed citizen aboard, but it did have a fourteen-year-
old seaman, now out on his second voyage, named Samuel Comstock.

In 1809 Congress repealed the embargo and Jefferson signed the
Nonintercourse Act, which forbade trade only with England and
France. By 1811, when the Comstocks moved, the city was on its feet
again.

Several years before the move to New York, Nathan had sent his
oldest son away to school. His choice of school was part of a plan that
the father hoped would sweep Samuel through formal education
right up to a college degree, an exceptionally high goal for a
Nantucket parent to set at that time. The school was a new and
highly regarded academy just established by the Friends' New York
Yearly Meeting. Nine Partners School in Dutchess County, founded

in 1795, was modeled on Ackworth, a large Quaker boarding school founded by the London Yearly Meeting and viewed by eighteenth-century Friends as embodying the most developed thinking in Quaker education. Nine Partners School stood on a site in what was Washington, New York, at the time and is now Millbrook.

Samuel did, in fact, turn out to be a good learner in the course of a fragmented and erratic education, but he had to learn in his own way. His days in successive schools were contests in which the schools almost always came out losers and Samuel a winner. From his last recorded schooling at the age of sixteen he retired virtually undefeated. William describes one of the Nine Partners schoolmasters, Mark Coffin, taking out his knife to trim a switch for use on the misbehaving Samuel. As he did so, the six-year-old's world-weary words to the schoolmaster were, "Ah! friend Mark, it will be of no use; father has used up a whole poplar tree on me, already; but to no purpose."

It may be easier to picture Samuel's fellow Nantucketer and fellow student, Lucretia Coffin, later Lucretia Mott, the celebrated women's rights activist, as a Nine Partners student than Samuel. (Lucretia was nine years older than Samuel and had been promoted to assistant teacher around the time Samuel was enrolled in the school.) But Samuel is a constant anomaly and may have responded well, even happily, to textbooks such as *Mental Improvement or The Beauties and Wonders of Instructive Conversation*. Nine Partners was probably training Samuel as well as any school could have, even though this was the child about whom his mother prophesied, when pregnant with him, that he would be a person of extraordinary but ill-directed energies. And this was the child who, before leaving Nantucket, went to work on the family homestead with his favorite hatchet, lopping off every projection on the barn, downing fence posts, and felling the large poplar tree standing in front of the family's house. In any event this was the child who was now coming to New York.

Coming to the big city and succumbing to it tragically is a classic pattern in literature. But that was not the fate of young Samuel Comstock, whose opportunities for wildness and willfulness were quantitatively greater in New York, but whose wildness and willfulness were his own, already perfected and imported as part of his permanent equipment. He measured up to the metropolis.

New York was Everycity; it wore all the faces that it does today—elegant, squalid, refined, and threatening—and it was thriving even in spite of the two-year Embargo Act crisis and the fear of a looming war with England. Between 1800 and 1820 the population doubled from 60,489 to 123,706. (The population of Nantucket when the Comstocks left it was around 7,000.) Along the lower reaches of Broadway, or "The Broadway" as it was called, the poplars grew in front of elegant four-story homes, and the sight of promenaders evoked from foreign visitors favorable comparisons to European cities. By 1800 the street extended one mile north from the Battery.

The city's cultural societies flourished, and musical organizations abounded. America's leading playhouse, the Park Theater, presented such notables as John Howard Payne and in 1825 was to stage the first grand opera to be presented in America, *The Barber of Seville*. The New York Academy of Fine Arts was founded in 1802, and the New-York Historical Society in 1804. The city was the home of Charles Brockden Brown and Washington Irving and it was the place where John Trumbull and Samuel F. B. Morse painted. The recently finished City Hall heralded a new epoch in public architecture. The city had libraries and schools and newspapers and relief societies and fraternal organizations. The stock exchange had moved its meetings from under the buttonwood tree on Wall Street to the Tontine Coffee House. A small but revealing indication of New York's arrival at the status of metropolis was the publication in 1807 of Samuel Latham Mitchill's *The Picture of New-York*, the city's first guidebook. There was enough in the city now to call for a guide.

The enthusiasm of growth prompted an 1807 commission to lay

out a grid of streets extending up to an envisioned 155th Street in perfect, unvarying rectangles with no regard for hills or streams, thus
dooming the topography that would have been one of the city's greatest amenities. The most defiant alteration in Manhattan's surface was
just being completed when the Comstocks moved to New York, and it
was happening in their neighborhood: the filling-in of the city's
remarkable inland lake, the Collect Pond, which occupied five acres in
the area of present-day Canal Street. The city ordered the draining and
filling when it concluded that the pollution of the pond from effluents,
trash, and the dumping of dead animals had become irreversible.

Next to the pond lay the soon to be notorious Five Points (today
Baxter, Worth, and Park Streets). It was the neighborhood of the
city's poorest residents: workmen in the tanneries that polluted the
pond or in breweries or potteries, immigrants, free blacks, modest
craftsmen, and the city's unclassifiable poor. In time Five Points
became the fabled center of the city's vice and crime, best known for
its subhuman tenement, the Old Brewery.

There was much for a guidebook to avert its gaze from: poverty,
violence, dissipation, and disorder. The barefoot hot-corn girls wandered the streets chanting, "All you that's got money—poor me that's
got none! Come buy my lily-white corn and let me go home." There
were more than two thousand saloons by 1820, pigs ran in the
streets, and bawdy houses flourished in the red light district known
as the "Holy Ground." The barbaric entertainment of bull baiting
and bear baiting was extremely popular: dogs were released in a ring
to kill, or be killed by, the chained bear or bull. Although the well-
known gangs like the Forty Thieves, the Plug Uglies, and the Dead
Rabbits were not organized until 1825, there was enough unorgan-
ized mayhem from early in the nineteenth century, especially by rowdies picking random targets for beatings in public.

When the Comstocks came to New York, the water was bad, fire
was a nightmarish threat, and disease an even worse one. Aaron

Burr's Manhattan Company, chartered to provide the city with water, had sunk a well on Broadway near Spring Street and laid some wooden pipe, but it was to be years before anything like an adequate and healthy supply of water was available. The helplessness of fire-fighters emptying leather buckets into burning houses was familiar to New Yorkers and was to be demonstrated most dramatically when the great fire of 1835 destroyed over twenty blocks in a wedge of lower Manhattan bounded by Wall, South, and Broad Streets. No threat to the city's well-being, however, frightened New Yorkers more than the yellow fever epidemics. They came in waves; the one in 1819 was bad, but that of 1822 was the worst. So great was the fear of the disease that New Yorkers who could afford to left the city for a popular country haven: Greenwich Village. Among those families who closed up their city homes in 1822 and moved north until the epidemic passed were the Comstocks; this they did right before Samuel and young George were to leave for Nantucket to sign on the *Globe*.

When Nathan Comstock set up business in New York, he located in the whale oil center of the city, Front Street. For brief periods he was doing business on some nearby streets—Bancker, Oliver, James, and the Bowery—but most of his business life in the city was spent selling whale oil, sperm oil, candles, and even ambergris on Front Street, mainly at 191 Front. In 1857, two years before the Drake well in Pennsylvania brought petroleum out of the earth and signaled the end of the whaling industry, there were at least seventeen oil and candle merchants on Front Street and at least twenty-two on nearby streets.

The Comstocks' eventual home was on Market Street, roughly a half-dozen blocks away from the whale merchants' stores. When the Comstocks moved in, the neighborhood proper, even though it was only a few blocks south of Five Points, was one that mixed comfortable residences and active businesses.

Samuel's parents sent the eight-year-old to a Quaker school near his home, this one conducted by the Friends' Monthly Meeting on Pearl Street. When Samuel entered the school, William was sent along with him. At last Samuel had to take him some place. This was probably William's first school, so he had the edifying opportunity of learning from his older brother just exactly what one does in school. For example, when confined to a second-floor classroom for disciplinary reasons, one jumps from the window down to the street. Samuel sprained his ankle that time. When confined to the same room a second time, one learns from experience and does not jump from the window, but picks up a pair of tongs and smashes a hole in the door.

Out of school Samuel was equally exemplary. He was nine when he joined and became a leader of a group of neighborhood boys who had christened themselves the Down Towners. Night after night Samuel, carrying his big homemade wooden shield and wearing his "coat of mail," sneaked out of the house to rendezvous with the Down Towners and meet in battle the rough boys from the shipbuilding area of Corlears Hook. The scars on his arms and legs stayed with him all his life. William returned to the subject of the juvenile gang wars in his novelette, *Mysteries of New York*, where his account of a conflict between the Down Towners and the Corlears Hookers, aided by their allies from other gangs, reads like battlefield reporting; the armies grow to number in the hundreds. When the Down Towners chase a group of Corlears Hookers who have locked themselves in a deserted house, the leader of the pursuing group orders his lads to break off a rotting pillar from the piazza and use it as a battering ram to break down the front door.

Samuel's parents did not leave him in the Pearl Street school very long, for they soon resolved that it was time to transplant him again; the choice was back to his first school, Nine Partners. But every new stratagem was failing, and the stay at Nine Partners this time was a short one. In the middle of winter Samuel set out with an older student to return to New York. One can only wonder if the older student was as far gone in unrealism as Samuel: return to New York how? The first leg of the escape was walking to Poughkeepsie, miles away. Then, what else but to put on the ice skates that they had carried with them and start skating down the frozen Hudson. When the authorities at Nine Partners noticed the truancy, they dispatched two men from the school in a sleigh to retrieve the boys, but the boys actually skated on through the night and were not spotted by their pursuers until the next morning. The driver took the fugitives into the sleigh, swung the horses around, and headed north to the school. But once the boys were there, the authorities granted their wish to return to New York— they were expelled as hopeless cases and sent to the city by conventional conveyances.

Daunting as the prospect was, Samuel's parents had to find another school for him. Again it was a Quaker institution, this time a boarding school at Cedar Swamp, Long Island. The venerable headmaster of that institution has the distinction of being the only school authority on record to control young Comstock. His first attempt to discipline Samuel, who was his rebellious self from the start, was the misguided one of overpowering the boy by force of numbers and locking him up in the smokehouse. Naturally that did not work. Visiting the smokehouse to check on the prisoner, the headmaster found the building empty and boards smashed out of a rear wall. Samuel had escaped into the woods. This time his strategy was not to run away but to build a fortress of sorts, which he imagined he could hold out in. The plan was as fanciful as his escape from Nine Partners had been and was just as doomed even if no one tried to apprehend him. But the headmaster's response this time was remarkably sage: he sent two girls out to Samuel's fort to persuade him gently to return to the house. That worked; Samuel yielded, went back with the girls, and for the next four weeks, until he left to return home, was a model student.

Back in New York Samuel loved to play war games and to lead

neighborhood boys in parades, trench battles (the trenches were dug in the family's backyard), and courts-martial, where the accused were sometimes cats and dogs, duly "executed" by toy cannons. At the age of twelve he carried pistols and daggers and kept them under his pillow at night—very un-Quakerish sport. His father, fancying that a reading of *Don Quixote* would show Samuel the foolishness of imaginary battles, gave him a copy of the book, only to find the boy enchanted with the story. The Don became a role model.

If one freeze-framed Samuel at this point in his life, he would look a good deal like Tom Sawyer organizing Huck Finn and his other unimaginative companions to ambush Spanish merchants and rich Arabs with their two hundred elephants. While the companions saw only a Sunday school picnic, their leader, Tom, kept the fantasy play going; there *were* elephants and soldiers and treasure—some magicians had made the scene look like a Sunday school picnic. But there is a difference between imagination and pathology. Tom Sawyer, if Mark Twain had followed him into adulthood, would have stopped playing. Samuel Comstock was not destined to stop. The plateau of mood, imagination, and grandiose fantasy on which every stage of his life was acted out did not change with growth; as far as his personality went, chronology was irrelevant: he was an adult as a child and a child as an adult. The inability to know the limits of game was going to keep him playing when the moves were no longer game moves—to any sane observer.

At the age of thirteen Samuel ran away to sea, almost. William says that his brother had formed an acquaintance with an Irishman at the fortification of Harlem Heights and headed off with him to find a ship in Philadelphia to sign on to. That is a Samuelesque escapade, all right, but the arresting thing about it is not the running away to sea but what happened before the flight to Philadelphia. Who was the Irishman, and how did Samuel come to know him?

New York City, already tense over developments in the War of

1812, was alarmed when by the summer of 1814 a British naval force had begun to assemble off Sandy Hook in apparent preparation for invasion. Mayor DeWitt Clinton appealed to the people of New York on August 2, 1814, to work on building up the fortifications in Brooklyn Heights and Harlem Heights; a committee of defense was formed a week later and rallied masses of citizens to turn out with shovels and pickaxes, first in Brooklyn and then, on August 20, in Harlem. Organizations, including the Patriotic Sons of Erin, and individual volunteers, even children and women, labored with a camaraderie born out of panic to build the fortifications along 123rd Street against a British landing (which, in the end, never came). It was easy to make new friends in the solidarity of the moment, but the friendship of Samuel and the Irishman with whom he was carrying earth to the fortifications raises questions. William, who is mainly interested in reporting the running away to sea, refers only to "an Irishman whom he had before formed acquaintance with, at the digging of Harlaem Heights"—not an Irish *boy* but an Irishman. The use of *before* is suggestive of an acquaintance that had endured for some time, as well it may have, for Samuel was eleven years old in August 1814 and, if William is correct, thirteen when he set out to run away. That would mean more than a year had gone by between the meeting of Samuel and the Irishman, making for a rather long and even strange friendship. Were they Huck Finn and Jim? The Irish occupied a social position close enough to blacks to make Twain's couple comparable to Samuel and friend, except that in general blacks would have been viewed as more benign than the Irish and safer as companions. It was scandalous enough for a young man from a family like Samuel's to befriend an Irishman; running off with one would be unthinkable. But, in Samuel's life the unthinkable becomes thinkable.

Through the night of Samuel's disappearance, his mother kept vigil for him. His absence was alarming even for a family hardened to his behavior. Around noon the next day a Frenchman appeared at Nathan

Comstock's office and explained that an interesting young man had attracted the attention of people at a hotel in Elizabeth, New Jersey. No one believed the boy's story, that he was walking to Philadelphia on business for a brother. (Nothing is said of the Irish companion.) The good people of Elizabeth were able to keep the boy confined and eventually get a confession from him. Nathan asked a Quaker friend, who was on his way to New Jersey on business, to collect the boy and bring him back. Why did Samuel not sign on a ship in New York and spare himself the walk? Probably because he knew he could not get away with it. He must have known that no ship in the port would have him and that he would probably be recognized and reported to his parents. But Philadelphia, being sufficiently remote, verged on an imaginary place, and in imaginary worlds one can do anything. Confidence in imaginary possibilities was an enduring part of Samuel's thinking; in the end that confidence was boundless.

The running away paid off, though. If nothing but a life at sea would do, Samuel's father told him, he could have it. The next day the elder Comstock contacted the firm of Hicks, Jenkins, and Co., who agreed to take the greenhand on their Liverpool trader, *Edward*, captained by Josiah Macy. It took a lot of persuading by Captain Macy, for the owners were dead set against the idea, possibly because of the boy's age but more likely because the owners had heard enough about Samuel to mistrust him. Dressed as a sailor, in duck trousers and tarpaulin hat, Samuel was in his glory; he delighted in showing himself off to all company. That included the Quakers who turned out for meetings in Pearl Street—and there was a special delight for Samuel in defiantly provoking them. Their reactions to the boy were, to put it mildly, censorious; the boy's reactions to them in turn included an invitation to one of the distinguished elders to administer, as brother William puts it, a certain act of endearment to the rear of his person.

The Liverpool that Samuel was sailing to had been compared with

New York by more than one English traveler at the end of the eighteenth century. "New York, for instance, is a perfect counterpart of Liverpool: the situation of the docks, the form of the streets, the state of the public buildings, the inside as well as the outside of the houses, the manners, the amusements, the mode of living among the expensive part of the inhabitants—all these circumstances are as nearly alike . . . as possible," wrote Thomas Cooper, an English educator. All of which does not say much about the experience of a greenhand working his way to the city.

Herman Melville began his career as a sailor in much the same way as Samuel Comstock—same ports, same kind of ship, same length of voyage—and Melville does tell something about the experience in his quasi-autobiographical novel *Redburn*. The hero of the novel is a naive greenhand, mocked by the older seamen, ordered about roughly, given revolting duties, terrified by the high rigging, and overcome by seasickness, who in the course of the brief voyage learns the sea language, comes to perform well on the masts, and gains the respect of his mates. Melville was nineteen when he sailed in 1839, and Samuel was thirteen when he sailed in 1816. Melville was probably not as sensitive as his fictional young hero Redburn (although Melville wrote home that he was homesick in Liverpool); Samuel Comstock, for sure, was not that sensitive. Or greenhand-ish; nautical terms, orders, and gear he would have been at home with, and he could hardly have waited to get into the rigging.

It is provocative to picture Samuel Comstock in the Liverpool that Melville encountered, that is, that Redburn encountered. It was a social horror; one scene in the novel, of a mother and her children starving to death, stays in the reader's mind, and although Redburn had mixed experiences, Melville emphasizes his encounters with the squalor, beggary, and vice of the city: "Old women, rather mummies, drying up with slow starving and age; young girls, incurably sick, who ought to have been in the hospital; sturdy men, with the gallows in their eyes, and a whining lie in their mouths; young boys, hollow eyed and decrepit; and puny mothers, holding up puny babes in the glare of the sun." Again: ". . . the lowest and most abandoned neighborhoods frequented by sailors in Liverpool. The pestilent lanes and alleys which, in their vocabulary, go by the names of Rotten-row, Gibraltar-place, and Booble-alley, are putrid with vice and crime; to which, perhaps the round globe does not furnish a parallel. . . . These are the haunts from which sailors sometimes disappear forever; or issue in the morning, robbed naked, from the broken door-ways." If Samuel saw what Melville saw, it was with different eyes, and if Samuel issued in the morning from Booble-alley, he would not have been deploring it or warning his mates about it.

Nathan Comstock may seem irresponsible for letting his wild thirteen-year-old son go to sea, especially in the wake of an attempt to run away from home, but it is likely that he would not have allowed it on any other ship than the *Edward* and under any other captain than Josiah Macy. Nathan probably put his son in the care of Captain Macy with the same feelings he would have had in enrolling him under a good teacher, for Josiah Macy was a moral force: he was devout, generous, solicitous about his men, temperate, and decorous; he had never been heard to utter a curse in the course of his twenty-two years of command, and his men avoided curses in his presence. Macy was very successful as a shipowner and a captain, bold in defying the War of 1812 blockades and endlessly resourceful in trading cargo in difficult and unlikely ports, but the strongest impression left by his own autobiography and the testimony of others is that of an upright and kindly man. The explorer Captain Benjamin Morrell writes about Captain Macy in his book *A Narrative of Four Voyages, to the South Sea*:

I was justly considered a very "wild youth." How long I should have continued in this thoughtless career of folly it is not easy to determine, had not Divine Providence raised up for me a faithful friend and adviser in the person of Captain Josiah Macy, master of the ship Edward of New-York, belonging to Samuel Hicks and himself. On a voyage to Calcutta, this worthy man, who is a pattern for all ship-masters, took me from before the mast, and by his watchfulness and fatherly advice directed my attention to more manly and useful pursuits; nor did he remit his guardian care until he saw me master of a ship.

Thus was I diverted from the path of indiscretion, which too often conducts to ruin, by the unsolicited friendship and benevolent feelings of an entire stranger, who long acted towards me the part of a parent and a tutor; labouring incessantly to supply the glaring defects of my education (or, more properly, my want of education), and to eradicate from my mind the seeds of folly, and plant in their stead the seeds of useful knowledge; and finally, putting me forward in the world as a man of business, and thus securing me an honourable rank among my fellow-citizens. Heaven grant that I may feel properly grateful for such inestimable favours.

On all the world's oceans there were probably no two people as disparate as the captain of the *Edward* and the future mutineer, but the material for the making of another Benjamin Morrell was not to be found in Samuel. Nathan may have sensed that but hoped.

On his return from Liverpool Samuel exchanged his sea clothing for the latest fashions, which did not meet with any more approval in the Quaker community than his sailor garb had—except for one segment of that community, the girls. In romantic affairs he was eminently successful. Or, as his brother put it, "I do not know that he was particularly susceptible of pure disinterested affection, but he possessed a superabundance of something which the fair sex seemed to consider a very agreeable substitute." One of the girls he targeted was a devout Methodist, a fact that produced an instant conversion in Samuel, who became a regular member of the girl's Methodist congregation, conspicuous for the loudness of his amens and hallelu-jahs. He was still, it may be noted, thirteen on his return from Liverpool.

Idle for some months, he diverted himself by climbing up to the eaves of a house and jumping into the tops of nearby trees and by running along the gutters of the building four stories above the ground. In lieu of work in the rigging, these stunts would have to do—and they had a gratifying effect on onlookers. But he was soon to be in the rigging again. This time parental permission must have been easier to obtain; Samuel had turned fourteen, and nothing is said of his return to school after the voyage of the *Edward*. Back to sea may have seemed the least of available evils.

This second ship of his was John Jacob Astor's *Beaver*, the largest ship that Samuel would ever serve on; it was 447 tons and 111 feet long. Built in 1805 by the distinguished shipbuilders Eckford and Beebe at the foot of Clinton Street on the East River, it was the ship that Astor had used to finesse a voyage to China during the time of the Embargo Act. When it sailed in June 1817, it is not likely that Samuel or any of the other hands on the ship knew that the declared destination of Canton was a cover for the delivery of $140,000 worth of munitions to the Chilean rebels who were fighting their eventually successful war of independence against the Spanish royalists. When the *Beaver* put in to Talcahuano harbor for water and supplies, the Spanish authorities stopped and searched the ship, condemned its cargo, and pressed the ship into service for voyages up and down the coast. For the crew the seizure of the ship meant time in the Talcahuano jail, five months according to William.

The officers of most American ships in Chilean and Peruvian coastal waters during the war of independence were so mentally pre-pared for seizures of their vessels that they could treat the events as business, but Samuel was infuriated. On days when he was given liberty from confinement and allowed into town, Samuel carried his indignation into the streets and insulted so many of the townspeople that he often ran back to his hospitable cell at full speed before a hail of stones.

Samuel probably could have returned to the *Beaver*, and indeed wanted to, for he had heard that the ship would go to Lima, which was one city he was anxious to see. Lima had a certain disreputable allure for foreign seamen. But he had to make a decision: Nathaniel Bunker, the *Beaver*'s mate, approached Samuel with news about the Nantucket whaler *George*, which had come into Talcahuano. Captain Fitch was taking on crew, and Bunker told Samuel that he was going to quit the *Beaver* and sign on the whaler. Would Samuel be interested? Despite all that he knew about whaling, Samuel had never served on a whaler. But his answer to Bunker was yes. The ship would carry him back to Nantucket, where relatives whom he had probably not seen for seven years would take him in; that was a plus, and the whole experience would be worth a try. And then there was the well-known responsiveness of Nantucket girls to young men who had lowered for a whale.

In fact, Samuel never lowered for a whale on the *George*, for the ship, according to its log, had taken its last whale about a month before it met the *Beaver* at Talcahuano in early May 1818. The *George*, when it reached Nantucket, had 2,106 barrels of sperm oil, all of which had been taken before meeting the *Beaver*.

Lowering or not, Samuel's stint on the *George* introduced him to life on a whaler. Now he was finally on one of those ships that he had known and studied at Straight Wharf on Nantucket. The experience had an effect on him that he was not ready for: he came to hate whaleships and their officers with an intensity that he never got over. That is what William reports, and there is evidence that Samuel meant what he told his brother, and no contradiction to it in the fact that he was to serve on two other whalers after the *George*. In a strange sense, the very choice of joining the other two whalers may have owed something to his hatred of them. They became just the right setting in which to heap more fuel on his rage, and he basked in that rage. However Samuel described his feelings to his brother, William was the right one to talk to, for William's contempt for whalemen and for Nantucket was as fervent as his brother's, as he makes abundantly clear in his story of his brother's life and in *A Voyage to the Pacific*.

It was a warm, pleasant summer when the *George* arrived back in Nantucket, paid out its lays, and discharged its crew. Samuel, who would be sixteen in the fall, received a cordial welcome from his great-aunt Eunice Mitchell and her daughters, his cousins Lydia and Maria, but there was a cloud over the reunion, for those good people were called upon to offer the returning seaman their condolences. On April 30, about two and a half months before he reached Nantucket, his mother had died in New York. His grief was deep and genuine, for—so it seemed to William—Samuel had been devoted to his mother. How long he stayed on Nantucket before returning to New York is unclear, but if what William tells us about that period is correct, it was long enough to fall in love.

In a more normal nature, Samuel's mourning or his love would not have been profound, but to borrow some Melville phrasing, to pass from a normal nature to Samuel, it is necessary to cross the deadly space between. It was "a little red-cheeked Nantucket girl." Did the courtship begin within weeks after learning of his mother's death or within days? Did Samuel tell her of his mother's death, and to what effect? And did the girl tell Samuel why her cheeks were red? It was not the glow of health, but the "hectic flush." She was, like Puccini's Mimi, radiant from that supreme nineteenth-century romantic enhancement, consumption. Yes, she died. Whatever one makes of the symmetry of a mother's and a sweetheart's death—we are listening to William tell the story—Samuel's part in it is in character. The unruffled maintenance of conflicting emotions was one of Samuel's gifts; it served him well—no, it served him ill—all his life.

Back in New York Samuel entered his fifth experiment in schooling, again under Quakers. It was apparently at the Henry Street School, for his teacher was Goold Brown, the former master at Nine Partners.

Enough is known about Goold Brown to suggest that Samuel was lucky to be one of his students. Brown, who had been teaching at Nine Partners when Samuel was first a student there, was a teacher with fresh perceptions and early in his career had been an assistant to the Quaker educator John Griscom. Griscom, a disciple of the progressive and influential Swiss educational theorist, Pestalozzi, advocated cultivation of the child's reason and imagination more than his powers of memorization. This emphasis put him at the opposite pole from the thinking of Lindley Murray, a Quaker, the son of Robert Murray of Murray Hill, and the author of *English Grammar* and *English Reader*; Murray, whose view of students' powers of rational thinking was considerably jaundiced, taught that memorization of rules was more important than an understanding of grammar. For two generations his books were among the most widely used and, for better or worse, formative school texts in America. Goold Brown described Murray's examples of parsing as "so verbose, awkward, irregular and deficient" that they were of no help to the students. Brown published his own *Institutes of English Grammar* in 1823, a few years after he had had Samuel Comstock as a student.

It may be that Samuel was exposed to the best teacher in the city and spared the baneful influence of the Murray tradition. And what followed from having the best schooling available? Maybe some benefit no one knows of. In any event all that has been handed down about the relations of Samuel and his teacher is an anecdote about their respective responses one day to a barrage of snowballs and shouts that some neighborhood boys directed at the school building,

disrupting classes. Master Goold opened the door and spoke to the
rowdies, who replied insolently; student Samuel rushed out the door,
laid into the crowd, and sent them scattering. For this support
Samuel was not rewarded; rather he was advised by Friend Goold
that what he had done was scandalous for its violence. Whatever
Samuel felt about the whole episode, William, who had as acid a view
of Quakers as he did of Nantucketers and whalemen, recorded an
emphatic reaction to it:

> Goold [believed] that if the assailants hit him with a snow ball on
> one cheek, it was his duty to turn and receive a patch of mud on
> the other. Such are the principles of the Quakers—but, unfortu-
> nately, the anger which they are forbidden to express by outward
> actions, finding no vent, stagnates in the heart, and, while they
> make professions of love and good will to their opponents, the ran-
> cour and intense malevolence of their feelings poison every gener-
> ous spring of human kindness. It is not theirs to unsheathe the
> sword or poise the lance, but they make use of their influence and
> false pretensions to respectability to ruin the reputation, standing,
> and hopes of those they hate—pursuing their adversaries even
> beyond the grave, and blasting widows and orphans, "in a quiet
> and sober manner." Notwithstanding their smooth professions,
> they are the most proud, aristocratic, selfish and spiteful people on
> the face of the earth.

And Samuel? How did he see the religious people who had been family, educators, and society to him from birth? The stereotype that
comes most readily to mind is that of the youth raised in devout circumstances who repudiates his religious faith and heritage and leads
a self-indulgent and vicious life. Oddly, that does not fit Samuel.
While he bridled at the stiff-necked ethos of some of the Quaker
community, there is no evidence that he shared the deep resentment

felt by his brother. Indeed, as we shall see, a strange vestige of faith lingered in Samuel down to the end.

In the fall of 1818 Samuel turned sixteen. A year would intervene between his return from Talcahuano in the *George* and his next voyage. This was the year of his attendance at Goold Brown's school on Henry Street. It was also the year of his visits to another address, about three blocks from his home. On Lombardy Street, opposite Mechanic Alley, a sign over a house door read euphemistically "James Jackson, Boarding and Lodging." Here Madame Jackson and her red-nosed pimp minded one of the city's best-known brothels, and here Samuel became a regular. How he met the cost is not clear, but a couple of years earlier he had discovered that judicious thefts from his father's store would bring in spare change.

The year went by, and Samuel told his father that he wanted to go to sea again. Make it a whaler, the father insisted—whalemen spend less time in port than other sailors and hence are less exposed to opportunities for dissipation, a rationalization that came from God knows where. It was a hopeless irony, which the poor father may have pondered, that the notable port city in which his son was living while at home presented more opportunities for dissipation than most of the foreign cities at which any ship he was serving on might touch.

CHAPTER TWO

PORT LIFE AND A
SINKING STAR

Father had his way: it was a whaleship. Samuel wrote to Captain Shubael Chase in Nantucket and was offered a berth on the 317-ton whaleship *Foster*, which would be going out on its first voyage. There was something out of character about Samuel's compliance with his father's wishes in the matter, and something equally out of character about Samuel's compliance with his father's advice to get a new coat to wear to Nantucket. It should be a Quaker coat, Nathan said, and Samuel bought one. He was signing up for work that he hated and wearing clothes that he hated. He could overlook his clothes and even his work—other things claimed his attention.

The *Foster*, which sailed from Nantucket July 22, 1819, was to be out for thirty-three months. This was the only whaling voyage that Samuel sailed on from beginning to end. He was sixteen when he left port and nineteen when he returned. Three years is a long time; in the confinement of the ship and in the company of men he was contemptuous of, it was a very long time. Swirling around Samuel and incubating inside him while the *Foster* sailed for whales was a complex of bloody fantasies and anarchic strategies, some of which he talked about on his return home.

Even before he said anything, however, his family was shocked by his appearance. "His face and neck [were] nearly as black as an indian's," William writes, "while there was nothing left in his eyes of the frank and open expression that characterized them. There was a deep, subtle, and mysterious expression about them, which I thought very repulsive. His sister noticed the change, and remarked to me that he had 'a *bad* look'. His manner, however, was not like his appearance. There seemed to be no shyness or reserve, no feeling of conscious guilt in his soul. He was as cordial, bold, and reckless as ever; and seemed to feel himself perfectly at home." William was surprised that he did.

Eight months passed between the *Foster*'s return and the *Globe*'s sailing. During most of that time William, who was preparing to go to sea for the first time himself, talked more frankly and deeply with Samuel than ever before. Tales from the days on the *Foster* were part of the talk, but part of it was a cluster of dark thoughts that Samuel took out of wraps in front of William, confident that he had the right audience.

Samuel knew when he was being understood, but the communication had to flow both ways between him and William. Encouraged by a brother whom he knew to be a wit, a cynic, and sometimes, surprisingly, a philosopher—that much is clear to a reader of William—Samuel spoke freely, for Samuel himself had the wit of a raconteur, as people who enjoyed his company had remarked several times, and had as well a perverse profundity. One of the brothers was hysterically fixated and the other passionately curious, and they formed each other's thinking. Therefore, the one who lived to put the story on paper was part of the story himself. Apart from a long account of one episode, the picture of Samuel on the *Foster* comes in a few short flashes that light up his psychic landscape like lightning in a storm.

One of the lightning flashes: among the crewmen of the *Foster* were two boys, John Cotton and John Lincoln, whom Samuel came to like; they seemed to be a cut above the gross types that he expected to encounter on a whaleship. As his friendship with them grew, Samuel felt free to spring a disturbing proposal on them: he liked the captain, but he did not like the mate—he thought the mate should be flogged. Would his two friends join him in laying on the stripes? From a practical point of view the idea was outlandish. What did he expect the captain to do? What did he expect the other officers and, for that matter, the crew to do? Naturally Samuel's two friends did not support the idea, so he dropped the plan, probably without recognizing the shock he had produced in the boys. Samuel was always blithe about his outrages. There were gaps in his sense of consequences. William could have, and may have, told him that even in imagining the flogging, he was treating as a mere personal grievance something that in fact was mutiny.

Another flash, which raises a question: Samuel was frequently seen on deck in rain storms without a jacket, walking about and talking to himself. Where did that come from? Samuel told William that? Maybe he did.

By stages he told William something that overshadowed everything else. For a long time he had been contemplating what it would be like to live for the rest of his life as the only white man among the natives of a Pacific island. He was sure that he would quickly be elected king. Once in power he would make the island a pirate kingdom, launching a native navy that would capture every vessel in sight. His exploits would turn him into a fable; he would gain immortality as the terror of the South Seas. He even, at one point in the voyage of the *Foster,* tried to get started on establishing his kingdom. Resourceless as he was—and what difference did that make?— he asked Captain Chase to put him ashore at Easter Island. Samuel would take it from there. The captain naturally refused, assuming, no doubt, that he was saying no to a discharge request, while in fact he was saying no to a delusion.

Soon Samuel was speaking to William more to the point about his obsessions. That desert island—he knew how he would become its monarch. He would sail for the Pacific, kill the captain and officers of his ship, take it over, land at an island inhabited by savages, murder the rest of the crew, become the king of the natives, and turn them into his army. William, who for once was not the perfect audience, discounted Samuel's fantastic schemes. His brother was capable of much, but there were limits.

Samuel, the student of *Don Quixote*, was even capable of the picaresque. In the longest single episode in his account of his brother's doings, William follows Samuel through a night and a day in Valparaíso during the *Foster*'s stop there. The account ends with an ominous link to events that would later unfold on the *Globe*, about which Samuel, ironically, could have known nothing at the time he was telling the story to William. The account stands as light relief and can be discarded only with the same consequences as discarding the drunken porter scene in *Macbeth*. This may be one of the moments when William is dancing like Hippoclides, but Samuel, like William, was an engaging storyteller, and if there is historical enhancement in the telling, it may be Samuel's work.

The *Foster*'s visit to Valparaíso put it in one of the most important and interesting ports in the Pacific. The city had a sizable English-speaking community, an American consul, and frequent *entradas* and *salidas* of American whalers and merchant ships. It also had sections celebrated among seamen for the ready availability of the most popular of pleasures.

Samuel's time ashore began with a visit to a neighborhood of shady renown, which was reached by climbing a long hill called, presumably only by visiting sailors, Main Top. Partway up the hill Samuel met one of the well-known denizens of the area. Her name was Chicochee; she was four feet tall, dressed in her finest, and carrying a guitar. She was then at the peak of her popularity, although later reports made her out to be an object of some derision on the part of sailors, who had named her Jack O'Clubs. The small figure hailed Samuel, "Halloo Jack! where are you going?"

"You don't call yourself a woman, do you?" he replied.

"Come to my house and see."

"If your house is built in proportion to the size of its tenant, I shall not be able to get into it."

"Oh, yes, I see you, how 'tis, very well. You go up the hill to see Indian Queen. All the damn Yankee go to Indian Queen. Come, John, go home with me."

That was all Samuel needed to know. He started up the hill again. Chicochee called out, gestured threateningly, and pulled a knife out of her bosom but did not follow him. At the top of the hill Samuel inquired about the Indian Queen and quickly found her house.

Entering the house he was confronted by an array of elegant furnishings in derelict condition: a shelf of fine wine glasses with their bases broken off, a decanter missing its neck, rare-looking chairs too fragile to sit on, a picture of the Virgin Mary missing one eye, and a broken mirror with only a fragment of glass left.

The only occupant of the room, a rough-looking black man seated in a corner, bowed but said nothing. Soon a girl entered. She struck Samuel as having a bearing lighter and more graceful than that of any Spanish girl he had seen. There was mildness in her eyes; her lashes were long, and her complexion browner than was usual in Chile. She asked Samuel to be seated. From her attitude toward the negro it became clear that he was her father. He was a soldier of Bolívar's, he said, who had obtained a leave to visit his daughter. They talked about Bolívar and other things until a rustling sound outside threw a hush over the room. To Samuel it sounded like wind brushing the side of the house, but the Indian Queen suddenly grew tense and stared at the door. As it opened, the three people in the room saw a pair of flaming black eyes against the dark night. The Indian Queen sprang to her feet, drew her knife, and plunged at the small figure, who also had a drawn knife, as she threw herself through the doorway. It was Chicochee.

The two women fought like wild cats. While Samuel made an effort to stop them, the black man restrained him—it was against the rules to interfere. But as soon as blood was drawn, the father of the taller combatant declared the battle settled. Although neither of the women would have abided by his call, and the fight probably would have ended fatally, Samuel and the other man were able to separate the two. Soldiers had gathered outside in response to the uproar, something, the black man indicated, that would mean jail for all four of them, not just the two women. With that said, he kicked a hole in the thin wall of the house and told Samuel to follow him out the new back door.

Samuel did follow and froze when he got through the wall: they were standing at the edge of a high cliff. One false step would send them falling through the darkness. Inside the house, the soldiers were struggling to control the two women, who kept fighting, scratching, and screaming. As the arms of the law led them out of the house, leaving it empty, Samuel suggested to his companion that it was now safe to crawl back in. The other neither moved nor answered; he was glaring darkly at the young sailor and seemed to be weighing something in his mind. As Samuel backed up against the wall of the house, the black man drew a long knife and asked him for his money. At this point the would-be robber had his back to the cliff edge. Samuel groped in his pockets, pretending to look for money, and then suddenly threw all of his weight against the man with the knife, who fell backward off the cliff, letting out a scream that pierced the night. Samuel heard a loud crash below and then only silence.

Samuel's impulse was to head for his ship as fast as possible. He descended into town past glowering members of the watch posted at intervals along the hill road. Once he reached the waterfront he was less anxious, sufficiently less anxious in fact to head for a still-open dive that caught his eye. It was called "Hit or Miss," and inside it the crewmen of a newly arrived English brig were carousing. Although a little cool to the newcomer at first, they soon yielded to Samuel's easy manner and made him part of their group. If he would stay the night, they told him, they would take him off to his ship in the morning. As the drink flowed, their tales came out; they had been smugglers and pirates and loved the vicious side of life at sea. Samuel found everything about them congenial; they were kindred spirits.

One of these men, John Oliver, became particularly friendly to Samuel and took him aside to ask him what he was doing and what he planned to do. Samuel told him the main thing that he had just done—killed a man. Oliver was intrigued; he listened with great interest to the whole story of the women and the police raid and the cliffside assault, then made a nervy suggestion: let's take a stroll over to the calaboose to see what we can find out about the two women who were arrested. Samuel was as nervy, and despite the evident folly of going near the one place in town that he should stay away from, he agreed. It may have been the drink, but it was also the Comstock character plain and simple. Folly was a magnet to him.

The two men actually got past sentries, who were probably asleep, and entered the prison yard, but there they were discovered. Oliver broke into a run and made it out through the gate, but several soldiers seized Samuel and brought him into the guard room, where a clownish scene ensued involving the lieutenant of the guard, the jailer, and a bunch of half-asleep soldiers. It may or may not have had something to do with Samuel, the new prisoner, but Comstock was unable to interpret the loud exchanges, laughter, and wild gesticulations. It ended with the jailer beckoning Samuel to follow him.

They passed through a square room with an earthen floor, on which two women were asleep. Both leapt up when the jailer's lantern lit the room; they were Chicochee and the Indian Queen. The jailer was leading Samuel to a door on the far side of the room, but the Indian Queen ran to them and begged the jailer to return Samuel to the guard room. He would be killed, she said, if he was put in with the convicts. The jailer merely laughed and crossed to the double doors leading to the inner prison, unlocked them, and gave his prisoner a glimpse of one of the most squalid sights he had ever seen: amid the vermin and heaps of filth, approximately fifty rag-clad wretches were stretched out on the bare ground; the stench was overpowering. It took Samuel an instant to make up his mind; he sprang past the jailer and ran for the guard room, but the jailer's yell was heard, and Samuel found himself encircled by bayonets in the outer room.

He was led into the loathsome inner room, where the convicts, who had heard the disturbance of his attempted escape, got to their feet to see who the new guest was—that is, all except one dark figure in the corner of the cell who looked more like a pile of rags than a person. Samuel's membership in the prison fraternity was celebrated by a barrage of insults from several of his fellow members until one prisoner with some evident authority silenced them. Eventually Samuel fell asleep, but toward morning he was awakened by someone stepping on his foot. He awoke to see an upraised knife poised over his chest; his sudden awakening and moving were enough to make the assailant retreat. Where he retreated to was the corner he had been crouched in when Samuel was brought into the cell; he was the pile of rags, and in the dim light of the one candle that lit the whole room, his face could hardly have been made out even if he had not been trying to conceal it. Samuel did not sleep anymore that night.

In the morning the convicts, except for the newcomer, were led out to work; even at this point the pile of rags kept his face covered. Alone in the cell, he found that he could talk through the door to Chicochee and the Indian Queen in the adjoining room. The latter was able to tell Samuel who his would-be assailant was: "Have you forgot him so soon? That is my father." Obviously some explaining was needed. Her father, the Indian Queen said, was in prison on a charge of breaking and entering, in a rather singular fashion. A certain Señor Phillippi, whose house was at the base of the cliff on which the Indian Queen's house stood, complained that in the night the negro had made his way into his house by crashing through the roof. When the guard came to arrest him, the housebreaker told them that two Yankees had robbed him and thrown him off the cliff—he even showed them his bruises from the fall—but this was obviously too fantastic a story for the forces of the law to accept, for, among other things, the arrested man was found to be a deserter from the army and therefore not to be believed about anything.

For Bundle of Rags the unexpected appearance in the same jail cell of the troublesome Yankee who had started this whole misadventure was too good an opportunity for revenge; he would stay concealed, which was why he did not get up with the others when Comstock was brought into the cell, and wait for the right moment to strike.

The through-the-door conversation with Chicochee and the Indian Queen had explained most of what Samuel wanted to know. Was her father ashamed of having tried to rob him? Samuel asked the Indian Queen. Chicochee interrupted, "All men rob in this place. When rich folks rob, they don't make any noise about it; but when poor folks rob they put them in the calibouse." The rich man's technique is extortionate pricing, she explained. At which point the guard appeared and informed Samuel that he was at liberty, and "our hero" bade the ladies adieu and returned to his ship.

Time's sleight of hand, which can deal coincidences sparingly or lavishly, dealt a big one that night in Valparaíso: John Oliver, the seaman whom Samuel Comstock met in the "Hit or Miss" and found so congenial that he fell in with his dangerous lark of visiting the prison, had a bigger role to play in Comstock's life than either would have guessed as they drank and talked, and a bigger role than Samuel could have foreseen as he was telling the story to William. Three years later Oliver would resurface as a crew member of the *Globe* recruited out of the blue in mid-cruise. This time he and Samuel Comstock would be involved in more than pub crawls and pranks. This time their companionship would be fatal.

Another coincidence that, unknown to anyone, cast a shadow occurred December 21 and 25, 1820, when the *Foster* spoke the *Globe* at 4°50' S/105°40' W. No one knew that the *Globe* would be Samuel's next ship, and that its mate, Thomas Worth, would be Samuel's next captain.

The *Foster* returned April 12, 1822, with 1,624 barrels of sperm oil, which it discharged in Edgartown, not Nantucket; sand buildup in the Nantucket harbor often led full ships to use Martha's Vineyard instead. Samuel crossed over from the Vineyard to his native island and in his usual blunt and unceremonious fashion turned his attention to the girls. For the first time without lying he could boast to the exacting Nantucket lasses that he had struck a whale; that guaranteed his eligibility. The first was a Methodist girl, whom he pursued as he had his earlier Methodist love, but this time he laid on the piety so heavily that some speculated he was going to enter the ministry. "The people of God I do admire," and "I hope my sins are washed away," he intoned. The Methodist girl and her family considered that Samuel had made a commitment to her. It was no threat to this attachment, indeed it was perfectly understandable to all involved, that he should leave Nantucket to visit his family, who were anxiously expecting him in New York. It would be just for a while. He sailed from Nantucket in a packet. On board was a pretty English girl. Before they arrived in New York, Samuel had proposed to her.

Back home Samuel surprised his family not only by his disturbing appearance but also by some good news: he was finished permanently with whaling and the sea. He would work for his father in the whale products business. The family felt better about Samuel after that announcement, and his father was especially happy to have him in the store at that time, for Nathan was moving the business from 242 to 191 Front Street; Samuel could superintend the move. He would also be a replacement for William, who had been working in the store but was now preparing to go to sea for the first time.

Samuel as store clerk was not going to be a success. The job's chief reward was the "brisk mulatto girl" whom Samuel found whitewashing the wall of the counting room. He sent her down to the basement for a pitcher of water and followed her there. After an unduly long stay, the two came up; the brisk girl took William aside and whispered in his ear, your brother is a real devil.

Samuel's real business these days was not the store but girls and fantasies. The fantasies were the desert kingdom schemes that he had been talking about with William; the girls were legion. To the Nantucket girl whose family anticipated a marriage, Samuel sent a letter explaining that his decision to leave whaling for good would make it "inconvenient" for him to marry her. Meanwhile he took his English fiancée to various entertainments and tried to relieve her dissatisfaction over the continual postponement of their wedding (claiming that he had to overcome objections from his father); he also glibly reassured her of his innocence—he played naive—when she caught him on the street with a woman of doubtful reputation.

Predictably, he tired of the life of a store clerk. He could not even pretend: life in business was insupportable. He had begun to think more and more about the navy; whalers he hated, but there was romance in the navy, especially in naval battles and deeds of daring. The navy, of course, was no place to carry out his scheme to kill his officers and find an island for his desert kingdom, but his imagination had room for more than one design, provided that they were exciting. He was filled with admiration for Lieutenant Commandant William Burrows, captain of the *Enterprise*, who in 1813 gave American morale a great boost by defeating the British brig *Boxer* in a celebrated battle off Portland, Maine, but who died of injuries incurred in the battle. He was buried ashore next to Captain Blythe of the British ship, who also died in the battle, a detail that heightened the romance of popular versions of the story. Burrows, who was twenty-eight when he died, was exactly Samuel's kind of hero. Samuel adopted "B.," for Burrows, as his middle initial.

Fortuitously, as 1822 wore on and Samuel's loathing for the oil and candle business grew, a navy ship tied up at a wharf not far from the store. The vessel, described by William as a "Patriot frigate" but not further identified, was probably one of the many ships sold in New York during the 1820s to the navies of Nueva Granada (later Colombia), Venezuela, Ecuador, or one of the other emerging Latin American nations. Whether it was a frigate in strict rating by the number of guns it carried or whether it was a warship loosely called frigate, it was an awesome vessel to Samuel. He hung around it and struck up an acquaintance with the officers, who finally offered him a position on the ship. This was almost too good to be true. Would his father agree to his leaving the store and returning to the sea? Father agreed. Samuel, who had already done some serious reading about things a ship's officer should know, like medicine and surgery, now threw himself into the study of navigation and tactics. And almost certainly Spanish—he would have had to acquire at least the shipboard language in Spanish, and he could have, for he was a fast independent learner. His dream was coming true.

But it did not come true. Some of Nathan Comstock's acquaintances, whom William describes as "miserable quaker bigots," denounced the father for allowing his son to serve on a ship of war. The pressure succeeded, and Nathan withdrew his permission; he would not approve of his son joining the navy and he would not put up a penny toward the purchase of the necessary outfits that Samuel would have to buy before joining the ship. Furthermore, he laid down the law about Samuel's finding a position in business if he wanted to stay in his father's good graces at all.

In retrospect things seem so clear. If Samuel had been allowed to join the navy, all his prodigious drive toward action, all his fearlessness, and all his resourcefulness would have been given full play but within a discipline. His impulses, which were waiting to be used rationally or irrationally, would have been civilized. The "bad look" would be replaced by the clear and frank appearance that his family remembered. In the movies maybe.

What Samuel did do in the wake of his crushing disappointment was an explosive act of rage, the targets of which were everything and everyone, himself included. The bitterest thing he could do to the world that had just denied him his keenest wish was a self-destructive act: he would go whaling again. This was one of those moments when father and son were planetary distances apart. Nathan was relieved, even cheered, to hear that his son would sign on a whaler. It was at this point that Nathan promised Samuel that if he would go to the Pacific Ocean "and conduct himself well," he would buy a ship on his son's return and give him command of it. Conduct himself well? Samuel was like an iron pot with noxious contents that should never be stirred up; now in the steam of rage over being denied the chance to sail on a naval vessel, he could not have even grasped the concept of conducting himself well.

William, who was already at sea on his first whaler when Samuel chose to return to whaling, was appalled when he learned what his brother had done. "At that moment," he wrote, "the star of Samuel Comstock sunk in blackness forever!" At the time William wrote that, he had seen Samuel's story played out to the end, but he did not need the wisdom of retrospect; his premonitions were accurate.

Immediately after his announcement, Samuel left for Nantucket to find a ship. He was in a desperate state of mind and would probably have taken the first ship he came upon. The *Globe* was there; it would do. The business was quickly concluded. He was offered, on the basis of his experience, a boatsteerer's berth; he would be a ship's officer, immediately below the third mate.

He returned at once to New York to prepare for the voyage. He packed a chest with items that would have made no sense to an ordinary seaman—pistols, daggers, swords, powder and ball, a case of surgical instruments, a medicine chest, and garden seeds—but that were provisions for the kingdom-to-be. The garden seeds were for the introduction of agriculture on the chosen island.

Whether the family observed any of this packing or not, they seemed insensitive to the real state of Samuel's mind. Nathan Comstock even yielded to the pleas of fourteen-year-old George, who for some time had been begging to go to sea, and decided that this was the right time to let the boy begin his whaling career. Young George in the family's view would have the protection of an older brother. The ironies are poignant. Describing the climax of the mutiny a little over a year later, George calls Samuel "a brother in flesh but not in heart for if he had been he would have put away this wicked design thinking it would ruin me forever for little did he think I would ever get home to tell the fatal news."

CHAPTER THREE

I HAVE THE
BLOODY HAND

Shortly after Samuel and George had taken their final departure from New York, a singular circumstance occurred. The family had been induced to leave the house in the city and retire to Greenwich, on account of the yellow fever, where they remained until late in the fall. Before moving back to town, two maids were sent to get the house ready for their reception. While the two girls were at work in a front chamber, a seabird flew in at an open window, and continued his course until he reached the partition at the back part of the room. When he wheeled, flew back to the window and went off, leaving two distinct streaks of blood on the ceiling, extending the whole length of the room. When our hero's father mentioned the fact to a visitor, the latter replied, "If thou wert inclined to superstition, thou would be likely to imagine that was some omen relating to thy two sons who are about going to sea in the ship Globe."
—WILLIAM COMSTOCK, *The Terrible Whaleman*

The 293-ton *Globe* was a "lucky" ship, the term was currency for a whaleship that came back full of oil from a relatively short cruise without adverse incidents. It was built in 1815. On its first voyage, which lasted a bit over two years and two months, it set a record as the first whaleship to return more than two thousand barrels of oil. Its second voyage, in 1818, when it discovered the whale-rich "Off-Shore Ground" west of northern Peru, and its third, in 1820, were just as successful. On all three of these voyages the captain was George Washington Gardner, a respected whaleman who could doubtless have retained command of the *Globe* for its fourth voyage but was offered a new and larger ship, the *Maria*, which was under construction and nearly finished in shipyards at Higganum on the Connecticut River. In the middle of July 1822, a couple of months after returning from the *Globe*'s third voyage, Captain Gardner loaded the ship with gear that would be needed on the *Maria* and turned it for the moment into a transport for a week's trip to Higganum. The *Globe* had begun to look somewhat "rough," as one of its seamen noted. With no main topmast up, it even looked like a ship in distress as it moved along the Connecticut coast; a passing ship hailed it and asked if it needed assistance.

But this was July, and the next sailing would not be until December; there was enough time for refitting back in Nantucket. That work was going on when Samuel Comstock dropped in to sign on as a boatsteerer before going back to New York to organize himself for the voyage. When he returned to Nantucket, he had fourteen-year-old George in tow.

During these days before sailing, Samuel paid several visits to a Nantucket widow, Mrs. Plum, with whom he enjoyed talking. There was something about her that made her a good confidante. Last evening, he told her on one of these occasions, he had been walking up Main Street "thinking on certain subjects." Suddenly he was so overcome by emotion that he had to sit down on the steps of a house. A woman who knew him came by and asked what was the matter. Nothing much, just a little faintness, he replied. Nonetheless she stayed with him and walked him to his boarding house. On another occasion Mrs. Plum asked Samuel about the surgical instruments he was carrying. What were they for? To have at hand in case they were needed, he replied. Would he be up to the job of cutting off a man's leg? she asked. Yes, he answered, "or his head either." I've heard young men talk before, she said. They love to be extravagant; you're just like the rest of them.

When the time came to sail, the *Globe* crossed over from Nantucket to Edgartown on Martha's Vineyard to take on provisions.

The Vineyard was a congenial place to sail from since it was home to about half the *Globe*'s company. Captain Thomas Worth, at age twenty-nine the oldest man on the ship, was a Vineyarder. He had been first mate under Captain Gardner on the *Globe*'s previous voyage. William Beetle, the first mate, was a Vineyarder, as were Second Mate John Lumbert (in some records Lumbard, Lambert, or Lombard), Third Mate Nathaniel Fisher, and one of the boatsteerers, Gilbert Smith. Six of the seamen were from the Vineyard: Stephen Kidder, his brother Peter Kidder, Columbus Worth (first cousin of Captain Worth), Rowland Jones, John Cleveland, and Constant Lewis.

From the manifest in Appendix A it is evident that half of the crew were teenagers, not an unusual figure on a whaler of the time but one that nonetheless became a circumstance of the mutiny. The question, why did the crew stand for the takeover of the ship, is easy to ask, and was asked, but it can only be answered existentially. The average age of all on board the ship at the time of sailing, officers included, was around twenty. No picture of the mutiny captures the reality of events unless it shows boys' faces. Boys are ready for hardship and hazard if the hardship and hazard come with precedents and rationales, but even adult experience is not preparation enough for outlandish and irrational evil. And none of these boys, none of the original crew except Samuel Comstock himself, was going to join in the violence of the mutiny, although one, Rowland Coffin, was suspected of prior awareness of Comstock's plans and of questionable chumminess with the mutineers after the takeover of the ship. All the actual mutineers around Comstock were later recruits to the ship.

Two of the crewmen who were going to sea for the first time, William Lay and Cyrus Hussey, would leave their names prominently on the *Globe* story; their book, *Narrative of the Mutiny, on Board the Ship Globe, of Nantucket,* which was written with the help of another hand, was to become the most popular account of the mutiny and its aftermath. Halfway through the story, Lay and Hussey have the stage all to themselves—they become the story.

During the time that the ship was being provisioned in Edgartown, Samuel had a chance to socialize with some of the Vineyarders, to all of whom he came across as convivial, witty, and likable. Captain Worth was watching him approvingly. From the start the captain, who seemed to combine an educated intelligence with a capacity for heavy-handed shipboard discipline, saw Samuel as his kind of seaman. Samuel realized this and knew how to play to it. Indeed, in the days spent waiting to sail, he played to everyone including the captain's bride of six months, who was easily amused by Samuel's conversation. So perfectly did he adapt his manner to the various Vineyarders that when the story of the mutiny broke on the island, part of the shock came from the naming of Samuel, the last member of the crew that any of them would have suspected of such an enormity.

The *Globe* sailed on December 20, 1822, weathered a severe two-day storm, passed the Cape Verde Islands by January 9, and on the seventeenth crossed the equator. Then whaling began: on the twenty-ninth, lookouts sighted whales, boats were lowered, there was a chase and a kill, the try-pots were stoked, and the *Globe* sailed on, seventy-five barrels richer.

Samuel's hatred of the ship and the shipboard work was intense. He cursed his luck at not getting to join the navy ship his heart had been set on. He cursed the whale oil, which, he said, irritated his skin and gave him boils. At the same time he was one of the best hands on the ship; he jumped to commands and was intolerant of anyone who was not as lively. When he found greenhands asleep on the deck during their watches, he splashed cold water on them. This made him sufficiently hated by some of them, but he was indifferent to the hostility of his victims and he watched with calculated pleasure as his credit with the captain grew.

It was clear to everyone on board that Samuel had moved into a favored position with the captain. In a hearing before the American consul in Valparaíso, one of the crewmen, Stephen Kidder, was asked if there had been any sign of mutiny on board the ship between its departure from the United States and its second departure from Hawaii. "No," he replied, "Constant Lewis was once put in irons for differing with Comstock the Boat Steerer and let out next day and the Captain struck the Cook another time on account of Comstock also." Other accounts have it that the cook was punished for being drunk, but punishment for that may well have been at Comstock's behest. Comstock was the captain's man; "differing with Comstock" meant trouble.

The *Globe* passed the Falkland Islands on February 23 and on March 1, four days before it rounded Cape Horn, spoke the New Bedford whaler *Lyra*, Captain Reuben Joy, which had been out seventy-two days, one day longer than the *Globe*. No other ship was going to share the *Globe's* story as the *Lyra* was. It was not merely that the *Globe's* and the *Lyra's* captains were extremely companionable—when they met some months later off the Japan Ground, they agreed to sail in company, a familiar practice in whaling that entailed hunting together and dividing the luck and the oil—but it was the third meeting of the two ships that wrote the *Lyra* permanently into the *Globe* story. Captain Joy was on board the *Globe* socializing with Captain Worth just hours before the mutiny erupted; the *Lyra* was so close to the *Globe* that if the mutiny had taken place during daylight hours, it might have been possible for the *Lyra* to get some sense of what was happening on board its partner.

The *Globe* cleared Cape Horn on March 5 and moved north with remarkably bad luck, coming in sight of whales only once on the way to Hawaii. The lack of sightings was remarkable and ironic, for its route was through the Off-Shore Ground (5° to 10° south and 105° to 125° west, between northern Peru and the Marquesas), which not only was one of the richest whaling grounds in the world but also in a sense was the *Globe*'s property. When Captain Gardner, on the *Globe*'s second voyage in 1818 discovered it, it was teeming with whales. Gardner gave the ground its name, and in two years word of it had circulated like a bulletin through the whaling community, bringing ships galore to the area. Thomas Worth, as first mate on the *Globe*'s third voyage, saw the merits of the area when the ship worked it intensely and successfully for eight months before leaving it abruptly for the Japan Ground, which had been discovered about a year after the Off-Shore Ground, and where it was equally successful. But now that Worth was the *Globe*'s captain, the whales were boycotting the ship.

On May 1 the *Globe* was off the big island of Hawaii near "Karakakoon" (Kealakekua), where, George Comstock noted, Captain Cook had been killed. Hawaii would soon be a major stop for replenishing provisions and crews, but it was only four years before the arrival of the *Globe* that the first American whalers had stopped there. The day was calm and the ship stood off about ten miles from shore under light sail. Late in the afternoon the masthead watch called out black fish off the lee bow. As the black fish drew nearer, they turned into canoes, which at nightfall came up to the ship with loads of potatoes, sugar cane, yams, coconuts, bananas, and fish. The *Globe* bought these provisions with the Pacific trader's coin of the realm, iron hoops. The whaleship had come prepared to do business: it is hard to exaggerate the value that natives of Oceania put on iron—it was like gold. Natives possessing pieces of iron slept with it under their heads. Around 1730, one of them said to a missionary, "Our yearning for iron is as strong as your longing for heaven."

The *Globe* went on to Oahu, where it was in port less than twenty-four hours before heading for Japan. It sailed for the first two days in company with the *Palladium* of Boston and the *Pocahontas* of Falmouth, both of which had been out a year more than the *Globe* and both of which were to return with two thousand barrels each. A tally like that would have improved morale on the *Globe*, and morale was beginning to need improving, first because the six hundred barrels that the *Globe* took on the Japan Ground were not enough for the time spent, and second because of complaints about the food.

Bad luck with whales weighs on the minds of the crew: it means a long cruise, which means a long time away from home and a long time away from pay. On the Japan Ground the *Globe* met five Nantucket ships, the *Sea Lion*, the *George Porter*, the *Enterprise*, the *Paragon*, and the *Phoenix*, all of which were doing well and were going to return with between fifteen and twenty-five hundred barrels.

The problem with the food began five days after the ship left Oahu for the Japan Ground. The amount of meat served the crew was very irregular, sometimes twice as much as they needed, sometimes half what they needed. The fault lay not with the captain, who wanted the crew to have the standard ration of three barrels of meat a month, but with the steward, who made an unequal division. Those in the crew who were inclined to grumble, however, blamed the captain, not the steward. The grumbling lasted until the ship was back in Hawaii in late 1823, and abundant provisions were taken on board. A more enduring complaint that lasted all through the voyage, however, was that regardless of the quality and quantity of the food, the crew was not given enough time to eat. That complaint peaked right before the mutiny.

While still on the Japan Ground the *Globe* had a gam with the 413-ton *Enterprise*, on the deck of which something happened that was insignificant at the time but would come to life again during the mutiny and add one more bit of viciousness to the tragedy. A party from the *Globe*, including Third Mate Fisher and Boatsteerer Comstock, had gone on board the *Enterprise*. In a playful mood, which the spirit of the occasion encouraged, Samuel approached Fisher and challenged him to a wrestling match. Fisher was the more athletic of the two and had no difficulty winning the match. Samuel was enraged and punched Fisher, who easily went after him again and laid him on the deck. "I'll see your heart's blood for this," Samuel said, but Fisher paid no attention to the threat, something that enraged Samuel even more. The humiliation never abated in Samuel's mind.

By October 1823 the *Globe* had abandoned the Japan Ground and returned to Oahu. From there Second Mate John Lumbert wrote a letter home; it is the only surviving document written in the course of the voyage. Its poignancy is great, for Lumbert would be dead in less than three months.

WAHOO SHIP GLOBE
[]EMBER THE 8 1823

Most [ ] and affectionate parents it with the grate ist pleasure that i have an oppertunity to inform you of my health which is good at presant and ihoap these few lines will find you health and sperits with all thay comforts of life which is all that we can wish for i hear that the barclay has gone home and if Thomas is thare [ ] [ ] to write me thomas haden has gone likewise i should wright to them boath but i exspet that thay will both begon before this get thare all tho the pay is small to beat round cape horn whare whales are wild and scatered and oil 40 cents per galon allto ouer luck small we are about aleven months out 600 barels i [think] that i have dun [m]y part it is along time since i herd or seen enny of you which makes me ankcious to hear from you tell sephronia July that thay must write to me and all the rest of you i am in north pasifick ocean along distance from home but our ship goes well and we have [ ] that will make her [walk] Capt worth is afine man and mr. beetel is afine man and I amiswell contented as ever I was in my life pleas to give my best respects grandmother and nancy and all thay rest [ ] too and to [parneal] and all his famaly [ ] and so i must remain your dutifull son

John Lumbert

It was in Honolulu that the *Globe* experienced its first desertions. Six men left the ship without authorization and one, John Cleveland, was discharged. The deserters were Holden Henman, Jeremiah Ingham, Daniel Cook, Paul Jarrett, Constant Lewis, and John Ignatius Braz; the last named appeared in records as Prass or Pray, impossible names for the Azorean boy and probably corruptions of the common Portuguese name, Braz. It is notable that with the exception of Braz none of the deserters was from Nantucket. Two of the runaways were caught and put in irons, probably in the prison of the fort that stood on the water's edge at the end of present-day Fort Street, in sight of the anchored ships. One of the two had slender enough hands to slip out of the manacles; he released the other, and both escaped.

Captain Worth needed replacements for the crew members lost, and as all captains knew, recruiting in foreign ports was a lottery. There was no way around it, though, if the ship was short of hands. The risk of getting riff-raff or worse was always greater when the pick had to be made from beachcombers and deserters from other ships, some of them supplied by harbor crimps, a Dickensianly seedy form of lowlife. There were foreign recruits, including island natives going to sea for the first time, who were not disreputable and proved to be good seamen, but the shrewdest captain could never be sure what he had signed on until the cruise was under way.

One of the *Globe*'s Hawaiian recruits—small world, much too small a world—was John Oliver, the same who had been the companion of Samuel Comstock in their colorful adventures in Valparaíso three years before. Comstock and Oliver renewed the bond they had formed at the "Hit or Miss," and admitted to their close society three other Hawaiian recruits, Silas Payne, William Humphreys, and Thomas Lilliston. Oliver was from Shields, England; Payne, from Sag Harbor; Humphreys, a black man, from Philadelphia or New Jersey; and Lilliston, from Virginia. Also signed on in Honolulu were Anthony Hanson, Joseph Brown, and Joseph Thomas. Hanson is described as an Indian and is in various sources said to be from Barnstable or Falmouth. Brown, from the islands, is not even named in the main sources but is recorded merely as "the native," or, as George Comstock calls him, a Woahoo [Oahu] Indian—*Indian* at the time was a common term for a Pacific islander. Neither Hanson nor Brown participated in the mutiny.

Thomas is the most curious figure among the new recruits. None of the main sources of the mutiny story—neither George nor William Comstock nor Lay and Hussey—include Thomas in their lists of the Honolulu replacements, an omission made more notable by the fact that in the wake of the crimes on board the *Globe* Thomas was suspected of some association with the mutineers and, in fact, was the only man prosecuted for involvement in the mutiny. He was acquitted when tried, but remains an ambiguous figure.

Did bad treatment by Captain Worth cause the desertions in Hawaii? The severity or fairness of captains in handling their men is an issue that has come up repeatedly in stories of whaleships with fractious crews and frequent desertions, and in most cases judging the captain is not easy. Was Herman Melville's desertion from the *Acushnet* in 1842, which gave him the material for his first novel, the result of bad treatment by Captain Valentine Pease or was it a lark? Desertions took place on well-run ships, and seamen stayed with badly run ones. The fact that six of the *Globe* crew deserted all at once on arriving in port suggests that the grumblers had been talking their complaints out and building up each other's resolve to make the break. Six months of unsatisfactory food and hardly enough time to eat it could have done the trick.

While glimpses of Captain Worth's treatment of his men are inconclusive, he was spoken of more favorably than not by the non-mutineers and, of course, was spoken of with the highest praise back on Nantucket. It counts for something that Second Mate Lumbert characterized the captain in his letter home as "a fine man." It also counts for something that an impartial observer like Michael Hogan, the American consul in Valparaíso who investigated the mutiny, wrote to John Quincy Adams, then secretary of state: "It does not appear that there was cause to complain of the Captain of this Ship, which is uncommon, for in Justice to truth, my experience for upwards of three years in this Port, has proved to my conviction that the Masters of Merchant Ships trading here are oftener in error than the sailors, who by severe, inconsiderate and unfeeling treatment are driven to insubordination and desertion."

In the long view of the events on the *Globe*, the only uncontrived complaint against the captain seemed to be length of meals. While the food improved once the ship provisioned in Hawaii, the time allowed to eat it did not. When the men went down to meals, they would scarcely have food brought down before the second mate would appear shouting, "Where are you there, forward? Come out of that or I will be among you." If they did not leave the food and start up to the deck immediately, the first mate or even the captain would come cursing and threatening to break their backs.

Captain Worth had some ready responses to crewmen who complained of hunger: he told them to eat iron hoops, or he took a handful of pump bolts and crammed them in the complainers' mouths. Both of these actions may be made to seem hostile and tyrannical but also, if the whole context is grasped, may be little more than rough official horseplay, and not enough to make Worth less than "a fine man."

Samuel Comstock, of course, was delighted with every instance of the captain's rough usage, even if he knew it was not serious enough to complain about, for he could put a spin on it that made it serious enough; it was easy enough to stoke hostility to the captain if one were adept at firebuilding. Almost any move or command from the captain could be made useful to the mutineers' purposes.

The problem on the ship at this point was not any of the captain's discipline but the poisoning of morale by most of the new crewmembers taken on in Hawaii, that "rough set of cruel beings," as George Comstock calls them, "neither fit to die or live." They magnified every cause for resentment. They sent a campaign of hostile talk circulating throughout the forecastle, complaining about the food, even though the food had greatly improved, and about the usage of the captain in general. The feeling generated was much uglier than the mood of complaint had been when the ship was on the Japan Ground.

Leaving Hawaii around the end of December, the ship crossed the equator, searched for whales around latitude 2° south, and then moved north toward Fanning's Island (Fanny's Island in George's account), one of the Line Islands, which are strung out between Hawaii and Tahiti on the eastern edge of what is today the republic of Kiribati. The fact that no whales were raised in this cruising may be partly attributable to the indifference of the new hands to any whaling at all, their only agenda being conspiratorial. Comstock tried cautiously to sound out some of the original crew for sentiments that would make them members of his band: to William Lay, when he was alone with him in the masthead, he said, "Well, William, there is bad usage in the ship—what had we better do, run away, or take the ship?" Lay answered evasively and tried to get to the second mate and tell him what he had heard, but did not fin¬d an opportunity. It became clear to Comstock that he could count on no one but Payne, Oliver, Humphreys, and Lilliston. (Joseph Thomas reported in his deposition in Valparaíso that he had heard Comstock say that his first attempt at mutiny had been before the new recruits joined the ship in Hawaii, "but the men to aid him failed.")

Then one day, January 25, 1824, the captain, cursing and threatening, ordered the men out of the forecastle to pull on the fore brace. He singled out one of them, Joseph Thomas: if he did not come up in more haste the next time, he told the seaman, he would knock him to hell. It would be a dear blow for him if he did, Thomas replied. The captain swung at him, but Thomas, ducking the blow, ran forward until he was seized by the mate, who brought him to the captain. The captain held him by the neck and grasped the main buntline and commenced whipping him. The crew who were not aloft stood in the waist, the widest part of the ship, watching the punishment in silence except for one seaman whom George refers to as Rowland—presumably Coffin, not Jones—who asked those near him "how they could bear to see the man served that way." The crew went off to the forecastle muttering and talking desertion. Silas Payne said that if the captain flogged anyone else, they should tell him to stop. "One of the boatsteerers," George writes, "came and told us to revenge it that he would see us out." One of the boatsteerers, of course, was George's brother Samuel, who was testing the mood of the crew to see if the moment for an uprising was at hand. The crew was shocked by the flogging and the sight of Thomas's bruised back—Thomas said that he had been struck thirteen or fourteen times—but the feeling among many of them was that this was not the time to start a quarrel with the officers.

For some of them, however, what had just happened was the last straw, not the flogging by itself but the turmoil of bad feeling among the ship's company that surfaced as the men watched. Desertion became a live question now. Several of the crew, George Comstock among them, resolved that if they came to Fanning Island, which they were fairly near, they would desert and hide out in the woods until the ship sailed.

"I had been very well used by the capt," George writes, "and had nothing to complain of but foreseeing that there would be some noise yet between the crew and officers I was determined to leave the ship to get clear of so much turbulence and dissention." The talk among the men ready to desert was that they would take one of the boats during the watch headed by Samuel Comstock, that is, the second watch, from 10 P.M. to 2 A.M., for Samuel had spoken with enough threatening innuendo about the ship in general to convince them that he was a safe bet to cooperate with a desertion attempt. Fanning was a far from ideal spot to set up any encampment and not a logical place to expect rescue from, but the whole question of desertion became moot.

Thomas, the seaman who had been flogged, was on his way to supper when Samuel Comstock approached him and, as Thomas puts it, "spoke a blunt word to me about the officers." Would he, Samuel asked him, "go down in the cabin with him tonight?" In view of the state of things on the ship that day, the words carried the most sinister suggestions. Thomas temporized and told Comstock that he had been ordered forward to supper and would tell him by and by. Although this account is confirmed by several other crew members, there may be some disingenuousness in Thomas's using it as a defense; Peter Kidder and others were convinced that Thomas did know, once Comstock had spoken to him, what was in the works. At the very least Thomas would have known that he had heard something he was obliged to report to the officers.

The whipping of Thomas took place in the morning and made it a day like no other. On one level of the ship's company there was a conspiracy to desert, and on another there was a conspiracy to kill. For the deserters it was a matter of the right place; for the killers, a matter of the right time.

The would-be deserters were probably not close enough to the right place for an attempt; the ship's position that day is not recorded, but on the following day it was about 120 miles north and a few miles west of Fanning. In addition, though, the decision not to jump ship could have been affected by a premonition, or more than a premonition, of what was going to happen during the second watch, when they were planning to make their move. If Joseph Thomas, in spite of his later denials, knew that a mutiny was coming during

Comstock's watch, did anyone else know? Several of the crew accused young Rowland Coffin of later saying things that made them suspect he had known something of the mutiny plans. (He was also accused of being, after the mutiny, the chief informant to Comstock about what was going on among the crew.)

For the mutineers the time was right. The hostility on board the ship over the flogging of Thomas was too opportune to pass up. Midnight between January 25 and 26 was to be the moment.

But for the officers it was a social day. The *Globe* was once again sailing in company with the *Lyra*, and Captain Joy had been rowed over to the *Globe* for a gam; he was on board most of the day. The two captains confirmed their plans to sail together for a while. For that purpose they would observe their present course until the middle of the night and then tack together, the signal for doing so being a light that the *Globe* would show. The boat sent from the *Lyra* to pick up its captain arrived before he was ready to leave, and the men from the boat came on board the *Globe*. Samuel, who was splicing the foresheet, looked at the setting sun and said to the *Lyra* men, "That sight reminds me of the saying of a Roman General on the eve of a battle—'How many that watch that sun go down, will never see it rise again!'"

With the departure of the boat from the *Lyra*, the night watch was set. The three watches were manned by the ship's three boatcrews: that of boatsteerer Gilbert Smith had the first watch, which ended at 10 P.M.; the crew of the waist boat headed by boatsteerer Samuel Comstock had the second watch from 10 P.M. to 2 A.M.; the third boatcrew, which was assigned to stand watch from 2 A.M. to 6 A.M., was headed by Third Mate Nathaniel Fisher. George Comstock did not belong to any boatcrew, doubtless because of his age, and was one of those who kept the ship during lowerings for whales, but for purposes of standing watch he was considered part of the waist boat's crew and therefore belonged to his brother's watch.

The evening was warm and pleasant, and the first watch was uneventful. The ship held to its northerly course, as did the *Lyra*, which was still easy to see in the gathering dusk. Midway through the watch, around 8 o'clock, Captain Worth came up from the cabin and spoke with Gilbert Smith; he ordered reefs to be taken in the topsails and gave Smith the orders for the night: stay by the wind until the third watch came on duty at 2 A.M., at which time the ship should tack and set a light for the *Lyra*, so that it could match the tack and stay in company, as the two captains had agreed earlier in the day. Captain Worth stayed on deck for about an hour; there was no foreseeable need for him to come up again until morning, for Smith would pass the orders on at 10 o'clock to the boatsteerer in charge of the next watch, Samuel Comstock, who was responsible for passing them on to the head of the third watch, Nathaniel Fisher. When the captain went below, around nine o'clock, he found his stateroom too hot for sleeping; he did not go in but climbed into a hammock rigged outside it.

Darkness had descended on the ship by the end of the first watch at 10 o'clock. The wind was low and the seas were calm. The ship was sailing more slowly now with sails reduced. Smith passed the captain's orders to Comstock, and the first watch crew walked to the forecastle and went below. There was moonlight, but on the ship the only spot of additional light was from the binnacle, the illuminated wooden housing of the compass, and that hardly dispelled the darkness. Comstock's watch collected on deck, and Samuel ordered one of them, his brother George, to take over the helm. His duty, George knew, would last two hours; his relief would take over at midnight.

At some point after he had taken the helm, George heard indistinct voices coming from around the mainmast, but near as that was, he could see no one, nor could he make out what was being said. There was, however, a tense and excited tone to the voices. They did not seem to be people from his watch, for if they were just attending to the ship's business, they would have no reason to whisper. As George strained to catch a word, he was startled to hear a very clear voice right in his ear: "Keep the ship a good full. Why do you have all the head sails shaking?" Samuel had crept up close to him without George's seeing him and was speaking with an urgency that matched that of the voices around the mainmast. George tried to comply, but Samuel came back to him several times cursing him for having the ship up in the wind. Keep the ship "a good full," he ordered; that is, keep the sails full of wind. There was something odd about his brother's excitement and the hushed voices in the waist. What was happening on the ship?

Samuel's orders about full sails were not a subtle navigational concern but a terribly practical one for the mutineers. They wanted not a sound to be heard on the ship lest it awaken the officers. If the sails were full of wind ("a good full"), they were firm in place, but if not, they would flap with enough noise to awaken those asleep. George told him that the ship was already a full point (11¼ degrees) from the wind. "Mind what I tell you," Samuel told him and took the helm himself to turn the ship to two points off the wind. George reflected that it was his duty to obey without questioning the order, for it might have come from the captain, and he tolerated his brother's interference, for his two-hour spell at the helm was almost over. But Samuel's behavior was beginning to be not merely strange but disturbing.

Normally at the end of his helm, a seaman in George's position would pick up and shake a rattle that would alert his relief, and someone from his watch would come to take over for the remaining two hours. George had hardly begun to shake the rattle when his brother ordered him to stop. "It is not my helm, and I want to be relieved," said George. "If you make the least damned bit of noise, I will send you to hell," Samuel replied.

George watched as Samuel lit a lamp and went down to steerage.

When he thought Samuel was out of sight, George picked up the rattle again, but before he could shake it, his brother came up next to him and threatened to kill him if he made a sound. This time George did what he was told; now he wanted to shake the rattle not to be relieved of his duty but to have someone else beside him. George stayed with the helm and listened for sounds from any quarter; one he heard was made by something heavy being laid on the vice bench near the cabin gangway. It was impossible to see clearly, and George did not know what made the heavy sound. Later he learned that it was a boarding knife, a sharp-pointed, double-edged tool for cutting blubber; boarding knives were between two and four feet long and two or three inches wide.

Up to this point George is an eyewitness, but for the brief climactic events of the mutiny he relies on the sounds that reached him at the helm and, more important, on an account that he received from the leader of "these murderous treacherous deceiving and unfeeling wretches," his brother. The details of the killings are relayed from the killer to the horrified but faithful reporter, George, and through George they have come down to all subsequent accounts. A few details come from others on the ship, but the killer's blithe confession, which he would never think of as a confession but as a boast, is the main narrative of the most horrific moments of the mutiny. Samuel talked freely—*unsparingly* would be a better word—to George. Shortly after the mutiny he said to his brother, "I suppose you think I regret what I have done; but you are mistaken—I should like to do such a job every morning before breakfast."

Samuel Comstock, Silas Payne, John Oliver, William Humphreys, and Thomas Lilliston moved so silently away from the mainmast and toward the cabin that George did not see or hear them. One member of the watch did, though: sixteen-year-old Columbus Worth, the captain's cousin, had seen the four men go aft and had caught sight of the hatchet in Lilliston's hand. He was so terrified at the sight that he went forward to hide, not in the forecastle but huddled into a space by the bowsprit.

Payne carried the boarding knife and Humphreys the lantern, which he apparently kept covered until they were in the cabin. At the cabin gangway Lilliston broke away from the group and ran forward, wanting nothing to do with the planned killing. He had believed, he said later, that the conspirators would never actually attack the officers and he had gone along with them just to look brave. He later acknowledged that he had had a knife and a hatchet in his hands.

In a moment there was a thud, which George heard on deck as distinctly as he had heard the boarding knife being laid on the vice bench. Comstock, who was the first of the four into the cabin, slipped past the captain's hammock, mounted the transom—the athwartships timber at the ship's stern—to give himself some elevation above the sleeping man, raised the axe until it touched the carline at the top of the cabin, and swung viciously. The very first stroke came near to cutting the top of Captain Worth's head off, but Samuel followed it with a second.

Payne, who had been waiting to strike the first mate with the boarding knife as soon as the captain had been attacked, stabbed Mate Beetle on cue, but the wide-bladed knife was stopped by ribs, and Beetle woke up. "What, what, what, what, what is this?" he exclaimed. "Oh Payne; oh Comstock don't kill me. Have I not always. . . ." Comstock interrupted him, "Yes, you have always been a damned rascal. You tell lies about me out of the ship, will you. It's a damned good time to beg now you are too late."

Beetle struggled desperately, grabbing Comstock by the throat, bumping into the others, and knocking down the lantern carried by Humphreys, which went out. In the darkness and confusion Comstock dropped his hatchet and called out for another one; his call was a weak gasp, for Beetle was choking him. Payne felt around and by chance put his hand on the hatchet, which he gave to

Comstock, who swung hard, hitting Beetle in the head and breaking his skull. The mate fell into the pantry and lay groaning.

Oliver, according to George, was "cruising round putting in a blow when it came handy," but it was Comstock who was doing the killing. Leaving his partners to guard the door of the stateroom behind which Second Mate Lumbert and Third Mate Fisher were listening in alarmed silence, he went on deck to relight the lantern at the binnacle. George was waiting there, now at least half aware of what had happened below. George asked his brother if he intended to hurt Gilbert Smith. Yes, he would kill him; had George seen him? George said he had not; he felt sure that his brother's threat was serious. By now George was in tears. "What are you crying about?" Samuel asked him. "I was afraid that you all were going to hurt me," he replied. "I will hurt you if you talk in that manner," said his brother. George stifled his tears and fell silent, fearing for his life.

Meanwhile the noise from the cabin had awakened Boatsteerer Gilbert Smith, who came up on deck without any clothes on to see what was happening. When he made out that there was a disturbance in the cabin, he went below and dressed. He went aft and looked down the cabin gangway; all that he could make out was Samuel Comstock holding the boarding knife and standing at the door of the second and third mates' stateroom. Waving his hands in the air, Comstock was saying, "I am the bloody man; I have the bloody hand, and I will be revenged." This line became Comstock's mantra, and he repeated it in the course of the massacre. It was hysterical, but it was also theatrical. Revenge? He was going to let Third Mate Fisher know that he was getting revenge for the humiliation he suffered in the wrestling match on the *Enterprise*, and he may have had a grievance against Beetle (if he ever got to the United States, he would be the death of Beetle, he had once told Gilbert Smith). But "revenge," like the "bloody hand" line, is stage language, or words from the backyard childhood games on Market Street.

From where he was standing, Smith heard Lumbert repeatedly asking Comstock through the locked stateroom door, "What is the matter?" Comstock did not answer. Lumbert would give Comstock anything he had, he said, if Comstock would only let him go on deck and go into the forecastle or jump overboard. If Comstock even paid attention to what Lumbert was asking—to be allowed to jump overboard—he probably did not reason out what was behind it: Lumbert was not offering to commit suicide—he was looking for a chance to swim to the *Lyra*, which was about three miles away. Could he have found the *Lyra* if it was showing no lights, and even if it was, could he have swum that far? For Lumbert the risk was better than certain death in the cabin, but the plea was idle, for Comstock was deaf to everything his victims said to him unless he could make their words into a taunt.

Where were the captain and Mate Beetle? Smith wondered. Absurd as it would seem, the thought ran through Smith's mind that they were sleeping through all the commotion. The noise had been enough to awaken Smith, but maybe the captain and mate were heavy sleepers. He could not see the bodies, just a few feet away from him, and he could not see the splattered blood.

He turned away from the cabin, went forward looking about the deck, and managed to find, in spite of the dark, Columbus Worth hiding by the bowsprit. Worth told him about seeing Lilliston with a hatchet and coming up to hide in the best place he could think of. Did he know what was going on? Smith asked him. No, he did not. They may kill you if they find you here, Smith said, and led Worth to the forecastle.

Cyrus Hussey, who was asleep below, recalled Smith coming to the gangway and calling out, "Who is there below?" What did he want, Hussey asked. "There is a terrible time in the cabin," Smith replied, "they have aroused me out with the noise." Smith went aft again and came back to the forecastle, and told the now completely awakened men that the mutineers had knives and guns and that the officers were begging for their lives.

Smith was thinking clearly, but the idea of what was happening paralyzed the men; they were imprisoned by confusion and terror. They could only wait in the dark, hot, cramped quarters and listen. Suddenly they did hear something: musket fire from aft. "I will never see my father again," Columbus Worth burst out.

The scene that Smith had witnessed in the cabin was still being played out. After relighting the lantern Comstock had gone back into the cabin with two guns to attack the second and third mates, who were still behind their stateroom door. Second Mate Lumbert, who had been questioning and pleading with Comstock, asked him through the door if he was going to kill him. "Oh, no, I guess not," Comstock replied in a joking manner. Estimating where the two mates were in the room, Comstock fired through the door and hit Third Mate Fisher in the mouth. Was either of them hit? Comstock asked. Fisher told him where he had been hit.

Whether Lumbert opened the stateroom door or the killers forced it open, Comstock, holding one of the guns, which had a bayonet, lunged through it at Lumbert but tripped and fell into the stateroom. Grabbed by Lumbert, Comstock was able to break free but dropped his gun in the process. Fisher picked up the gun and held the bayonet at Comstock's heart. For a moment everything froze. It could have been the end of the mutiny, but Comstock extricated himself from the hopeless situation in a fashion that was absurd enough to fit his life and luck and no one else's: Comstock told Fisher to put the gun down, and Fisher did, hoping that his life would be spared if he complied.

Immediately Comstock seized the gun, turned on Lumbert, and ran him through several times with the bayonet. Lumbert cried, "Oh, Comstock! I've got a poor old father with six little children at home!" "Damn you, so have I!" Comstock replied. Comstock was inarticulate with fury and throughout the massacre had no retorts but throwing others' words back at them.

He told Fisher that he too must die and, in particular, die to pay for the offense that Comstock had been cherishing for months. He reminded Fisher of "the scrape he had with him in company with the Enterprise of Nantucket," the humiliating wrestling match. That Fisher had forgotten it made Comstock seem unimportant; that was infuriating. Comstock ordered Fisher to die like a man. Fisher turned about, saying that he was ready; he died instantly when Comstock fired into the back of his head.

Lumbert, bleeding from his multiple stab wounds, begged Comstock for water. "I'll give you water," he said, and stabbed him again. The wounds seemed impossible to survive, but Lumbert was still clinging to life.

When another musket shot, the one that killed Fisher, was heard in the forecastle, Smith started for the deck. Don't go up, the others told him. Hide out down here or go aloft. Smith told them, however, that he would face the mutineers boldly "and if his life was to be took he would ask for ½ an hour to exercise in religious duties." The first person he met was William Humphreys, who was holding the lantern. What is the matter, Smith asked. You'll know shortly, Humphreys replied.

Smith went aft and found George Comstock, who was still crying. The same question and the same answer: What is the matter? I don't really know, said George. Smith returned to the forecastle. Soon he heard Samuel Comstock on the quarterdeck giving orders to Oliver to call the crew up to make sail; Smith was the first on deck and the others followed.

In the dark the deck was a mass of vague figures shifting about and heading toward the masts. Where is Smith? Comstock called out. Here I am, Smith replied and walked up to meet Comstock next to the mainmast. Are you for us? Comstock asked. "Yes, don't kill me;

I'll do anything you want if you will only save my life," Smith answered. "Damn you, I will say what you will do. Go forward and set the fore top gallant sail and flying jib." He put his bloody arms around Smith's neck. If Samuel Comstock had been serious when he told his brother that he would kill Smith, he had his chance now, but he had just been making fierce talk. William Comstock explains Samuel's view of Smith in a fashion that has no logic but considerable plausibility:

> The reader may be curious to know what enlisted the sympathies of the man of blood so much in favor of Smith; and I should be remiss in not informing him, as by so doing I shall develope a distinguished trait in my hero's character. Smith was a religious young man; and with all his faults, our hero entertained a high respect for sacred things, and a superstitious awe of pious persons. He told George that if he had killed Smith, God would have avenged his death, and that while Smith was with them, the Almighty would smile on their enterprise for his sake. It is surprising that nothing could shake his faith in Orthodoxy. I once labored hard to convince him that the doctrine of endless punishment was derogatory to the character of the Almighty. "Don't try to argue me out of a belief in hell!" cried he passionately, "I tell you there is such a place; but that is not going to frighten me. If I go there, as very likely I shall, I will kick and squall and bear it as well as I can. But you can't persuade me that there is no such place."

Smith, the Kidders, and Thomas set the two foresails, the flying jib, the main topsail, and the spanker. Hussey, who was ordered to loose the mizzen topgallant, went aloft, looked out over the moonlit sea, and saw a body floating alongside the ship—it was either the captain or Mate Beetle. The sight and the turmoil below made him stay aloft after the sail was set until Comstock called out, "Who is [it] that I sent aloft to loose the mizzen top gallant sail?" Hussey had to come down.

Even after the sails were set, most of the men did not know what had happened to the captain and first mate. What had happened, in fact, was that the captain had been killed instantly, but the killers' rage against him had not abated. They ran the boarding knife through his body and drove it home with a blow from an axe; it entered below the stomach and came out the neck. They struck his head again with the axe. Mate Beetle, in spite of stab wounds and a fractured skull, was still alive. Both, however, were thrown overboard through the cabin windows. Mate Beetle died in the ocean in the dark of night.

William Lay had gone aft to see what was happening just as Comstock was ordering, "Haul them fellows up and throw them overboard," referring to the second and third mates. Silas Payne joined in to play officer and, spotting Lay, said, "You have been a damned coward all the time, come down & haul them." When Lay saw the two bodies lying in the stateroom, he could not move. "Here—take the candle if you are afraid of them, and I'll haul them out," Payne said. Payne called up to the deck for rope. One rope was tied around the neck of Fisher, who had had his brains blown out, and the other rope around the feet of Lumbert, who like Beetle had survived in spite of his massive injuries. Lumbert was dragged naked to the place where blubber is cut in the center of the ship. He had strength enough to say, "I thought you said you would spare my life." Comstock replied, "Damn you, I'll spare your life." When an effort was made to throw him overboard, Lumbert grasped the plank sheer, the top plank covering the gunwale, with his hands. Comstock called for a hatchet but did not use one, instead kicking Lumbert's fingers until he lost his grip and fell overboard. Seeing that Lumbert, despite his multiple stab wounds, swam quickly once he was in the water, Comstock called out, "Lower away the boat—he's alive—he swims."

The cranes were swung out and the boat partway down, when Comstock countermanded the order: "Hoist her up again; he has a pretty good wound; he won't live." What had dawned on Comstock, and probably everyone on deck around him, mutineer and innocent, was that the likelihood of Lumbert swimming to the *Lyra* was virtually nil, while the likelihood of the boat, once in the water, heading for the *Lyra* was great. By the moonlight, Smith, standing at the mizzen, watched Lumbert swimming an amazing number of strokes, then lost sight of him. Joseph Thomas said that Lumbert swam two or three rods in the direction of the *Lyra*.

Comstock summoned the crew and announced that he was the new captain and that his orders would be obeyed under penalty of death. He had already ordered sails set; with the reefs ordered by Captain Worth shaken out, the ship had unusually heavy sail for moving at night. The orders seemed to reflect panic, as if there was a need to get away from something. The mutineers did indeed want to get away from the *Lyra;* in the mizzen rigging they set the agreed-on light to signal the *Lyra* to tack, but kept the *Globe* on a different course and quickly lost the other ship. But the panic went beyond that.

Comstock ordered all hands except the helmsman below; Smith went with the rest. The sea was calm. It was about 2 A.M. The second watch was ending; the head of the third watch was dead, and the members of that watch were not on duty but in the forecastle with the rest of the crew. The mutineers were alone on deck; they were the third watch that night.

With the light of day Monday morning, January 26, the cleanup began. It was a scene of gore and havoc. The captain's blood covered the cabin table and deck. His brains, or Third Mate Fisher's, were splattered across the cabin floor. Cleaning up meant carrying up to the deck whatever could be moved, washing away the blood, which ran diluted into the scuppers, and, down below, scrubbing the deck and the bulkheads. It was devastating work for the men, who were habit-uated to the extremely messy cleanup after the trying-out of whales and were anything but fastidious. But human blood was different.

During the day light breezes came from the east-southeast and built up until about 2 P.M. The course of the ship was roughly south by southwest, and by Tuesday, January 27, it was about two hundred miles south of the scene of the crime, having passed a few miles west of Fanning Island. Comstock, who a few years before had been denied his chance to join a navy ship, was playing navy now. The first work he ordered for the day included cleaning the muskets and guns that the ship was carrying, making cartridge boxes, and preparing in general for battle with another ship. The new officers of the ship under Captain Comstock are variously named in different accounts: Payne first mate, and Oliver and Humphreys—or vice versa—second and third mates. George Comstock is listed as the new steward in brother William's account. Oliver was regarded by the crew as such an ignorant and contemptible figure that Samuel Comstock's addressing him as *Mister* Oliver struck the men as one of the minor absurdities of the new situation.

Comstock drew up laws for the ship's company. Seamen embark-ing on whalers were used to signing ship's articles, which bound them to a code of conduct, but Comstock's laws were no ship's articles. He ordered the crew aft and had them sit on a spar on the quarterdeck. If there was anyone, he told them, that they would rather have as cap-tain than him, they had a right to choose that person. That demo-cratic rhetorical flourish was not a risky offer on Comstock's part: he held a cutlass as he spoke and had a pistol ready beside him. But, Comstock continued, if they did want him to be the captain, they would have to conform to laws that he had drawn up; any who could not bring themselves to sign the sheet should move to the other side of the deck. Terrified that such a dissent would mean death, no one crossed the deck. The laws required that anyone who saw a sail and did not report it at once or anyone who refused to fight another ship would be shot or hanged or boiled in oil in the try-pots, where the blubber was rendered down. Shades of the once popular cartoons of the missionary in the black tub over a kindling flame surrounded by grinning stick-figure natives dancing in grass skirts, Comstock's caricature sanction was never carried out, but everyone signed the laws and affixed his seal—black seals for the mutineers, colored ones for non-mutineers.

The laws reflected the preoccupation of the mutineers with encounters with other ships. Even the morning after the killings, before Comstock had imposed the laws, Humphreys had ordered William Lay aloft to look out for sails and announced his own special sanction: if anyone on deck reported a sail before the lookout called it out, the lookout would be shot.

It was some business of George Comstock in his new role as steward that led to the next violent act on the ship. One day—or several days, depending on the account followed—after the mutiny, George, who had occasion to go into the cabin, found Humphreys, the new purser, loading a pistol. When George asked him why, he said that he had "heard something very strange and he was going to be ready for it." George went immediately to inform his brother, who summoned Payne to come with him to the cabin. In the cabin they found Humphreys still standing with the pistol. He had heard something, he told Comstock, that had made him fear for his life. Asked what that was, he gave answers that were unclear and, George says, "suspicious." Finally Humphreys said that Gilbert Smith and Peter Kidder were planning to take the ship. Comstock told Humphreys that he thought he was lying because he did not come to him and report his suspicion.

Comstock called Smith and Kidder into the cabin and questioned them about Humphreys's charges; he cited the laws that he had drawn up for conduct on the ship, which included the death penalty for anyone who did not report seditious talk, but it was easy to convince Comstock that the charges against Smith and Kidder were lies. Cyrus Hussey reported that Comstock also questioned him and Rowland Jones about what Humphreys had said. Comstock then said that he would hang Humphreys in the morning but "would go through the form of the law for sake of being right but that he would choose such judges as would condemn him." Comstock, Payne, and Oliver shook hands on the decision to hang Humphreys.

The court, complete with jurors, was convened. Some accounts state that there were two jurors, but there is reason to accept those that say there were four. Stephen Kidder, in his deposition before Consul Hogan in Valparaíso, named Payne, Oliver, George Comstock, and Rowland Coffin. Gilbert Smith gave the same list except that he named Joseph Thomas instead of George Comstock, a significant difference. There is no figure in the whole *Globe* drama who has left a firsthand picture of himself as perfectly as George Comstock; anyone who reads his "Narrative" would have to go through mental contortions to imagine him concurring in a death sentence on Humphreys.

In the days following the mutiny Comstock and Payne were to divide the night watch between them, sleeping and relieving each other alternately; this was apparently out of mistrust of Oliver, but, Stephen Kidder reports, on the night after Humphreys's arrest, Comstock, Payne, and Oliver all walked the deck. In the morning six of the men, one of them Stephen Kidder, were called into the cabin and issued muskets, then sent on deck to encircle the seated Humphreys and present their bayonets to his heart. Smith and Peter Kidder sat on a chest behind the defendant; both were called to testify, as was Humphreys, "who was asked a few questions which he answered but low and unlikely."

Comstock made a speech to the assembled company, implicitly anticipating the verdict, but adding that if Humphreys were found not guilty, then Smith and Kidder, whom he had accused, would be hanged in his stead. There was no question, however, that the verdict had been established the night before. The jury found Humphreys guilty.

William Comstock reads the whole episode as a contrivance of his brother's to kill Humphreys not for his behavior with the pistol but for another reason: "He was much averse to having a black man on board—he always felt a strong dislike to colored persons—and was therefore willing to lay hold of any pretence to set Humphreys aside."

Humphreys was set aside with dispatch. Comstock ordered Payne to tie Humphreys's hands behind his back, and a watch that Humphreys had bought of Captain Worth was taken from his pocket. A cap was put over his head, he was taken to the bow, and the cap was pulled down over his eyes. Comstock had ordered two men to rig out a studding sail boom; a block was attached to it. Comstock took a rope, slushed the end of it in grease, and tied that end around Humphreys neck. He had Humphreys sit on the rail before the forerigging and ordered all hands to take hold of the rope, and he said that if any of them flinched, he would cut off their heads.

Comstock told Humphreys that if he had anything to say, he would have to say it damned quick. Comstock had sent one of the men to fetch the ship's fourteen-second sandglass; Humphreys would have just that long to make his final statement.

Comstock stood with the sandglass in one hand and his cutlass in the other. Humprheys began, "When I was born, I did not think I should ever come to this," but then the sand was in the lower half of the glass, and Comstock swung his cutlass to strike the ship's bell. The crew ran aft with the rope, and Humphreys was snatched up to the yard and died without a struggle. How long he hung is unclear, but it was at least fifteen minutes. The body was cut down and thrown overboard, but, some reports have it, there then occurred one of those mischances that seem symbolically appropriate to the mutiny. The line that was left attached to Humphreys's body became fouled aloft, and the body, like a haunting figure in a Poe story, was being towed alongside the ship. A runner hook, a heavy tool used for hoisting in blubber, was attached to the body to sink it, and the dragging rope was cut. Humphreys descended to the watery grave he shared with his officers. Humphreys's sea chest, when opened, was found to contain sixteen dollars in specie that he had purloined from the captain's trunk. It was all over by 9 A.M.

Humphreys's defense, that he had heard Smith and Peter C. Kidder plotting to take over the ship, was one of the weakest he could have presented. It seemed thought up, none too quickly, on the spur of the moment; it was hesitatingly and stumblingly presented; and it accused two of the most unlikely and peaceable members of the crew of planning a mutiny within the mutiny. Smith was, after all, accommodating to the new command, and Kidder, George notes, was "a man very easily scared." Comstock could hardly have failed to find them innocent of Humphreys's charges after a brief examination. If anyone was plotting to retake the ship, it was not those two. But, much as it would have astonished Comstock and the other mutineers, Humphreys was probably right. Peter Kidder's interrogation by Consul Hogan in Valparaíso ran as follows:

Q. Was the plan of retaking the ship conceived on board & when—
A. It was determined on before the ship reached the Isld
Q. Who was the principal person that projected recapturing the ship—
A. Mr. Gilbert Smith—

Hogan is not known to have raised these questions with anyone else among the escapees, something that suggests he had already learned that Kidder was one of the planners and that Smith was the chief planner.

One of the commands from the new captain was strikingly wanton and at first glance surprising, even in this theater of surprises. After the hanging of Humphreys, Comstock ordered the crew to throw overboard many of the ship's supplies and even the valuable casks of oil still on deck. Empty casks were thrown overboard or burned; fluke ropes and rigging were flung into the sea. The act, which would outrage any whaleman or shipowner, probably owed something to Comstock's plan to turn the *Globe* into something as close as possible to a warship, but it may also have been intended precisely as outrageous and contemptuous: the mutineers were discarding their identities as whalemen. Not only was the ship not to pursue whales again, but also the very signs of the work that Comstock hated so much were to be destroyed. It was retaliation on the chief mutineer's part against every abuse that whaling had made him suffer since he served on the *George* six years before. The fact that the oil meant money was not an issue, for the new master of the *Globe* was committed to something that would take them away from commerce in oil forever. In fact, the destruction of the casks was somewhat symbolic, for the officers contented themselves with getting rid of only those still on deck; there was apparently no effort made to bring up oil from below—and the *Globe* still had 372 barrels on board when it finally returned home.

Another order from the new captain was to paint the ship black wherever the name *Globe* appeared. That meant on the stern and wherever it was branded on the spars, oars, and buckets. William Comstock characteristically exploited that black repainting of the ship in his 1838 novel, *A Voyage to the Pacific*, where the *Globe*, renamed the *Ark of Blood*, makes a brief melodramatic appearance, commanded by a captain "like Lucifer, fallen from Glory, and bound to Hell!"

With Comstockian grotesquerie Samuel ordered a memorial service for the repose of the souls of the murdered officers. Gilbert Smith was ordained chaplain for the occasion and delivered the scripture passage and the hymns.

Captain Comstock introduced a distinct novelty in the ship's orders: the crew were to eat with the officers in the cabin. Whether this was more to let the crew hear what he had to say or to let him hear what they were saying, some of the things that the crew overheard were not exactly designed to improve morale. Every morning Payne and Oliver complained of nightmares in which the murdered officers appeared to them; Comstock told them that the captain had appeared in his dreams too, pointing to his bloody head. "I told him to go away," Comstock said, "and if he ever appeared again, I would kill him a second time!"

It was doubtless not at one of these meals in the cabin but during some chance proximity to Comstock that Anthony Hanson overheard Comstock, possibly talking to himself, make a threat that everyone on the ship would have taken seriously: ". . . before we got to the Islds I heard Saml Comstock say he would send some of them adrift in the boat." This was never done; it would not be too farfetched to say the reason was that Comstock could not afford to waste a boat.

The course of the ship lay with the prevailing winds for the next two weeks, except for one day: "The mutineers felt ugly and malicious as we had a headwind," George Comstock noted on February 11. The ship sailed south for the first day after the mutiny, then west along a course two or three degrees north of the equator, except for an unexplained little swerve around Howland Island, until it reached the Gilbert Islands and turned north. The shipboard discipline was as ugly as the mutineers' reaction to the headwind: they were "barbarous . . . generally to those of the crew that were not of their party," Peter Kidder reported.

On January 31 the captain was still ordering quasi-naval exercises: the crew was employed to make boarding pikes for use against any other ship. Here was a considerable irony: the *Globe*, which had such inexplicably poor luck with whales in the Off-Shore Ground and in the Japan Ground, was passing great numbers of sperm whales every day now that it was no longer a whaleship and was instead playing frigate. That luck, which was a mockery of the ship and no luck at all, lasted for over a week as the ship moved through the Gilberts and north to the Marshalls.

On February 7 the *Globe* sighted one of the Gilbert Islands (Kingsmills, as they were known at the time) bearing west by south. The ship stood in, and natives came alongside in canoes offering beads of their own manufacture, but they appeared to be hostile and the ship left them, ran along the shore, and at night stood off. George does not name the island but does record the next contact as "Marshalls Isle" (which in spite of the name is in the Gilberts, not the Marshalls).

Here occurred an encounter with natives that struck George with remarkable force. One of the ship's boats was sent ashore at this island but did not land when the natives attempted to steal from the boat. Instead those in the boat backed off and fired a volley of shots at the natives, probably wounding some, and then the *Globe*'s boat pursued one of the native canoes with two men in it and fired into it. When they came up with the native boat, George writes, they

> perceived one of them was wounded the poor native took up a bas-
> ket manufactured by themselves from a species of flags [*flax*] famil-
> iar to those Islands & a number of beads which he offered to these
> inhuman cruel brutish Americans and held up his hands to signify
> there was all they had he would give us that if they would not kill
> him Oh, how unfeeling must be they hearts of such wretches they
> cannot be called anything better no name no tittle is half revenge-
> ful enough if the righteous are scarcely saved where have and will
> these vile inhabitants of the earth go hell itself is not bad enough

no nor all the pains imaginable. The blood was seen to crimson the poor mans eyes grew dim alas he layed in the canoies bottom and we expect left this world which was as dear to him as to those who shed his blood—But after the devil gets full hold it puzzells a bright genious to get away let us leave this melancholy scene.

William Comstock, too, is moved in recounting the episode. After running through his brother's narrative, he continues in a tone of moral outrage that is hard to match in anything else he has written:

The omnipotent Jehovah looked down from his seraph girdled throne, and saw one of his unsophisticated children slain for mere pastime, and that moment passed His decree that the instigator of the foul deed should die by the same weapon with which he had slain his brother, and that the accessories should be cut off by the people whom they had wronged. The Destroying Angel bowed sternly as he received his orders, and posted down to Earth to blind the understandings and distract the counsels of those whom he was commissioned to destroy.

Instead of dulling their sensibilities to atrocities, the killings on board the ship seemed to have made George and William more acutely sensitive. It is their own blood brother whom they are now ready to consign to hell, and the anonymous murdered native in his canoe whom they call brother.

On February 10 the ship moved out of the northern reaches of the Gilberts, leaving behind what had been the announced destination of the *Globe* from the time of the mutiny. The Gilberts had been a shot in the dark; what would the Marshalls be? The ship headed for the southeasternmost corner of the Marshalls, the nearest one to the Gilberts, and passed Nako and Knox Islands and arrived at Mili Atoll, which on their charts appeared as the Mulgrave Islands.

Judging by George Comstock's account, the *Globe* passed west of the little spur formed by Knox and other islands and anchored off an island in the main string of the atoll that looked like, and proved to be, a good place for provisioning. This first landing place cannot be precisely identified but may have been Lukunor. The provisioning included, according to George, "some of the women or girls and a large quantity of cocoanuts, some fish &c." The ship stood off during the night and in the morning, on February 12, sent the girls ashore and set out to cruise the south coast of the atoll.

George (and of course Lay and Hussey following George) recorded the stop a little too tersely to satisfy a natural curiosity about how this first encounter with the Milians went. How much communication was there? What was the mood of the natives? Did it take anything more than an invitation to get some aboard the ship? What kind of intentions were conveyed? Did the people on the ship see any canoes depart the landing site (which would have been carrying word of the strange arrivals to the high chief)? What kind of sexual generosity was involved? And why does George, the key source, mention only the girls, when Stephen Kidder says, "Comstock brought off several of the Natives, men & women, all very friendly. Kept them on board all night, gave each of the women one of the Captain's white shirts and the men other articles of the Captain's."

The twelfth of February was a day of no success either in finding a good anchorage or in spotting a point ashore that seemed to have arable soil. It was not a great distance that they were covering, a little over twenty miles east and west, so that they could have doubled back more than once in the course of the day. The ship stood off overnight and continued exploring the same area in the morning; only toward evening did they resign themselves to choosing "a long narrow Island" that they had doubtless passed and observed more than once. They were fairly close to shore. The lead revealed a depth of twelve fathoms, but on being dropped again, just a little farther offshore, found no bottom. The precipitous drop-off of the coast in all the coral islands of the Marshalls is frequently commented on. The hazard of these anchorages was that getting close enough to have the anchor reach bottom put the ship in danger of being swept onto the coral by an onshore wind. But so intent was Comstock to land that a delicate midpoint was chosen and the ship anchored about 110 yards offshore in seventy-two feet of water. A kedge, a small supplementary anchor, was dropped astern to keep the ship from swinging around to the coral shore. It was getting dark now; George reports, "The sails were furled the ship moored and we all retired to rest except an anchor watch but rest as it was not fit for brutes much more for human beings we lay deploring our fate yet glad to get out."

It was Friday the thirteenth.

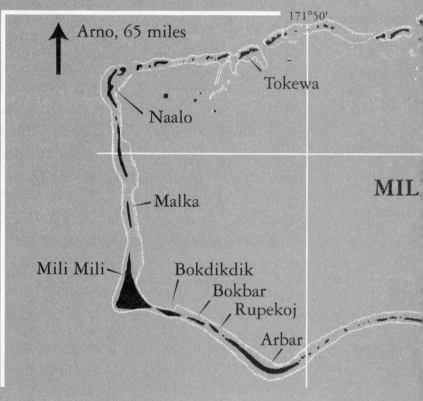

Arno, 65 miles

171°50'

Tokewa

Naalo

Malka

MIL

Mili Mili

Bokdikdik

Bokbar

Rupekoj

Arbar

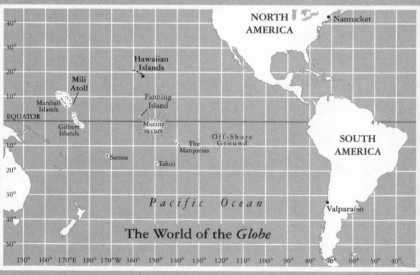

NORTH
AMERICA

Nantucket

Hawaiian
Islands

Mili
Atoll

Marshall
Islands

Fanning
Island

EQUATOR

Mutiny
occurs

Gilbert
Islands

Off-Shore
Ground

SOUTH
AMERICA

The
Marquesas

Samoa

Tahiti

Pacific Ocean

Valparaíso

The World of the *Globe*

150° 160° 170°E 180° 170°W 160° 150° 140° 130° 120° 110° 100° 90° 80° 70° 60° 50° 40°

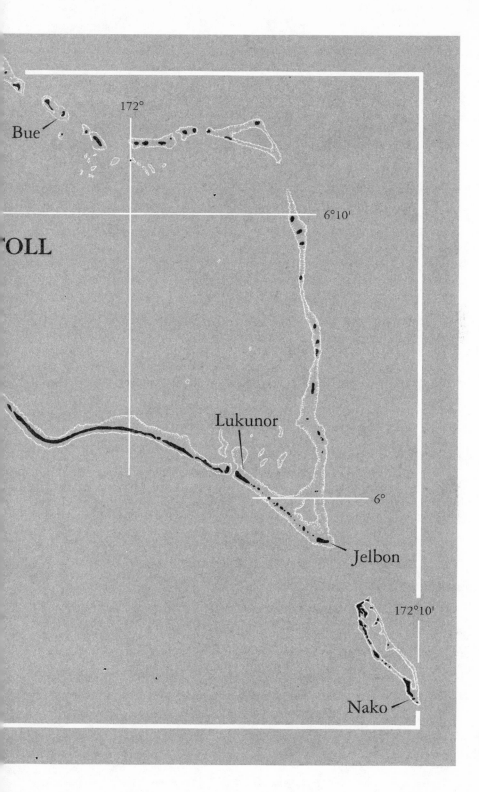

NO LASTING CITY

What the *Globe* people saw as they moved along the coast was a very white sandy and alluring shoreline, with the dense palm growth on the wider islands beginning well back from the water. For the crew the island meant a little—but just a little—relief from the tense and senseless flight of the last three weeks; for Comstock, however, the island was transfigured: it came into focus as the domain of its new white monarch. Everything that he had told William and that William wrote off as fantasy was on the point of fulfillment now: "he would take the vessel to some island inhabited by savages, and after murdering all his crew, join with the natives, teach them the art of war, and raise himself to the dignity of a king." Mili was destiny. Comstock's vision grew: In a few days—not in weeks but literally in a few days—the natives would be his regiment. And they would also be tending the plantation—he would take the seed packets out of his chest and teach the natives to plant them—no, that would not be necessary—they would simply turn into good field hands. In a few days no one would stand in the king's way. Everything was Comstock's.

On the morning of Saturday the fourteenth, Comstock sent a boat east along the coast to look for a better anchorage and also for signs of arable soil. The boat came back in the middle of the day reporting no luck, and around 2 P.M. was sent west toward the large island of Mili Mili; here too it found no satisfactory coast. Comstock decided that the ship would anchor where it was; he wanted Mili at all costs.

Early the next day, Sunday the fifteenth, Comstock and company landed as if they had tied up in Nantucket or Edgartown. This was home port now. The natives had come out of the woods and down to the shore to watch; what they saw was not a boat coming ashore but an invasion. None of the sources indicate that the *Globe* people regarded the natives as anything but folks from the neighborhood. But they were not; within hours of the ship's first sighting off the southeast, word had spread throughout the atoll that something truly extraordinary had happened. It was an event that called for a council of the chiefs and for intelligence gathering. That would have been the case even if the *Globe* had stood off and put no boat ashore, but the strange people from the strange ship had come ashore and now they were landing a hoard of inexplicable things from the ship. It is quite possible that the majority of the natives had never seen a square-rigged ship: Some of the elders may have seen the *Scarborough* and the *Charlotte* when Marshall and Gilbert stopped at the island thirty-six years before. And some may have seen the British merchant ship *Rolla* in 1803 when it tried unsuccessfully to put a boat ashore. Ships were rare and remarkable events even when there was nothing exceptional about them, but the *Globe* was like a visit from creatures of another species. A response had to be decided on as soon as it was clear what the reality of this visit was. Things were happening fast. The natives were calm and diplomatic, but their minds were spinning.

Who were these "Indians"? Mili was as much a mystery as most of the Pacific in 1824. Not only were the islands a lottery, but it seemed that the more that was known about them, the harder it was to generalize about the human welcome to be expected on them. In 1835 at Namorik Atoll in the southwest corner of the Marshalls, the Falmouth whaler *Awashonks* was boarded by natives, whose attention was caught by the ship's brightly polished cutting spades; these they seized, used one to behead the captain, and killed six and wounded seven of the ship's company. Otto von Kotzebue, on the other hand, was so well received in the northern Marshalls in 1815–1818 that he might as well have been among family—or so Kotzebue and his chronicler, Adelbert von Chamisso, would have it. From the time of Magellan there had been every variety of encounter between European and islander. Sometimes the natives were friendly, sometimes duplicitous, sometimes frightened, and sometimes belligerent. (The same could be said of the Europeans.) All expectations had to be tentative.

Throughout the sixteenth century, Spanish and Portuguese ships made spotty contacts with the people of the islands that were later to be called the Marshalls, but with the end of the century, the world passed the Marshalls by; the favored trade routes were thirteen degrees or more north of the equator. The Marshalls, of course, were not yet the Marshalls, and their southeast corner, Mili Atoll, was not named anything—by Europeans—until in 1788 it became "Lord Mulgrave's Range" and so appeared on charts like those the *Globe* used.

It was "Lord Mulgrave's Range" not because Constantine John Phipps, second Baron Mulgrave, had discovered it, but because the captain of the British ship *Scarborough* passing through the area

decided to name it for him; he was probably quite conscious of the paradox of memorializing Mulgrave, the great polar explorer, in so warm a place, six degrees above the equator. The captain of the *Scarborough* was William Marshall; sailing in company with him was Thomas Gilbert, captain of the *Charlotte*. When it came to memorializing, both of these explorers fared well: amid the vicissitudes of multiple western christenings and native rechristenings of islands through the centuries, the group that bears Captain Marshall's name is still the Marshalls, and Captain Gilbert's islands have remained the Gilberts although now pronounced "keer-a-bots" and spelled Kiribati.

A few months before arriving in those islands the *Scarborough* and the *Charlotte* had made history as part of the nine transports and two men-of-war that sailed from England in 1787 with convicts to plant the seeds of the future Australia in the barren and desperately cheerless penal colony of Port Jackson. This was the famous—or infamous—"First Fleet." Prisoners unloaded, the ships headed for Canton to pick up cargo for the return journey, most of them taking the obvious and direct route to the north and northwest. Marshall and Gilbert, however, ventured on the most circuitous route imaginable, heading away from China altogether and east past Norfolk Island, passing Fiji on the west, and finally turning north and coming to the lower Gilberts. They did swing west again, made it easily to Canton, and their route, which came to be known as the "Outer Passage," was actually soon preferred as safer by ships covering the same ground. On June 25, 1788, the *Charlotte* approached the atoll about to be named for Lord Mulgrave (Mili henceforward in this account) and made contact with the people.

The Milians had been waiting about two thousand years for the meeting. Whether it was by eerily brilliant navigation or unintentional and fortuitous drift, people from east and southeast Asia were populating the Pacific Islands by 100 to 200 B.C. It was an unmatched feat of migration, depositing human seedlings on a total

70 square miles of land spread over 750,000 square miles of water—those figures are for the Marshalls alone; they have to be extended proportionately to take in the rest of Micronesia (the Carolines, Marianas, and Kiribati) and even more to include Melanesia and Polynesia. It almost seems right that centuries should pass leaving the Oceanians as isolated in time as they were in space. But that was ending now. Captain Gilbert's invitation to a delegation of natives to come aboard the *Charlotte* was the opening up of Mili Atoll to the world. Not only did Gilbert and Marshall leave the earliest picture of its people, which would have foreshadowed the cast of characters of the *Globe* drama, but the two captains may have met the actual cast—some of the very same natives whom thirty-six years later Samuel Comstock and Payne and Oliver and Gilbert Smith and George Comstock and the Kidders and the rest of the crew would descend upon.

Geographically Mili invites the necklace-of-islands cliché used to describe many atolls; it applies somewhat, but Mili's rectangularity is more suggestive of a belt buckle. Except on the north side of the atoll, where a number of islands cluster out into the lagoon, and the southwest corner, where the main settlement of Mili Mili is situated, the atoll looks as if a rope had been dropped into the ocean and was floating there. At points it looks like a trail through the ocean where two people could not easily walk abreast. The outer limits of the atoll are less than thirty miles east to west and twenty miles north to south. At points, passage between ocean and lagoon is possible for relatively small boats at high tide, for example, over the reef between the north point of Mili Mili and Malka; elsewhere, as in the turbulent Tokewa Channel on the north side of the atoll, passage is possible even at low tide. In the winter (the *Globe* arrived in the winter) the seas are much higher, but even then the lagoon is relatively calm. Small boats, assured by their charts of sufficient depth of a passage between lagoon and ocean, have to calculate as well the winter wave heights, for the wave troughs in some of the passages suddenly drop boats to scrape on the coral.

Mili today is not in all its mappable details exactly the same as it was when the *Globe* arrived. Typhoons and tropical depressions erode and extend beaches, divide islands into two or more, or fuse separate islands into one. A typhoon that hit Mili on June 30, 1905, sent three huge waves over the atoll, the last and highest of these described as reaching the tops of the coconut trees. One small island was completely washed away, and islands in the Knox spur of the atoll were stripped down to bare coral. Relief boats had to steer through the debris and corpses floating in the lagoon. Less dramatic but as permanent are the changes wrought by the accretion of coral around the atoll rim. Passage to the lagoon becomes at points impossible for boats that could have cleared a few years before, and islands that were once separate are turned into one, even at high tide. One of the distinctive marks of a recently created island or extension of an island is the relatively low height of the palm trees that have just sprung up on the island. These often stand, silhouetted against the sky, in a single row, if the new islands are too narrow to support more than a line of trees.

The "long narrow island" off which George Comstock said the ship anchored was probably Bokdikdik. In its exploration of the south coast of the atoll, the *Globe* sailed west from the village where it had taken the girls on board, past the long curving island of Arbar, and past three smaller islands that lay between Arbar and Mili Mili: Rupekoj, Bokbar, and Bokdikdik.

The first task on board the *Globe* Sunday morning was to build a raft that would be floated ashore and made fast to the rocks and coral to function as a kind of wharf. At first one boat at a time came in to unload; then, as soon as the hasty carpentry was completed, an improvised catamaran made of spars fastened across two boats began ferrying material from the ship.

Comstock was ashore, and Payne was on the ship managing the off-loading. The whole scene looked like a delivery made by a supply ship to a colony that it visited four times a year. There was food: casks of bread, flour, and molasses; forty barrels of beef and pork; barrels of sugar, dried apples, vinegar, rum, coffee, tea, pickles, and cranberries; even a box of chocolate. There were pigs, for which a pen had to be built. Then the sails: a mainsail, a foresail, a mizzen topsail, a main topgallant, two royals, staysails, studding sails, and a spanker. Some of the sails were turned into a tent, which was to become the *Globe* settlement's administrative center. Coils of rope of many sizes, an anchor, spars, tools, and various gear piled up—even the two binnacle compasses, which it was pointless to have on land—directions were obvious on the atoll, and even if they were not, no one was going to carry those heavy pieces of ship's equipment on a hike along the narrow islands. Every chest of clothing on the ship was brought ashore. The crew worked like a colony of ants, and by late in the day the ship was more than half emptied and unrigged.

The frenzy of the work for a while forestalled thinking, but the big question that had to form in the minds of the crew, and could not be asked out loud without looking around, was, why are we doing this? It had been only three weeks since the mutiny, and the crew was cowed, confused, and resourceless. The fear of some of them was that one or two of their own number might be on good terms with Comstock, Payne, and Oliver. It seems clear in retrospect that no one was really in league with Comstock, Payne, and Oliver, whatever the mental posture of Rowland Coffin and Joseph Thomas, both of whom may have been no worse than self-serving, and of the mutineer manqué, Lilliston, about whom not a word is said from the moment of his desertion from the conspiracy to the moment of his death. The ten unquestionably innocent victims of the mutiny— Gilbert Smith, Stephen Kidder, Peter Kidder, Columbus Worth, Rowland Jones, George Comstock, William Lay, Cyrus Hussey,

Anthony Hanson, and Joseph Brown—can be forgiven for being tensely circumspect, for even if they trusted their confidants, they had to find a time to be alone and out of earshot. And even then, what were they to say? And would the confidant be up to the job of thinking things out or would he be too frightened to make any move?

Gilbert Smith was going to prove adept at covert and judicious strategizing with the crew. But things were coming too fast, and, besides, up to the landing on the island the crew had been completely absorbed in the simple matter of saving the ship and their own lives by preserving a vestige of good shiphandling sense at a time when the crazed officers were playing military games, throwing casks of oil overboard, and preparing to do God knows what.

The landing on Mili was one of the God-knows-what moments. Was this a permanent settlement? Then what? And whether it was permanent or temporary, why was gear that would be of use only on the ship, like the anchor and compasses, being taken ashore? What was going to become of the ship? Whatever dire speculations ran through the minds of the crew, there was no questioning in Comstock's mind what the future of the *Globe* was: as soon as the ship was completely emptied, he would run it aground and set it on fire. At least one among the crew, Stephen Kidder, realized this.

For the natives the spectacle was entrancing. They had never seen anything like it before. More important, they had never before received gifts to match the piñata shower of presents that Comstock made to them from the stores accumulating on shore. As he walked about giving orders to the shore party, he took lavishly from the ship's goods and gave prize after prize to the natives. The gifts included the best clothes from the chests, a curious present for people who were not going to wear them but a welcome one nonetheless, for they were valued for their cloth; within weeks the natives would have torn up the clothing and turned it into ornaments. Comstock's motive for lavishing the gifts on the natives was transparent: he was recruiting them. At a signal that was to be given soon, they would get their orders to kill everyone in the company except him. It was typical Comstock thinking: short-term practicality and long-term absurdity. Even a touch of realism would have led him to wonder what power he was going to have over the natives after the gifts ran out, not to mention what the traditional lives of the natives had been, what their inalienable culture demanded, and how their psychology would impel them to react to the strange white intrusion.

While the ship was being unloaded, Comstock assigned some men to the reconstruction of one of the boats, equipping it with a kind of deck. Then he turned his attention to city planning: he walked about the settlement, mentally laying out its features. This municipality in the palms was to be Comstock-ville, featuring specifically what? The only building that we are told he selected a site for was a church. Doubtless a benefice for Gilbert Smith. God bless our enterprise.

Payne, who was on board the ship supervising the off-loading, got word of what was happening on shore and was angered by Comstock's handling of things there. He sent word that rebuilding the boat should be left until the work of discharging the ship was completed. He was especially furious over the gifts to the natives and told Comstock that if he did not stop giving things away, he would drop what he was doing on the ship, come ashore, and put an end to Comstock's liberality. Comstock immediately ordered Payne ashore. When Payne arrived, the two of them went to the tent and fell into a violent argument. "I helped to take the ship," Comstock said, "and have navigated her to this place. I have also done all I could to get the sails and rigging on shore, and now you may do what you please with her; but if any man wants anything of me, I'll take a musket with him!"

It was a challenge to a duel, and Payne accepted: "That is what I want and am ready." The response was too fast for Comstock, and he deflected it saying, "I will go on board once more, and then you may do as you please." He went out to the ship promptly and as soon as he was on board, found the copy of the "laws" he had drawn up and had forced all on the ship to sign and append their seals to. Drawing his sword, he slashed it to pieces. It was a way of dissociating himself from everything the mutiny had been up to that point, just as the throwing overboard of the barrels of oil on deck right after the killings was a way of dissociating the ship from its whaling identity. The mutiny was over; now came the kingdom.

To all hands on board he threw out challenges to fight him and, as he was leaving the ship, called out, "I am going to leave you; look out for yourselves." At his most excited Comstock was also at his most vague and theatrical.

Payne came back ashore with Comstock, and the two went to the tent, still enraged. Comstock put a sword into his scabbard and said to Payne, "This shall stand me as long as I live." Comstock had made his cutlass the symbol of command and had, according to Stephen Kidder, worn it every day since the mutiny. The sword was childhood play still: he was with the Down Towners again facing the Corlears Hookers. Comstock took a knife as well as his cutlass and some hooks and lines and walked out of the tent. Outside he went up to a gang of natives and tried to make it clear to them that he wanted them to kill Payne. How much they understood, and whether any of the *Globe* people heard what he was saying, is unclear, but later in the day Comstock walked past the tent accompanied by a crowd of about fifty natives; they were heading for what Lay describes as their village, doubtless Mili Mili, about three miles away. (Estimates of distances in all accounts of the period on Mili seem to be frequently exaggerated.)

Payne, alarmed that an attack by Comstock and his native forces was imminent, went on board the ship and selected some of the men to come ashore for the night and form a guard around the tent. He set some of them as sentinels, armed them with muskets, gave every-

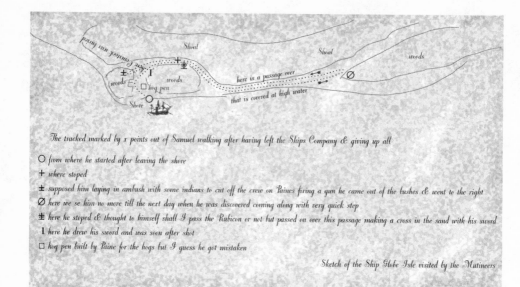

The tracked marked by x points out of Samuel walking after having left the Ships Company & giving up all

O from where he started after leaving the shore
+ where stoped
± supposed him laying in ambush with some indians to cut off the crew on Paines firing a gun he came out of the bushes & went to the right
Ø here we se him no more till the next day when he was discovered coming along with very quick step
‡ here he stoped & thought to himself shall I pass the Rubicon or not but passed on over this passage making a cross in the sand with his sword
1 here he drew his sword and was soon after shot
□ hog pen built by Paine for the hogs but I guess he got mistaken

Sketch of the Ship Globe Isle visited by the Mutineers

Rendering of a map attributed to George Comstock
showing Samuel Comstock's last movements

one a password, and told the sentinels to shoot anyone who approached and could not give the password. Nothing threatening occurred through the night, however.

Payne knew what he wanted to do. He had asked Gilbert Smith if he would kill Comstock; Smith declined. But Oliver, who had been on the ship overnight, came ashore in the morning and joined Payne, who had a number of muskets ready. Payne, Oliver, and at least two others, who are not named, stood waiting in front of the tent with the muskets. They did not have long to wait; Comstock soon walked out of a clump of bushes toward the *Globe* camp. This was Tuesday, February 17, the third day on the island,

The map above, attributed to George Comstock, follows the mutineer's last movements. When Samuel Comstock caught sight of the armed force in front of the tent, he drew his sword and moved with a quick pace toward them, but as the muskets were raised and pointed at him, he waved and shouted, "Don't shoot me, don't shoot me! I will not hurt you!" It was too late. Shots rang out; some went wild but one hit Comstock on the right side of the chest and went through and out near the middle of his back, and another went through his head. As Comstock lay on the ground, Payne, afraid that he might be merely feigning death, approached and swung an axe down on the back of his neck, nearly decapitating him. It was almost like the killing of Captain Worth. Comstock was twenty-one years old.

William's description of his brother's burial is the only ample one, and it is, in every way, related in the distinctive voice of William:

All hands were now called to attend the funeral of their late commander. He was sewed up in a piece of canvass. A grave was dug, by order of Payne, five feet deep. The body was then wrapped in the American flag, and lowered into the grave. His cutlass and every article of dress which he wore at the time of his death, was buried with him, excepting his watch. Muskets were fired over him, and Gilbert Smith read the fourteenth chapter of Isaiah, by order of Payne, who now assumed the command. When the grave was filled, the surviving mutineers required of every man that he should dance upon it, to show his approval of Comstock's murder, and his allegiance to the new authorities. They all complied excepting George Comstock, whom neither threats of death, nor promises of friendship could compel to make an exhibition of triumph at his brother's death. It will be recollected that George was at this time but fifteen years of age. Samuel had been a sort of protector to him; and indeed, the man who murdered the Captain and officers of the Globe was not an unnatural brother.

Something died with Samuel Comstock: the whole island kingdom project. It was an organization held together by a perverse imagination and irrational expectations, but held together it was, up to the moment that the shots rang out. Samuel Comstock was a malignant narcissist. He was a sociopath. Until they destroyed him, these traits enlightened him and gave him purpose and, in consequence, gave the whole ship's company a frightful and loathsome purpose. With the extinguishing of Samuel Comstock's life, everyone—mutineer and victim—was left in the dark.

Payne did not order any further duties for the day but sent Smith and five others on board the *Globe* as shipkeepers, a major miscalculation on his part. What Payne did not know was that for two days Smith had been surreptitiously questioning some of the crew about their interest in escaping in the ship; George Comstock must have been one of Smith's fellow plotters, for Joseph Thomas said that he had proposed retaking the ship. These fugitive conversations were not easy to carry off, but Smith had a sense of whom he was talking to, and he was probably the most respected member of the crew— one could trust him with a confidence. Smith was Starbuck to Comstock's Ahab, and the men recognized that.

The five whom Payne sent out to the ship with Smith were probably not all parties to his plotting, but once aboard they threw their lot in with him. Several of the crew who had been approached by Smith had agreed to join the escape effort, and some of them were prepared to swim the three hundred feet out to the ship at the right moment. Smith knew how scanty the gear and supplies still left on the ship were, but he was ready for the risk of sailing with what little there was. One of his main concerns was that one of the two binnacle compasses that had been brought on shore was indispensable to the voyage. At some point after the big Sunday off-loading, Smith managed, without being detected, to conceal one of the compasses in a boat and get it on board the ship. To keep the absence of the compass from being noticed, he smuggled the cabin's hanging compass on shore and put it in place of the binnacle compass. (The hanging compass was mounted upside down above the captain's bunk, so that he could look up at any time and see the ship's direction. An upside-down compass would be impossibly awkward to use on deck.) The swap worked.

It was late in the day when the six men went on board the ship. The five other than Smith were George Comstock, Stephen and Peter Kidder, Anthony Hanson, and Joseph Thomas. They were a mixed crew: George Comstock, unquestionably honest and reliable, was the kind of crewman that Smith wanted, but he was in a wretched state of mind over his brother's murder and the whole mutiny. The churlish Joseph Thomas was probably one of the last crew members that Smith would have invited to join the escape, but he was one of the party that Comstock had sent out to the ship, so Smith was stuck with him. Thomas was the only *Globe* survivor to be seriously suspected of involvement in the mutiny, and on the escape voyage he was to prove shiftless and insubordinate.

Around 7 P.M. Smith's crew started liberating the ship. Smith brought up on deck the few weapons that he found below: a musket, three bayonets, and some whale lances. Some of what the men on board were doing could be seen from shore, so it was necessary to do only what would seem explicable to those looking out at the ship, work like clearing the running rigging, and leave the more obvious moves for dusk. Above all, this meant that the sails could not be set until the last minute. On the windlass Smith put a greased handsaw to cut the cable and abandon the anchor; no effort was to be made to raise it. A hatchet—there was only one left on board—was put near the mizzenmast to be used to cut the stern moorings. It was darker now as Smith and one other went up the foremast and loosed the fore topsail. Two other men were loosing the main topsail and the mainsail, but none of the sails were shaken out because the bunt gaskets, which held the center parts of the sails, were left tied. At a signal these would be loosed and the sails unfurled. The men were working with cover of darkness now, but only for a while, for the moon was rising. A decision had to be made: There were more men ashore who were counting on swimming out to the ship at the right moment, but the moonlight was threatening to give the escape away. The minute the sails were set, it would be clear on shore what was happening. Smith knew he would be leaving some ashore who wanted to join the ship, and whom the ship sorely needed, but at 9:30 he made his move. It took less than two minutes to saw through the cable and cut loose the anchor. The wind was from off shore and swung the ship out from the island and toward the open sea. Someone cut loose the kedge, the small anchor dropped at the stern to prevent the ship from swinging around toward the coral shore, and the crew set the sails. A raft alongside holding iron hoops was also cut loose. The *Globe* sailed into the moonlit night with one-third its normal complement of sail and one-fourth its normal crew.

Near the tent two men stood watch; around 10 o'clock, minutes after the ship's getaway, they awakened the camp with the cry, "The ship has gone, the ship has gone!" Some knew exactly what had happened, but some who were not privy to Smith's plan speculated that the ship must have merely dragged anchor in a strong wind. For those who had the full picture of what had happened, especially those who had missed their chance to make it to the ship before sailing, the prospect was frightening. Even though experiences on the island for these few days had been agreeable, they knew they were trapped there. What were the odds of a ship coming by and landing a boat? And if they could sail off in a boat from the *Globe*, sail to where? Another island just like the one they were on?

When, in the morning, it was clear that the ship had not just drifted off, Payne was apoplectic with rage. His fear was the exact opposite of that of the innocent crew: he imagined the *Globe* reporting the mutiny and the United States government sending forces to seize him and Oliver, a logical enough scenario from a modern vantage point but not exactly the kind of thing there were precedents for in the 1820s. Comstock, if he were alive, would not have been as alarmed as Payne; the Pacific was not policed. But Payne's alarm would have been vindicated.

Payne ordered that one of the whaleboats be built up with a deck; he explained that he was worried that the natives might make them leave the island. The explanation did not go over well, for there was a most natural speculation that that boat was not intended to convey all nine people left on the island, but rather Payne and whomever he chose.

The natives continued to be friendly, spending a lot of time at the *Globe* camp, bartering food for iron, and even sleeping around the camp. For two days life was agreeable to the point that work slackened and both the leaders and the crew did some casual exploring and rambling. There was no question that the atoll was turning out to be as pleasant as one could have hoped—if one were there voluntarily. The sand was white and almost powdery; the beaches on the lagoon side were broad and inviting. The temperatures were comfortable, and the nights peaceful; from time to time one would hear the coconuts fall with a "powff" sound as they hit the fine sand. Overhead the stars were almost unnaturally bright—almost, a later visitor said, like a planetarium display. By sunrise clouds had formed over the lagoon-like buildings built on the surface of the water. In an hour or two after dawn the cloud buildings lifted from the water into the sky without losing their shape; their bottoms were planes parallel to the surface of the lagoon as if they had been stacked up on tables of various heights.

On Thursday the nineteenth Lay and others made a foray to a village of twenty or thirty families east of the *Globe* camp. There they became a visiting carnival for the natives, especially the women and children, who cavorted around them gleefully; everything about the white-skinned visitors, especially their talk, provoked howls of laughter.

The next day turned into time off as well. Payne was going to set some men to work on rebuilding the boat, but changed his mind and let the men take a *jambo*, as the Milians would call it today, a rambling excursion around the island. Lay and others went to Mili Mili, where they were received hospitably and where they entertained the natives with a display of musket firing. Bad policy, Lay later thought, for the natives could not fail to be uncomfortable about strangers with such extraordinary weaponry. They showed nothing but amazement, however, on this occasion. One of the older natives invited Lay to stay over for the night, and Lay did until the rats got to be too much for him and he left to return around 10 P.M. to the *Globe* tent, escorted by several of the natives.

Payne and Oliver and two or three others set off in a boat for some exploring and stayed overnight in a village where they clearly had been well received, for they returned in the morning with two women from the village, who struck the four or five men back at the tent as being "diverted" by their adventure. Payne was more than diverted; he was at a crest of good feeling and confidence, so much so that he did not post a guard around the tent in the evening when he retired with his bride.

If a guard had been on duty, he would have seen no incursions on the camp during the night but one desertion. When Payne awoke in the early morning from an unusually sound sleep, his bride was gone. Fiercely angry, he called Oliver and Lilliston, gave them muskets and took one himself, and set out for the village the girl had come from. The sun had not yet risen when they arrived there; sunrise is around six o'clock every day of the year, the atoll is so close to the equator. Payne and his raiders spied from bushes until the village began to awaken; when they spotted the runaway bride, the three men sprang from the bushes and fired a blank shot from a musket. The natives fled with Payne in pursuit, firing over their heads. He caught up with his unfaithful woman and dragged her back to the *Globe* camp, where he flogged her mercilessly and put her in irons.

Payne's sense of public relations was ineffable. He was a gross fool for throwing away one of the most amicable native connections that he could have made anywhere in the Pacific. He had already seen native hostility in the Gilberts and should have been counting his blessings over the reception the *Globe* people received on Mili. On Monday the twenty-third, the day after Payne imprisoned his woman, the camp discovered that the tool chest had been broken open and rifled during the night; a hatchet, chisel, and other things were missing. Payne fell into another one of his rages. He ranted at the natives and warned them that he would have revenge if the missing items were not returned. An unusually large number of natives milled around the camp and visited the tent during the day. Payne was misreading the situation completely; he was so obsessed with the loss of tools that he did not realize that the theft had a larger meaning: the *Globe* people were no longer friends—they could not be after the mistreatment of the abducted woman. When Payne fulminated over the theft, the natives listened with a great show of sympathy and regret, but their cordiality was, from that point on, a pose. Anything could happen now.

In the evening some natives arrived at the camp, one of them carrying half the stolen chisel. Payne angrily told the native that he needed the whole chisel, not half of it. He put the native in chains and told him that in the morning he would have to take some of his men to the stolen goods and identify the thieves. The imprisoned messenger was anything but happy about his reception, but the natives who had accompanied him did not seem distressed in any way. What should have occurred to Payne was that the chisel episode was a piece of reconnaissance: the half-chisel (which was probably broken with rocks and intended as an insult) would give the natives a chance to test reaction and detect what planning was afoot. As the natives were to prove on a later occasion, they were very good spies, and masters of deadpan. The chisel party was taking notes.

The next day, Tuesday the twenty-fourth, was to be the most momentous day since the mutiny. In the morning Payne assigned Rowland Jones, Rowland Coffin, Cyrus Hussey, and Thomas Lilliston to go to the village, find the stolen hatchet and its thief, and bring back both to the camp. Neither Payne nor Oliver chose to be part of the mission. The native who had delivered the half-chisel was unshackled and put in charge of the raiding party, so that he could point out where the hatchet was and who was its thief. The four crewmen were given muskets with bird shot, since, Payne assumed, it would suffice to show the muskets *in terrorem* and would be unnecessary to load them with balls.

The four raiders did secure the hatchet and were on the point of returning when a large number of natives confronted them. They were carrying stones. It was useless to point the muskets, which, even if fired, would terrorize no one in a group like this. The four men backed off; that was the cue for the attack to begin. As they ran for the tent, all four were hit by some stones; Rowland Jones fell behind, was overtaken, and instantly killed.

Everyone in the tent picked up arms and waited. Outside the tent a group of natives had gathered and were conferring together. After a while they walked over to one of the tied-up boats and began wrecking it. Payne had to act at that point. He approached one of the chiefs, sat down on the ground with him for a while, then went back to the gathered natives and conferred with them for nearly an hour—whatever conferring without a common language meant—signs work for exchanges of gifts and requests for water, but not for a summit conference. Payne felt, however, that he had communicated, for when he came back to the tent, he told the others that he had reached an agreement with the natives. It was complete capitulation, but nothing else would have sufficed; the natives were to have all the *Globe* property, even the tent, and the eight remaining *Globe* people would submit to be governed by the chiefs and to adopt the native style of living. William Lay was appalled at the thought that he and his six innocent companions were now trapped between two enemies, one as bad as the other, and what he kept thinking was the worst part of it was that he and his mates were innocent of any of the murderous deeds on the ship or of any other wrongdoing.

The new owners of the *Globe* property did not waste any time in seizing it; the natives roamed around the camp picking up whatever they fancied. Some of them began tearing the tent down. Precisely at this moment an older native couple came up to Lay, took him firmly by the hands, and led him fifty feet or more away from the camp. He did not know their designs and feared the worst. At the same time he sensed that he was being helped in some way and for reasons that he could not fathom. The only thing he could think was that he had done some kindnesses to the old woman, taking her side when some of the other natives had been teasing her. But if the couple were saving him, not leading him to his death, what about the others? What was going to happen to them? Especially what was going to happen to Cyrus Hussey, Lay's best friend?

Then pandemonium broke out. Shouting and screaming, the natives charged at the *Globe* men with stones and spears. The attackers were not only men, but women and even children, all armed. The seamen ran off in any direction they could. Two of them, Lilliston and Joe Brown, one of the Hawaiian recruits, fell within six feet of Lay, who watched as the natives smashed their skulls with rocks. Columbus Worth, the young seaman who was a cousin of Captain Worth, was pursued by a woman at least sixty years old who brought him down with a spear and then stoned him to death. Lay watched as Payne was led off by two natives, who, Lay thought, were going to save him, but one of them smashed Payne with a large stone, and when he attempted to run, hit him with another; he fell and was killed on the spot. Oliver was caught by natives in a clump of bushes and killed there. Seaman Rowland Hussey was also killed.

The old couple guarding Lay ordered him to lie down out of sight and then stretched out on top of him; this was partly to keep him from being seen and partly to shield him from watching the horrors. One native did spot him and came over to beat him with a handspike from the *Globe* gear, but the old couple would not let him get at Lay, and the native left after a few words to the old couple, the import of which Lay could not make out.

Lay's protectors led him in haste toward their village over coral causeways that cut his feet. They were anxious to outdistance pursuers if there were any. By noon they were at the home of the old couple; almost at once the hut was surrounded by an excited crowd of natives. Lay could not make out the mood of the crowd and assumed that they were there to kill him and that his protectors would be helpless to save him.

Suddenly he saw a group of natives walking up to the hut. A shock of astonishment and gratitude swept through him as he watched the procession move toward him. There in their midst was Cyrus Hussey. He looked safe and healthy, even though he had been bruised by stones in the morning, and he was being treated solicitously by the natives around him. The joy of the two good friends on being reunited was intense, but it was not enough to put all their anxieties to rest, for they were afraid that what they were enjoying at the moment was not a pardon from but a postponement of execution. The worst was as imaginable as the best, and what was the best that could happen now? They knew that when the sun rose that morning there had been nine *Globe* people on Mili, and now there were two.

They were the survivors but they were marooned.

CHAPTER FIVE

ETTO AMRO PAD
IOON ANEO

The day of the massacre was February 24. When Lay was led away from the scene by his two protectors, he could look back at Rowland Jones and Payne and Oliver and Lilliston and Joe Brown and Columbus Worth and Rowland Coffin bleeding into the sand. Nothing was clear to the two survivors; in their *Narrative* they rolled all of their feelings into one phrase: "superlatively miserable." But nothing was clear to the natives either. The whole situation was unprecedented. Violence the natives were capable of, like the hostilities that were threatening war at that very moment between the chief of the northwestern island of Naalo and an alliance of other chiefs of the atoll. And murder was not unknown on the islands. But this was an attack on the visitors from outer space, and not everyone was of one mind about it; in time they would hear from one of their chiefs that they had done an evil thing.

And the timing was bad. The dead bodies and the two survivors and the rubble of the *Globe* camp were going to need explaining to outsiders, for islanders from the far corners of the atoll would be arriving over the next three days for the celebration of a major ceremony. Some of them had heard about the ship and its strange people, but most had not. What were the chiefs to say to them? Who were the two men's masters, and how did they come to have the white men in their care? How did this affect relations between chiefs, especially when the two men were thought of as prizes? How would the two fit into the routine of island life? It was the middle of the first of two pandanus seasons of the year, and there would be harvesting to do, and there was always fishing. Would there be two new hands for the work? And would they want to work? And could they be trusted?

These were matters for the chiefs to speculate and rule on. The *irooj*, chief, was the authority on an island or part of an island and was frequently obliged to be in Mili Mili for councils or official business. Most of the time, an *irooj*, even if he was coming from one of the remote eastern islands, was able to travel to Mili Mili within a few hours. All the chiefs were subordinate to the *iroojlaplap*, or high chief of the atoll, whose official residence was in Mili Mili. At the time Lay and Hussey were on the atoll, the *iroojlaplap* was Luttuon. All through their stay, the ultimate determination of their fate in serious matters lay with the chiefs. At some point early on the chiefs decided that Hussey should be made a ward of Lugoma, an *irooj*. Lay was assigned to the unnamed old man who had saved his life, but the old man was poor and hardly able to feed him, so the *iroojlaplap* intervened and arranged his adoption by a native named Ludjuan.

The next morning, February 25, Lay and Hussey, whom the natives were anxious to keep apart, were nonetheless brought by canoe back to the scene of the previous day's slaughter. What hit the two men hardest was the sight of the bodies. They had to bury them, they knew, and communicated their desire to do so to the natives, who allowed them to dig graves and inter the mangled corpses. It was a lot of work, even though the soil was sandy, for there were seven to bury. And these dead, guilty and innocent alike, had been part of the flesh and blood drama that had tied them together for a month. It was a unique but potent intimacy that evoked, simultaneously, pathos and revulsion. Most of the bodies had crushed heads; Columbus Worth was covered with blood from stab wounds. Then there was Rowland Coffin, who had been suspiciously knowledgeable about the mutiny, but what did that matter now? What, in fact, did Payne and Oliver, whose viciousness did not even have the redeeming imagination of Samuel Comstock, matter? Gilbert Smith, if he had still been around, could have read a scriptural text over them as well as the others. And poor Joe Brown, who had signed on as one of the Honolulu replacements—Lay and Hussey did not know him well but could not help seeing him as one of the unluckiest. There was something brutalizing about the burial just as there had been about the cleaning up of the bloody cabin a month before; if Lay and Hussey weathered the experience with as much stability as they did, it may have owed something to their youth, their faith, or simply their terror of what was coming next. Mortal threats organize the psyche marvelously.

All around the two grave-diggers lay the relics of the *Globe* camp. The natives had stolen much since the day before and had pulled down the tent. When the two men completed the burials, they were sweating and worn out. They surveyed the despoiled camp to see if any food was left; there was, and the two indicated to their masters that they wanted to take some of it. The masters agreed and helped them load flour, bread, and pork into the largest canoe. They also brought into the canoe a blanket apiece, shoes, and books. The books included two Bibles; the natives would soon destroy Lay's, but Hussey would manage to retain his.

The canoes headed back to where Lay and Hussey had been kept the night before. Even though they were held in the same place, they were allowed little contact with each other. Two things struck the natives as suspicious: any conversation between them in their incomprehensible language and any looking at those disturbing items, their books. The men tried to explain that the books contained ideas that they wanted to think about, but the native reaction was a replay of the process by which the English word *glamour* (the power to enchant) derived from the word *grammar* (the power to read and write). The books looked like the instruments of dark arts.

All the way back from the *Globe* camp Lay was growing hungrier, and he longed to eat some of the pork and bread being carried in the canoe. Would his master allow him to break into the pork supply? The permission was granted, partly, no doubt, out of concern for his need, but more out of curiosity—the natives wanted to see how the white men cut and prepared pork. For the occasion they even made the concession of allowing Hussey to eat with Lay. The preparation that Lay chose was, to give it an enhanced name, pork stew—to be precise, pork boiled in a large shell. That meant making a fire: someone had to fetch an *eton*, a pair of sticks from a dry tree, one of which had a straight groove cut into it and was held more or less upright between the legs while the other was rubbed rapidly in the groove, producing a fine sawdust that caught fire. The water in which the pork was cooked may have come from the shell itself, for one of the water-collecting techniques on the islands was to put large shells under the roots of pandanus trees and catch the runoff. The pandanus has a trunk that begins several feet above the ground and sends a skirt of exposed roots with open space between them down into the earth. Shells near the bottom of the roots catch the dripping water. As Lay and Hussey settled into their meal of boiled pork, one of the onlookers brought them a tin cup with water, for the natives had noticed back in the *Globe* camp that the white men drank when they ate. A tin cup was not an island utensil; it must have come from the *Globe*'s stores.

For the next three days, as canoes arrived from remote parts of the atoll to prepare for a major ceremony, Lay and Hussey were a sideshow. Their pale skin was a marvel, and their clothing, in the popular view, was unnatural. Over and over again the visitors urged the pale people to adopt their style of clothing; at this point the two held out, but in time they would relent.

On the morning of February 28 (the last precise date that Lay and Hussey record until their rescue twenty-one months later), the natives ornamented themselves for the feast. Probably more ornamented, because of their tattooing, than any humans that Lay and Hussey had laid eyes on, they rendered themselves glittering from annointings of coconut oil and hung about them strings of *marmars*, shell necklaces strung on fine coconut thread fibers. The gathering place was a flat piece of ground a half mile from the village where Lay and Hussey were detained; that had to be Mili Mili, for no place else on the atoll could have easily accommodated the more than three hundred participants that assembled.

"Hideous" was Lay's word for the look of the crowd. He could have added *ominous* as well, for both he and his friend had one thing in mind as they approached the gathering place: it was going to be a cannibal rite, and they were the entrée. Tales of cannibalism circulated throughout the whaling fleets; the fear of it kept ships away from islands that would have otherwise been good victualling stops. This looked like one of the real cannibal moments. But the impression lasted only a few minutes, for it became clear that the occasion was a ritual dance, not a grimmer ritual.

There was still something terrifying about the scene, though. The dance was accompanied by the beat of drums and the strains of a chant. The *aje*, the small hourglass-shaped hardwood drums covered by the lining of shark's stomach, were played by twenty or thirty women who also supplied the chant. The music began low and gradually crescendoed like Ravel's *Bolero*; the three hundred or so dancers moved in an astonishing rhythm to it and joined in the sound; the effect was intense, breathtaking, and hypnotic. The women drummers were the *lejm'aanjuri*; they were well practiced, for it was their duty on the eve of battle to play the drums this way to *piniktak*—to urge on the warriors. To William Lay the vocal part of the performance was not music at all but yelling, and it was frightening. In what was a classic confrontation between the civilized New Englander and the representatives of a never-before-visited culture, the whole performance was not primitive art—it was hysteria. The dance went on through the day and ended in the evening. The visitors turned to their canoes to travel across the lagoon in the dark, but did not leave without another look at the sideshow: the oil- and sweat-coated dancers sought out and surrounded the two white men, not just to stare at them but to feel their skins. One of the weirdest things about the day was that Lay and Hussey had found themselves in the midst of a special time: it was as if two of the natives had been carried to as alien a place as Rio de Janeiro and just happened to arrive at carnival time. So, this was what life was like here? No, it's not what life was like, most of the time.

Lay, Hussey, and their masters returned by canoe to their village, where the day ended with a hearty meal, thanks to the *Globe* supplies on hand. The pork came out again, but this time it was cooked more palatably on a bed of coals; the natives still did not like it, but they did fancy the bread, which proved more popular than the two seamen would have preferred. The woman, Lay says, whom he called mistress "ate, to use a sea phrase, her full allowance."

All of this had happened in their first four days among the natives. In the months ahead, there was a lot of fitting in to do. The two would become used to the four native foods—breadfruit, pandanus, coconuts, and fish—and they would face periods of famine and drought when there would be barely enough of any of these to survive on. They would be forced to develop the skills of diplomats, never more so than when contending with native superstition. And they would be importuned to go native in their clothing and to have their earlobes bored and stretched. There was etiquette to learn for social occasions. There was even a quite practical toilet etiquette to observe: squatting at water's edge at low tide to allow the rising water to flush the waste out to sea.

The month of March passed with nothing recorded except an increasing unwillingness on the part of the natives to let the two men speak with each other. Then the bad news came—Lay says it was around April 1, Hussey says the end of April: they were to be separated.

What happened to the two from this point up to the time of their rescue is reported in a less than complete and sometimes contradictory fashion in Lay and Hussey's published *Narrative* and, to some extent, in the passage in Lieutenant Paulding's *Journal* where Paulding summarizes what Lay had told him. Of the nine chapters in Lay and Hussey's *Narrative,* only chapters 8 and 9 are attributed to Hussey; the rest are told in Lay's voice. Dating is not easy: the *Narrative* makes passing reference to April and July of the first year the two spent on the atoll, but it is easier to date events during the twenty-one months that they were living with the natives by references to the seasons of crops. (Breadfruit ripened from May to August and from November to January; pandanus's seasons were January to May and August to November.)

The separation amounted to no change of scene for Lay and to exile for Hussey. Lay stayed with Ludjuan on Mili Mili, and Hussey was taken to Lugoma's island, Lukunor, about twenty-five miles to the east, possibly the very community to which the *Globe* had sent boats ashore to take off women on its first coming to the atoll three months before. It would be another three months before Lay would see Hussey again.

Lay watched his supply of pork and bread, gathered at the *Globe* camp the day after the massacre, dwindle. He obtained permission, probably in early May, for another trip to the camp for food, and a canoe was readied for the purpose. The camp was near, even within walking distance, but the purpose of the trip was the transportation of a considerable amount of food and that would require the canoe. Entering the canoe, Lay had one of those moments of misgiving that were to recur all too frequently during his time on the island: The natives carried clubs and spears. Were they planning to do something to him? The experience was a replay of his anxiety a few weeks before over whether or not he was being taken to a cannibal feast. Shortly it became clear that they were just going fishing. The natives found a shoal of fish, waded around them, and killed a number with their spears. A meal of these fish was prepared as soon as the canoe tied up at the *Globe* camp; the natives cooked them on a bed of wood burned to coals and generously offered Lay a share, but he was not in a mood for dining, for he was upset by what he saw when he looked around the camp. The barrels of beef, pork, and molasses had been smashed open and lay rotting in the sun—for how long he could only guess— it could have been for weeks. In addition to the waste of food, every-thing else at the site had been vandalized: clothing was torn to bits, and the ship's instruments had been destroyed to make ornaments out of the parts. In spite of the pork's decomposing state, Lay put some of it, along with some of the clothing, in the canoe for the short trip east.

May and June passed. The natives destroyed Lay's books. Life was monotonous and lonely. Lay began to wonder whether, if his situa-tion was truly hopeless, he could adjust to it. Then a ray of light: Luckiair, the son-in-law of his master Ludjuan, came for a visit from his home on the island of Jelbon at the far southeastern end of the atoll. Lay and Luckiair quickly became friends, and when Luckiair was preparing to return, he mentioned that he would be passing near the place where Hussey was living. Immediately Lay asked Ludjuan if he could accompany his son-in-law; it took persuading, but Ludjuan finally agreed to allow him to go.

The trip began with another stop at the *Globe's* camp; the ship's provisions were even more deteriorated, but Lay nonetheless took some of the food. Luckiair headed for the northern side of the lagoon despite the fact that his destination was on the south side, and they camped for the night in a deserted hut on a small island. Lay brought out the questionable *Globe* food and cooked the pork and some wet flour on the ashes, and they retired for the night in the hut.

Faced with the continuing strong east wind, Luckiair decided to stay where they were for another day. They gathered breadfruit, which was just beginning to ripen, and made a more formal preparation of the meat than they had the night before—they cooked it as they would cook a large fish. Lay describes the technique: They dig a large hole in the ground, fill it with wood, start the fire, and then cover the burning wood with stones. The wood burns down, and the stones fall to the bottom of the pit. When the fire is out, the stones are covered with green leaves, on which the fish or meat is placed, and covered with another layer of leaves. Earth is placed on top of these, and the buried food is cooked by the radiant heat from the stones. The process, Lay says, preserves the juices of the fish; what it did for rotten pork he does not say.

Before the day was over, the weather cleared, and Lay and Luckiair sailed east again, arriving near dusk at the island of Tokewa. Here they were well received; loaded with gifts of breadfruit and coconuts, they left for the south side of the lagoon and Hussey's village, Lukunor. The reunion of the two, the first since they had been separated three months before, was extremely emotional but short-lived, just an hour. Lay told Hussey that the natives had torn up his Bible;

Hussey told Lay that they had torn up his clothing, which explained why he was wearing the native dress, a wide belt of artistically braided pandanus leaves with front- and back-hanging tassels. He was so painfully burned from exposure to the sun that he could not lie down in comfort; he had tried to explain to the natives that that would happen if he was not able to keep his clothes, but his command of the language was not as good as Lay's, and he could not convey the idea of sunburn to them. The natives had never heard of such a thing. Hussey had been employed in the breadfruit harvest and would have taken more part in the fishing but for the difficulty he had walking in his bare feet on the rough beaches.

Then the visit was over, and Lay and Luckiair were sailing east again to Jelbon. When they arrived, they found Luckiair's wife and child busy making a fishing net; in the evening Lay and Luckiair gathered breadfruit, out of which a dinner was prepared. It was a family feast, for Lay's status in Ludjuan's family was almost that of a son, so that he was virtually a brother of Luckiair's wife. The next day two native couples arrived from Lukunor with flour and a piece of meat, presumably part of the supplies that Lay had collected at the *Globe* camp and had left, intentionally or unintentionally, with Hussey's guardians. Lay's "vacation" in Jelbon lasted about a week.

Back in Mili Mili Lay was welcomed gleefully as if he had been absent for a long time. He describes a gift that he had been given by one of the chiefs: *jekaka*, which is the prepared version of *bob*, or pandanus. Pandanus, the fruit of which is a beautiful reddish orange, is arguably the most delicious of the island products. When not eaten fresh, it is preserved as something close to candy. The mode of preparation is to scrape the fruit finely and dry it in the sun, then put it into a cylinder of its own leaves (the cylinder is made by tying pandanus leaves around a piece of wood, then removing the wood).

It was around this time that Lay stopped wearing (but stored away) his American clothes for the same native style that Hussey had adopted, and with the same results: he was burned to a crisp. The folk in Mili Mili marveled at his red skin just as those in Lukunor had at Hussey's.

In Lukunor Hussey was given the task of working on the repair of a canoe, a more interesting assignment than fishing or picking bread-fruit because it introduced Hussey to the remarkable craft of Marshallese boat building. This was activity worthy of a seaman. There were three sizes of canoes: the smallest, the *korkor*, went out with one or two people in it and was used in the lagoon for fishing and traveling from one island to another; the larger *tipnol* carried up to ten people and could venture out into the open ocean; the very large *walap* carried forty along with food needed on extended voyages. They traveled at ten knots or faster and could easily outrace western boats.

The boats were an engineering triumph. They were made of boards cut from the breadfruit tree and painstakingly fayed into place. Perfect contours for watertight sealing between the boards were achieved by rubbing the edges to be joined with a burned piece of straight wood that would leave soot on the boards at points which were even slightly raised out of line. These bulges would then be worked down to a perfectly straight edge. The tools used on the wood were sharp shells (and for boring holes, sharks' teeth). The finished boards were literally sewed together with coconut fiber cords.

The canoes had sharp, narrow keels, and double-ended hulls that permitted a reversal of direction, not by coming around, but by shifting the triangular sail setting so that the back of the boat became the front. This took less than a minute. The hull was not symmetrical: one side was nearly flat, while the other bayed out in a normal boat contour. The outrigger, like the hull, made of breadfruit wood, stood far out from the hull and was connected by a platform that could be used for carrying goods (that did not need to be kept dry) or people; weight on the platform had a ballast effect on the boat, especially in rough seas. To tie up the canoes someone would dive with a line and secure it to a rock or a coral projection. Lay had watched natives go thirty feet down with their lines.

Although Lay and Hussey say relatively little about the canoes at any point in their *Narrative*, they were in them constantly and could not help developing a sailor's respect for them. It is likely that Hussey, who talks more about fishing than Lay does, learned how to handle the *korkor* that Lugoma fished from. Some of the trips between Lukunor and Mili Mili, on which fish and breadfruit were carried, would have been made in a *tipnol*, and on these Hussey may have acceded to the elevated position of handling steering oars and reversing sail, but he was very likely assigned to the middle place in the boat, the baler's position.

Some time, probably in August, after he had finished his work on the canoe, Hussey was invited to join a foray of folk from the village delivering a tribute of breadfruit and fish to the atoll chiefs, who would have assembled at Mili Mili. The best thing about the trip for Hussey was that it was his second reunion with Lay, but as before, the natives allowed the two little time together.

It was clear to Lay that the reason for not letting him and Hussey spend time together was not mainly that they would be conspiring— what, after all, could they conspire to do?—but that their communication with each other was offensive to the supreme god, Anit. Anit was going to be an influential figure in the lives of Lay and Hussey. Anit had to be consulted before big and small decisions and undertakings. He was consulted for such business as whether candidates for tattooing were ready for the rite (he would announce his approval by an audible tone or whistle); Lay and Hussey were bigger business than tattooing, and they raised a lot of questions for Anit. At the critical moment months later when Lay and Hussey had a chance to escape from the island, Anit was invoked by the *iroojlaplap*, and on his answer the rescue to some extent depended.

The ethnographer Horatio Hale, who visited Mili a dozen or so years after Lay and Hussey were there, left some early impressions of Micronesian theology that harmonize with the two men's account. The spirits that the Micronesians worship, Hale says, "are called at the Ladrones, *aniti*, at the Kingsmills, *anti*, at the Mulgraves, *anit* and *anis*, at Banabe, *hani* or *ani*. . . . They have neither temples, images, nor sacrifices. Their worship consists merely in praying and performing certain ceremonies."

The supreme divinity was theologically simple, even generic, but the theology of the afterlife was a bit more elaborate. A good capsule treatment of it comes from none other than Lay himself. He ends chapter 7 of his *Narrative* with a paragraph that rather remarkably anticipates and accords with the observations of later anthropologists: "With regard to a future state of existence, they believe that the *shadow*, or what survives of the body, is after death, entirely happy; that it roves about at pleasure, and takes much delight in beholding everything that is transacted in this world;—and as they consider the world as an extensive plain, they suppose the disembodied spirits travel quite to the edge of the skies, where they think white people live, and then back again to their native Isles; and at times they fancy they can hear the spirits of departed friends whistling round their houses, and noticing all the transactions of the living."

The detail is striking; even given Lay's rapid acquisition of the native language, the concepts in this passage are sophisticated ones for him to have picked up in discourse with the natives, yet in the two and a half years between his rescue and the appearance of his *Narrative* in print, Lay had limited opportunity to talk about the anthropology of religion with anyone in the Pacific or in New England, at least not anyone who knew something about it. There was, however, one person in the Pacific with a keen interest in native ideas of the afterlife, and Lay did meet him, the Reverend Hiram Bingham, the most renowned of the Protestant missionaries in

Oceania. When Lay's rescue ship, the *Dolphin*, reached Honolulu, Mr. Bingham sought him out to quiz him about Milian vocabulary (see the headnote to Appendix C); it would have been quite in character for the assiduous missionary to have talked to Lay and Hussey at length about anything that would prove useful to him in proselytizing. For Lay the conversation could have had the stimulating effect that any good intellectual talk would have—it would sharpen recollections and organization. All that is speculation. But if the reader thinks it a sound speculation, what will he make of the lines that immediately follow the above-quoted passage? "Singular as some of these notions and opinions may appear, there is much to be met with in Christendom equally at variance with reason; and I have heard from the pulpit, in New England, the following language: 'I have no doubt in my own mind that the blessed in Heaven look down on all the friends and scenes they left behind, and are fully sensible of all things that take place on earth!' " Not the words of Mr. Bingham. No voice as distinctive as a crotchet's, but whose? We are clueless, for nothing like this comes up anywhere else in the *Narrative*. The ghost-writer has lifted his mask for a moment.

So reunion number two ended; Lay went back to the routine of the harvest of breadfruit, and Hussey left with his conductors after a couple of days. Hussey's party headed not directly for Lukunor but for the northern island of Tokewa, where breadfruit was to be had in such abundance that the harvesters had to leave much of it to spoil on the ground. This route repeated the course taken by Luckiair and Lay when they came to Lukunor; it seems to have been a popular one, not merely for working the wind to advantage but for the avoidance of some shoals at low tide. At the same time that Hussey was working on Tokewa, Lay, at work with a group gathering a peculiarly large kind of breadfruit, heard a small boy who had run up to the natives say, "*Uroit a-ro rayta mony la Wirrum*"—the chiefs are going to kill William. Ludjuan, his master, saw that Lay had understood the words that were not intended for his ears. *"Riab, riab,"* Ludjuan insisted—it is false, it is false. The reassurance was not enough. Lay knew that there was something about him and Hussey that made the natives leery, even frightened of them. That night was a sleepless one for Lay, and the next day his agitation was too much to conceal from the natives: while working at the harvest, he burst into tears. When evening came he was no more successful in falling asleep than he had been the night before. Around midnight he overheard some of the natives saying that he was to be killed. When he confronted them and asked why, the natives denied everything; they were surprised that he had understood them. One of them who had been especially friendly to him in the past came over to his mat and stretched out next to him, assuring him that nothing would happen to him.

Nothing threatening did happen the next day; arrangements were under way for a harvest feast, and *bwiro*, cooked breadfruit with the taste of sweet potato, was being prepared for distribution to the chiefs. The feast marked the end of the breadfruit harvest, which meant for the moment the end of harvesting work for Lay; he was idle most of the time during the few days since he heard his death being discussed and thought it wise to stay out of sight in his hut as much as possible, especially since he sensed that he was under a new and suspicious surveillance.

Meanwhile Hussey was on Tokewa with his master, helping him to load more of the overabundant breadfruit. While they were at work, a canoe arrived with a message from "the highest chief" that Hussey was to be returned to Mili Mili and killed. This time the reason, which Lay had unsuccessfully been trying to pry from the natives, came out at once in the blunt announcement of the messengers that an alarming outbreak of disease (how widespread on the atoll is not stated) was attributed to the presence of the two *Globe* men among them.

The symptoms of the disease were swelling of the hands and feet, and in some cases the faces. Some young people had cheeks so swollen that they could not see for a few days. There were no fatalities, but the deformities were so shocking that it was easy to imagine that they were a prelude to death. When he was told about the disease, Hussey tried to explain that he and his friend could not have been the cause since no such disorder was known in his country. He could have saved his breath, for Lugoma did not need convincing, and back on Mili Mili, epidemiological arguments were not going to carry any weight: Lay and Hussey were the causes for preternatural reasons.

Lugoma wasted no time. Instead of returning to Lukunor to drop off the breadfruit he had been collecting on Tokewa, he bundled Hussey into the canoe and set off immediately for Mili Mili. His haste was not a sign that he was complying with the chief's order—he was going there in order to get answers. On landing, Lugoma went immediately to Luttuon to find out how he justified the death sentence.

Hussey and Lugoma's family stayed in the canoe while Lugoma (whom he calls "father") was conferring on shore. It was there that Lay, accompanied by his master Ludjuan, found his friend. On this third and unanticipated reunion they did not have to tell each other how they felt. With the death sentence hanging over them, they wanted time together, but as before, they were allowed only a few minutes to speak. Shortly after Lay walked away with Ludjuan, Lugoma returned to the canoe and explained to his family what he had told the chiefs: if they wanted to kill Hussey, they would have to kill him first. Hussey's grasp of the language was not good enough to take this in, but he was told of it later.

The night passed. Nothing but the decision of the chiefs stood in the way of Lay and Hussey being killed at any moment. Hussey does not say, but it is likely that he and his party slept on the beach at Mili Mili. In the morning Hussey asked his master for permission to visit

Lay and was readily allowed. He and his master's son set out for Lay's hut, but as they came up to it, Lay called out that Hussey should not come because the natives did not want them together. Hussey turned away, but to his surprise was summoned back, not by Lay but by Lay's master, Ludjuan. The young men talked death. Lay told Hussey that it was the design of the high chief to kill him; Hussey said that they were not only in the hands of the natives but also in the hands of God. Hussey went back to the canoe, expecting never to see his friend in this life.

Lay tried to defend himself "most solemnly" to the natives. Then he waited. The chiefs' verdict was not slow in coming: it was a reprieve. It was all to the good that no one had died of the disease, but that was not what saved the two young men from execution. As Lay learned, grave matters like the imposition of a death sentence required a unanimous vote of the chiefs. When the fate of the two men came up in council, one of the chiefs held out. That chief is not identified, but if Hussey's Lugoma had sufficient rank to be part of the council, he could well have been the one who saved the two from execution. In time the epidemic waned; when its victims began to regain their health, the focus on Lay and Hussey as its cause seemed to have been forgotten. But Lay could not stop thinking that the natives were capricious and volatile enough to replace one crisis with another.

The brief epidemic was dramatic and curious. It is possible to find a variety of exogenous causes of outbreaks of swelling: nutritional disorders like beriberi and kwashiorkor, and cardiac and renal diseases, which are not among the most likely causes of the symptoms observed; contact dermatitis can cause facial edema sufficient to encroach on the eyes, but the thickness of the skin on the hands and feet usually allows the extremities to be uninvolved.

A popular view in the Marshalls today is that the cause of such disorders is fish poisoning. Dr. Scott Norton, an authority on tropical medicine, suggests that the disorder may have been either ciguatera, poisoning caused by a toxin from plankton eaten by certain fish, or scombroid poisoning from spoiled fish. Both of these disorders have multiple symptoms, but the swelling is compatible with scombroid poisoning.

The whole melodrama of the disease and the threatened deaths of Lay and Hussey occupied little more than two weeks, for with the return of general health to the island, the chiefs were making preparations for the most important annual tribute of breadfruit to any authority on any of the islands, and those preparations had already been under way when the disease broke out. The tribute in question was to Labuliet ("La-boo-woole-yet" in Lay's account), the high chief on Arno, the nearest atoll to Mili, sixty miles to the north. The dispatch of the breadfruit to Arno did not exactly constitute international relations, but it was a diplomatic undertaking. Twelve canoes carrying the *bwiro* and about two hundred natives sailed for Arno to honor Labuliet, who maintained an overlordship from afar over Mili; his daughter (or granddaughter) was married to Luttuon, the *iroojlaplap* of Mili. Labuliet not only expected his annual tribute but threatened to wage war on Mili if it were not forthcoming.

The assembled flotilla may have been the largest Lay had ever seen. Since the preparations for the big voyage to Arno were being made all around him in Mili Mili, it is natural to wonder if Lay went along on it. The best reason to believe that he did not comes from Lieutenant Paulding's account of the *Dolphin's* stop at Arno after the rescue of Lay and Hussey, where the two Americans seem to be seeing the other atoll for the first time, and Labuliet seems to be seeing them for the first time. What then to make of Lay's statement, "After an absence of four or five days, during which time we exchanged civilities with numerous chiefs, we returned to *Milly*, and hauled up the canoes," or of Lay's phrase in the next paragraph, "About two days after my return . . ."? What is easiest to make of it is that the ghostwriter for Lay and Hussey did not get the story right at this point. Indeed, with the chiefs of Mili Atoll assembled in Mili Mili before and after the trip to Arno, it would have been easy for Lay to have "exchanged civilities with numerous chiefs." Lay does indicate that talk in this quarter led to his finding out after the return of the canoes that Labuliet, who had been told of the disease and of Lay and Hussey's being blamed for it, had issued his verdict: the contemplated executions would have been wrong since the affliction that had come upon them resulted not from Lay and Hussey living among them but from the displeasure of the natives' god over his votaries' killing of the seven *Globe* people. Thus, the highest authority that the islanders recognized definitively closed the question of who was responsible for the epidemic, and vindicated the lone chief who had held out against a death sentence. In any event, the fact that the disease had completely disappeared was taken to mean that the natives' guilt over the killings had been expiated, which, in Lay's view, was all too easy a self-absolution—he adds "!" after the word "expiated."

A couple of days after the return of the mission to Arno, a ship appeared off the coast of Mili Mili. The natives were in a flurry of excitement, which was nothing compared to the excited feelings that Lay was struggling not to betray. The chiefs who were still in Mili Mili after their trip from Arno thought that the ship was the *Globe* inexplicably returning. Lay knew it was not his old ship, but saw it as the first break in the clouds since the massacre six months before. Both Lay and Hussey imply that the ship appeared near the end of August. Lay and about three hundred natives went down to a vantage point, probably the southwest angle of Mili Mili, and watched the ship stand in toward land. Late in the day it took in its foresail and mizzen topgallant sails; there was every reason to expect to see a boat put ashore. But no boat was launched, and nothing further happened in the evening. Lay went back to his hut for a sleepless night; when in the morning he and Ludjuan went down to the beach, there was nothing to see but empty ocean. The ship of hope was gone.

The ship cannot be identified for sure, but if it had appeared only three months sooner than Lay and Hussey suggest, a first guess would be the French corvette *Coquille*, commanded by Captain Louis Duperrey. On May 26 the *Coquille* stood off Mili and sighted people ashore, but did not have any contact with them. It is possible that Lay and Hussey confused their chronology a bit and that they moved to August an event that had really happened three months before. If not, how was it possible for the *Coquille* to appear offshore and produce no reaction on the atoll that was worth recording? The ship that Lay and the natives did see created intense excitement; it was alarming for the natives and painfully hope-inspiring for Lay. It is almost impossible to believe that an event that created such turmoil in August would have been ignored in May.

The excitement ebbed among the natives, but the emotional force of a would-have-been rescue was still strong in the two seamen. They went back to their routines, fantasizing ships out of the blue. Routine meant work—fishing and harvesting. It also meant contending with entreaties of the natives to have their earlobes bored. The natives began ear cosmetology when a child was around four years old; sharpened sticks would make holes in the lobes, which were gradually lengthened by inserts until the ears reached almost down to the shoulders. Leaves were often inserted in the enlarged lobes as further decoration. It was considered a mark of great beauty, and the natives regarded the refusal of the Americans to have the operation done as something verging on ingratitude.

For Lay a more welcome communication from the natives was their sincere commendation of his command of the language. In roughly half a year he had become proficient enough to understand and speak with ease a language as heavy in consonants as Hawaiian is in vowels, alien in its syntax, and without English cognates. Good evidence of the achievement of the two men, Lay's especially it seems, is the vocabulary of Marshallese words printed as an appendix to their *Narrative* (see Appendix C of this volume).

Lay and Hussey give different accounts of their fourth reunion. Hussey says that he and his master left for Mili Mili as soon as they had been brought word of the ship. Lay has him arriving a couple of weeks later. Lay may have conflated two of Hussey's visits into one. On the first, Hussey says, he and Lay were allowed two brief conversations before he returned to Lukunor via Tokewa. On the next occasion, he says, he and Lay were together in a somewhat more relaxed setting than on previous occasions. Lay told Hussey that he was eating well and that the natives were considerate and shared food with him. There was a little exchange of food on this occasion: Hussey had brought Lay a basket of fish; keep them until nightfall, Lay asked, so that he would not have to share them with everyone he ran into. Lay picked up the fish after dark and brought them back to his master, who was pleased with the gift; in the morning Ludjuan gave Hussey some coconuts in return. When Hussey brought the coconuts back to the canoe, Lugoma asked him a bit suspiciously where they had come from—he did not want one of his people stealing.

Back in Lukunor Hussey settled into the routine of fishing, curing fish, and in short, being a servant. At some point his master was summoned to Mili Mili to face an investigation of the charge that he and Lay's master were planning to leave Mili for Arno, taking Lay and Hussey along to exhibit them as curiosities. The charge was worrisome, since leaving the atoll without permission was a serious offense. The two charged with the plot denied it altogether and were acquitted, but Hussey knew that they were lying, as he had often heard them talking about the flight to Arno. Hussey could have spoken up but chose to say nothing, for, quite apart from questions of loyalty, the whole matter could have turned into the next crisis.

It was probably late in 1824 when a severe famine struck the atoll. Hussey, who was in Mili Mili part of the time, speaks of a four-month drought that dried up the breadfruit trees so completely that it even killed some of them on the smaller islands. He had to listen to the ongoing and, for him, vital debate between the natives who felt the drought was sent to punish them for keeping Lay and Hussey on the island and those who felt that it was a result of the murder of the seven *Globe* people; Hussey, needless to say, sided vigorously with the latter opinion. The debate was all too reminiscent of the judgment blaming the two men for the swelling disease, although Lay and Hussey seem to have had more defenders this time.

Everyone moved into a survival mode. Hussey describes the boiling of the small branches of trees and the drinking of the juice as food. One day when his master was looking for Hussey to help him with fishing, he found him lying in his hut. What was the matter, Lugoma asked. He was too weak from hunger, Hussey told him. Lugoma cooked him a fish, which was, Hussey says, "not half enough." Back on Mili Mili Lay was getting by with half a coconut a day until he turned thief. Some of Ludjuan's coconut trees were heavily laden; at night when all were asleep, Lay would climb the trees, take one of the coconuts in his mouth by the stem and one in each hand, and shimmy down the tree. It took as much skill as working in the rigging. He was careful not to make noise by dropping a coconut, overly careful, in fact, since coconuts falling from trees are regular nocturnal sounds to which everyone is habituated—the sounds would not have attracted attention. But Lay was taking no chances. He carried his loot off to a clump of bushes to feast on them night after night, until Ludjuan began noticing a drop in his coconut inventory and said something about it. Then it was back to being hungry. Neither Lay nor Hussey made it clear why everyone did not have more access to coconuts; they were normally so abundant. On a typical day, especially if the wind has been strong, the lagoon is spotted with floating coconuts blown from trees on shore and carried by high tide out into the water; they are sometimes so numerous that they look like hazards to navigation, almost like reefs, but they are easily swept aside by the hulls of boats.

One particular coconut created a crisis *du jour*, when Lay picked it up off a fresh grave. Anit did not like that: only after a certain amount of time had passed following burial was a man (never a woman) permitted to do what Lay had done. The bunch of natives who accused Lay did not threaten to do anything themselves to him, but warned him that if he did it again, he would bring sickness and death not only on himself but also on the island. The bawling out required Lay's protestations of ignorance—he did not know that he was doing wrong—contrition, and promise of never again. He felt great relief when they left, for he was mentally prepared for serious trouble.

After four months the drought broke, and the rains came. The natives gathered in Mili Mili to sing their petitions to Anit to make the breadfruit crop abundant. Hussey describes the event in language suggesting that he was present in Mili Mili at the time. But chronicling every trip between Lukunor and Mili Mili and recording the days' events in general began to seem less important to both Lay and Hussey as the months passed. The two men were "members" now, and there was even less concern on the part of the natives to keep them apart. Lieutenant Paulding seems to contradict the *Narrative* when he quotes Lay as saying, "[The high chief] was very kind to me in every respect. They have always brought Huzzy [*sic*] to me, or taken me to see him once a fortnight, or once a month, and suffered us to pass the day together." That is certainly not the picture drawn in the *Narrative*, but it may be reconcilable with the *Narrative*, for most of the episodes recounted in the *Narrative* take place during the first year that Lay and Hussey spent on the atoll. By the second year the situation of the two had mellowed, and the benign permissiveness described in Paulding's account may have become the reality.

One day a party of natives from Naalo (Lay calls it Alloo) in the northwestern part of the atoll came to exchange gifts with the chiefs at Mili Mili and to enjoy a *bwiro* feast. None of them had ever seen Lay before, and they became damned nuisances. They clustered around him, felt his skin, and joked about its color and his intact ears. The telling thing about the episode is that Lay now felt entitled to be annoyed. This was not the first time the natives had been so blithely rude; earlier in his stay Lay would have taken it as one more happening in the alien and inexplicable world of atoll life, no worse and no better than all the other strange events that filled his days. But now atoll life was no longer so alien and inexplicable, and Lay had as much right as anyone on Mili to standard privacy and courtesy.

Lay entertained the natives from time to time by firing muskets and on one occasion the heavy swivel gun taken from the *Globe*, throwing the natives into a terror that turned immediately to hilarity. That is a little detail of daily life. The *Narrative* turns more toward such details as the second year on the atoll begins. It is revealing that now the two men are not relating this-happened-to-me reports but are telling what they have observed almost in the manner of travel books. Lay's chapter 7, in fact, is precisely that: The natives have broad faces, flat noses, and large mouths; they wear their hair long and tie it in a knot at the top of their heads, and the men have long beards; they love to dance in a manner similar to Hawaiians; they bathe a lot, and bathe their children from the day of their birth. When a person dies, the lamentation lasts for two days, day and night, and coconut trees are planted at the head and the foot of the grave. When not working, they visit, arriving and sitting down in silence without a word of greeting; after a pause the host brings out food, and when all have eaten, if there are leftovers, they "are very careful to secure them and carry them off when they return home; and the host would regard it as an imposition if his visitors were to neglect this important trait of politeness, and fashionable form of etiquette."

Hussey witnessed a murder. Two natives with whom he had gone fishing fell into an argument over a negligible matter; one seized the other's spear, broke it over his knee, and used the point to kill him. The dead man's parents laid him out on a mat and, Hussey says, with uncharacteristic understatement, "appeared to regret their loss very much." What threatened to be more bloody than the single murder was an impending war, which Hussey relates in a too-compact fashion. Bad feelings had grown between Luttuon, the *iroojlaplap*, and his brother Longerene, whose home was on the northwestern island of Naalo; Luttuon summoned his brother for a conference, which led to the adoption of a peace treaty between the two. A page later in his account, however, Hussey says he heard from some excited natives that Luttuon had killed several of the lower chiefs from Naalo, that Longerene had fled, and that war was about to break out. Luttuon summoned Lay and Hussey and informed them that they had been drafted: they were the artillery. They asked Luttuon if he had any powder for the muskets he wanted them to brandish. The powder was worthless, but the two men went through a charade of drying it in the sun, and the next morning joined the fleet of fifteen or sixteen canoes holding two hundred natives that sailed for Naalo. There, prepared to do battle, they discovered that the enemy had fled—Hussey does not name Longerene at this point, but he is the chief Luttuon's forces were pursuing (the peace treaty having apparently been revoked). The pursuit was a failure, and after a few days at Naalo the war party returned home. "We . . . heard no more of the war," Hussey says. The episode is treated so summarily that it is hard to get a picture of what was happening and even harder to determine what was going on inside Lay and Hussey. Did they know the whole thing would play out like a drill or an exercise? Or did they take seriously the possibility of killing or being killed? They were in the habit of taking things seriously, and the war looked like no small matter, but the authors bury this headline item in the back pages.

Etto amro pad ioon aneo—we have been a long time on the island.

For twenty-two months the future of William Lay and Cyrus Hussey had hung by a thread, and the thread was the *Globe*. If the ship made it anywhere, and if anyone at that anywhere had an idea about mounting a rescue and the resources to act, then maybe Lay and Hussey had a chance of not growing old as the odd white (each year less white) denizens of the atoll. Among Pacific stereotypes is the castaway who, willingly or not in the beginning, goes native in dress, adapts to the food, accepts tattooing, learns the language, joins tribal wars, masters crafts, marries a native wife, even becomes a kind of eminence among the islanders, and then after twenty years is discovered when a whaler or trader sends a boat ashore—for a rescue? Not always; sometimes the acculturation trap has closed, and the white man does not want to return.

Lay and Hussey wanted desperately to return. What was the fate of the *Globe?*

CHAPTER SIX

THE NEWS

When, on February 17, 1824, Gilbert Smith sailed the *Globe* into the dark with his crew of five, he made some right moves, whether he knew they were right or not. The ship carried a compass but not a quadrant; how much Smith knew about navigation is unclear, but he knew enough to feel the want of an instrument that would give him the altitude of the sun. Unless spare sail had been found below decks, the ship was operating with no mainsail, no foresail, no mizzen topsail, no main topgallant, no mizzen topgallant, and only one royal. The fact that there was a good deal of empty space on the masts may have been all for the good, for there were only six men to take care of everything, and one of them, Thomas, was a slacker if what Smith reported was true. Did they stand watches of two? Or lengthen the watches to twelve hours?

Smith's first move when the cable was cut and the *Globe* was ready to leave the atoll was to head to the east, retracing at first the course the ship had taken a few days before in coming to the atoll. There was a difference, though, for the *Globe* was now traveling at night past the Knox spur at the southeast corner of the atoll, a string of islands and reefs that is easy enough to see or infer in daylight but is daunting to deal with in the dark. Once away from Mili, the ship did not follow its old route through the Gilberts but headed south and crossed the equator. Whether by luck or by savvy Smith had chosen a course well suited to his purposes: the ship was carried past Samoa (known then as the Navigator Islands) and on to the east. Smith has left no record of landfalls between Samoa and South America, but his easterly route would have carried him into the vicinity of Tahiti if he moved a bit to the south and into the vicinity of the Marquesas if he moved to the north. These were natural places to stop for supplies; if the ship did not make any of these stops, it is evident that Payne and Oliver had left a good deal of food and water, enough to sustain six men for 112 days, on board the ship when they were overseeing the frantic off-loading on Mili.

The *Globe* in fact had food to give away. When, on June 5, 1824, it was at 34°19' S and had sighted the coast of Chile about thirty miles south of Valparaíso, it was spoken by a Chilean vessel, the captain of which described his ship as being in a state of starvation. This news led to an exchange that tells something about the state of fare on board the undermanned whaler: the *Globe* gave the Chilean ship twenty-one bags of bread and four pieces of beef, and the Chilean vessel gave the *Globe* a sheep and a peck of potatoes. The goodwill of the Chilean boat was also manifested in its sending some of its men on board the *Globe* to help it into port and in giving Smith a quadrant. These acts were more generous than effective, for, Smith states,

"Some of them [the loaned seamen] couldn't [help]" apparently because they were weak from starvation. And the quadrant, alas, "was of no use." The Chilean coastline was visible off to starboard, and Valparaíso was almost in sight to the north—the need for instruments was past.

On June 7, 1824, almost half a year after the mutiny, the *Globe* came into Valparaíso with a distress signal flying. The American consul, Michael Hogan, was notified and went aboard in company with several people, one of whom was Peter Dillon, a captain who was on a celebrated mission to determine the fate of the long-missing La Perouse expedition. Dillon, in his book about the cruise, briefly describes the *Globe*'s arrival in Valparaíso.

The thread that had been Lay and Hussey's lifeline had held. The news of the *Globe* mutiny was out. It was not up-to-date news, for Smith and crew reported what was the case the day they left: two of the mutineers and seven of the non-mutineers were alive on Mili Atoll.

Consul Hogan wasted no time in investigating what Gilbert Smith reported. Two days after the ship arrived, he took depositions from Stephen Kidder and George Comstock. A week later, on June 15, he questioned Peter Kidder and Gilbert Smith, and two weeks after that, on June 30, Anthony Hanson and Joseph Thomas. Smith's deposition was twice as long as any of the others and was ampler in details, including a few on the escape voyage, but by and large all the men, even Joseph Thomas, told the same story. On August 11, Hogan forwarded copies of the depositions to Secretary of State John Quincy Adams, to Commodore Isaac Hull (the head of the United States Pacific squadron) in Callao, and to the civil authorities on Nantucket "in order that Joseph Thomas who appears an accessary may be taken care of 'till such investigation takes place, as is necessary in the case." Hogan also took charge of the *Globe*, prepared it for the voyage back to Nantucket, and appointed a

Captain King as temporary master of the ship. The *Globe* sailed from Valparaíso on August 15, 1824.

Messages from the Pacific station to the United States took four months—a grave inconvenience at times to the navy command, which had to wait eight months for approval of requests, even lesser requests like appointment of subordinate officers and permission to send personnel home for court martial. All ships, commercial as well as naval, carrying news from the Pacific took roughly as long; the reports carried back on these ships appeared promptly in hometown newspapers and usually consisted of barrels of oil returned, ships met at sea or in port and the take in oil of those ships up to that date, and extraordinary events such as ships suffering severe storm damage. The news of the *Globe* adventure took the normal four months to reach Nantucket, but this was one report of a ship's return that did not contain any of the usual figures for oil on board (although it could have, for the *Globe* did in fact have 372 barrels of sperm oil below decks). On October 25, 1824, the Nantucket *Inquirer*, with inaccuracies (but probably fewer than might be expected), broke the shocking news:

> The Belle brought information that ship Globe of Nantucket, had ar. at Valparaiso, about middle of June, in charge of Smith, a boat-steerer, the crew having mutinied and killed the Captain, Thomas Worth and Wm. Beatle, and John Lombard mates. They took the vessel to the Mulgrave Islands, with the intention of remaining and took on shore such things as they might want—here they quarrelled among themselves, as to who should be capt.; shot the head mutineer, one Comstock, of N. York, a boat steerer, and afterwards hung the steward, suspecting him not to be friendly to them. Whilst most of them were on shore, Smith and a few others including several boys, who had been left on board, (and who had apparently joined the mutineers through fear) took possession of

the ship, cut her cables in the night, and left the Islands—falling in with another vessel, the mate came on board, and carried her to Valparaiso, and she was to proceed home, in a few days, in charge of Thos. Raymond. It was the intention of the mutineers to have burnt the ship—only 6 ar. in her at Valparaiso, and they were confined on board an English and a French vessel of war, there being no Am. national vessel in port. 11 were left on the island.

It would be twenty-two months, the same length of time that Lay and Hussey spent on Mili, before even an inkling that some had died on Mili and some survived made its way back to Nantucket. For nearly two years five families, those of Rowland Coffin, Columbus Worth, Rowland Jones, William Lay, and Cyrus Hussey, were in the dark about the fate of their young men. Someone with access to the *Globe's* manifest had written in its right-hand margin next to their names, "On Mulgrave Islands." So they were, the living and the dead.

On November 14, 1824, about three weeks after the article appeared in the Nantucket *Inquirer,* the *Globe* itself came into Edgartown. The story of what happened up to the time of the ship's escape was available now, but that story did not make it intact into print. The *Inquirer* wrote the next day:

> The only names of the survivors of the Mutiny, which we have been able to obtain, are, Smith (originally a steersman) and two sons of Capt. Kidder, of Edgartown. . . . It is further stated, that Capt. Worth was killed with an axe, while asleep in his birth, [*sic*] by Thain, a sailor shipped at the Sandwich Islands. . . . Comstock, the elder, was hung at Mulgraves' Island. The younger brother was compelled to assist at this execution, and on his remonstrating afterwards, was beat to death with billets of wood.

A week later, on November 22, the *Inquirer* wrote, "Having seen so many erroneous statements of the mutiny on board ship Globe of this place, and having ourselves published an imperfect account we are the more anxious to place before our readers the following, the veracity of which is indisputable." There followed a fuller and basically accurate account of the events.

In a separate article the paper reported that Joseph Thomas was brought before Nantucket Magistrate Josiah Hussey on November 18 on suspicion of murdering the officers. Thomas's examination was postponed first to the twentieth and then the twenty-second to wait for witnesses who were still on board the *Globe* in Edgartown. Thomas had obviously been brought promptly to Nantucket before the *Globe* crossed over from Edgartown. George Comstock may have been allowed to come over to Nantucket early, but Gilbert Smith and the two Kidders would not have been anxious to leave their families on Martha's Vineyard sooner than they had to; they may have been the only "witnesses" still needed for Joseph Thomas's hearing. The hearing took one or two days and was closed November 23, with Thomas being ordered held for trial in Boston at the next term of the United States Circuit Court in May. Less than a week later, on November 29, Joseph Thomas was committed to the Boston Jail, the alleged cause on the record being "Murder on the high Seas on board Ship Globe." A week later, on December 7, the list of Examinations on Criminal Complaints listed Thomas as charged with mutiny, not murder. In the end he was acquitted.

As promised, Consul Hogan sent one of the transcripts of the Valparaíso depositions of the six *Globe* escapees to the authorities in Nantucket; its presumed recipient was Magistrate Josiah Hussey. Whether the document was carried back on the *Globe* or another ship, it was in the magistrate's hands around the time the ship arrived at Nantucket; one of the first things the magistrate did was to allow the owners of the *Globe* to read the depositions and Hogan's cover let-

Thomas Worth, captain of the *Globe*.

The *Globe* arriving at Mili Atoll, frontispiece of William Comstock, *The Life of Samuel Comstock, the Terrible Whaleman.*

THE

LIFE

OF

SAMUEL COMSTOCK,

THE TERRIBLE WHALEMAN.

CONTAINING AN ACCOUNT OF THE

MUTINY,

AND

MASSACRE OF THE OFFICERS

OF THE SHIP GLOBE, OF NANTUCKET;

WITH HIS SUBSEQUENT ADVENTURES, AND HIS BEING

SHOT AT THE MULGRAVE ISLANDS.

ALSO,

LIEUTENANT PERCIVAL'S VOYAGE IN SEARCH OF THE SURVIVORS.

BY HIS BROTHER, WILLIAM COMSTOCK.

BOSTON:
JAMES FISHER, PUBLISHER,
No. 71 COURT STREET.
TURNER & FISHER, NEW YORK, AND PHILADELPHIA.

1840.

Title page of *The Life of Samuel Comstock, the Terrible Whaleman.*

"A Desperate Struggle Between Comstock and the Negro," from *The Life of Samuel Comstock, the Terrible Whaleman.*

"Dreadful Conflict Between Chicochee and the Indian Queen," from *The Life of Samuel Comstock, the Terrible Whaleman.*

"Comstock Running Lumbert Through the Body," from *The Life of Samuel Comstock, the Terrible Whaleman.*

"The Execution of Humphries," from *The Life of Samuel Comstock, the Terrible Whaleman.*

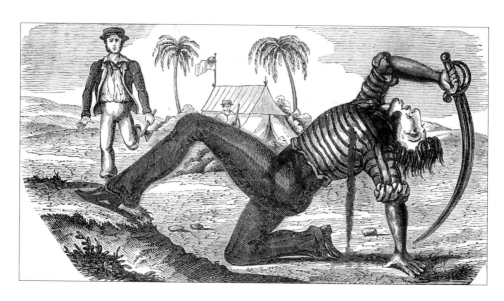

"The Death of Samuel Comstock," from *The Life of Samuel Comstock, the Terrible Whaleman.*

A

NARRATIVE

OF THE

MUTINY,

ON BOARD THE

SHIP GLOBE,

OF NANTUCKET,

IN THE

PACIFIC OCEAN, Jan. 1824,

AND THE

JOURNAL

OF A

RESIDENCE OF TWO YEARS

ON THE

MULGRAVE ISLANDS;

WITH OBSERVATIONS ON THE MANNERS AND
CUSTOMS OF THE INHABITANTS.

BY WILLIAM LAY, OF SAYBROOK, CONN. AND
CYRUS M. HUSSEY, OF NANTUCKET:
The only Survivors from the Massacre of the Ship's Company by the Natives.

NEW-LONDON :

PUBLISHED BY WM. LAY, AND C. M. HUSSEY.

1828.

Title page of Lay and Hussey, *A Narrative of the Mutiny, on Board the Ship Globe, of Nantucket.*

Hiram Paulding, first lieutenant of the *Dolphin*.

John Percival, captain of the *Dolphin*.

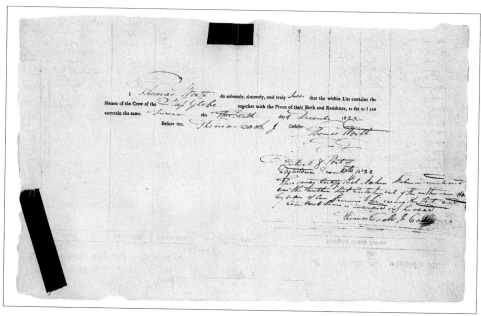

Manifest of the *Globe*.

Josiah Macy, captain of the *Edward*, the first ship on which Samuel Comstock served.

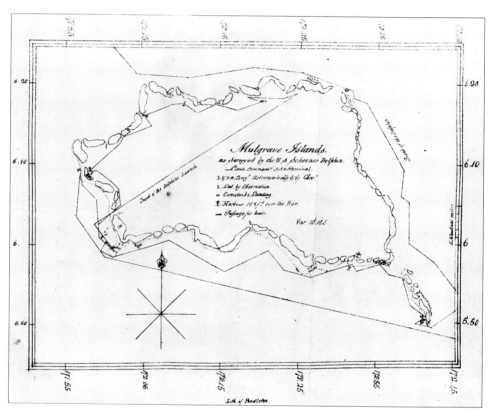

Mulgrave Islands (Mili Atoll) as Surveyed by the U.S. Schooner *Dolphin*; from Paulding, *Journal of a Cruise of the United States Schooner Dolphin.*

A Canoe and Natives of Mulgrave's Range, from Arthur Phillip, *The Voyage of Governor Phillip to Botany Bay with Contributions by Other Officers of the First Fleet and Observations on Affairs of the Time by Lord Auckland.*

"View of South Street from Maiden Lane, New York City" (1828) by William James Bennett. The wharfside from which Samuel Comstock, age thirteen, sailed on his first voyage, on the *Edward*, in 1815.

ter. One of the owners, Gorham Coffin, was also the uncle of Rowland Coffin, the seaman left on Mili who had been suspected by Gilbert Smith, Peter Kidder, George Comstock, and probably others of being close with the mutineers before and after the massacre. Gorham Coffin was outraged at what he read in the depositions about his nephew, and the thought that the document had been sent to the State Department, Commodore Hull, and, he assumed, the Navy Department angered him more. On November 29, a week after the *Globe* had reached Nantucket, Coffin wrote to Secretary of State John Quincy Adams deploring the fact that "Mr. Hogan suffered some of the men to give their suspicions as evidence of the Guilt of an orphan of Sixteen years of age." He was writing, Coffin said, "not wishing to extenuate his fault, if guilty, but to prevent if possible that aught may be set down in malice."

Coffin's anger against Gilbert Smith was going to endure and find expression in ad hominem attacks; it is easy to imagine what was said in meetings between the two. It is easy, as well, to construct the scenario of Coffin's meetings with George Comstock. Coffin wanted something in writing that would exculpate his nephew; what he got from George Comstock has the air of a much-negotiated statement. George did not retract any of his suspicions but furnished Coffin with a statement that, at worst, imputed unworthy motives to Rowland Coffin's accusers: "I George Comstock hereby certify that great jealousy was created against Rowland Coffin, from some of the Crew, in consequence of his being taken the most notice of by the Captain, previous to his death; & afterwards for being much noticed by Saml. B. Comstock."

Two days later, on December 1, Coffin wrote to Secretary of the Navy Samuel L. Southard with much the same message in support of Rowland Coffin, but added a rather ornate plea: "While Justice is stern, may not her sister virtue, mercy, be awed into silence, but be ready to extend her shield over those who have been forced to yield to necessity, with a drawn sword over their heads." Enclosed in this letter was one to Commodore Hull, which Coffin asked Southard to forward if he approved; the letter to Hull covered the same ground that the others did, but added a new detail: ". . . when their only expectation was that [the ship] would be burned, he [Rowland Coffin] was heard to say that those transactions were beyond his control, but that the stigma of them would be so great on their characters, should they ever return to their country again, that he had no desire to leave that island, except as a prisoner." This Coffin describes as "the only elevated sentiment reported to have been expressed by any one of the crew." It is easy enough to read the statement, however, not as an elevated sentiment but as an answer to feelers put out by others in the crew to the effect of "you carry some weight with the mutineers—do something about this."

Gorham Coffin wrote to Daniel Webster on December 22 making the same arguments in defense of Rowland Coffin's reputation as in the earlier letters, for example, that the crew were jealous of him because he worked hard and because he was "akin to the ship" (that is, he was related to the owners). But Coffin added a denunciation of the lack of courage shown by Gilbert Smith in not leading a capture of the mutineers and also introduced a request that a ship be sent to the Mulgrave Islands, where, he assumed, the remaining nine of the *Globe*'s company would be found. In a rather confused effort to weaken Smith's charges against Rowland Coffin, the uncle gives examples of things alleged to prove that Rowland was reporting to the mutineers, for example, that Peter Kidder complained to Rowland that they were fools to live under the regime of the mutineers and then found himself summoned by Oliver, who quizzed him on whether he had said that—obviously his words could not have reached the mutineers except through Rowland. Coffin's efforts to refute these charges are rather muddled, and he produces an effect opposite to what he clearly intended.

Reaction to the *Globe* news swept through the Nantucket community. A few weeks after the arrival of the ship in Nantucket, 142 "Merchants & others, engaged in the Whale fishery" sent a petition to President James Monroe reviewing the *Globe* events and requesting, first, an increased naval force in the Pacific in the light of the expanded operation of United States ships and, second, "that a vessel may immediately proceed to Mulgrave's island in search of those men." The signatories were a Who's Who of Nantucket whaling.

The petition and comparable appeals were not without effect. The mutiny had had a great impact. By the summer of 1825 the Department of the Navy had ordered Commodore Hull to send a vessel to the western Pacific to find the *Globe* remnant, whatever it was. Two years before, when the *United States* was on the eve of sailing for the Pacific, Secretary Southard had given Hull orders to cover not only the South American coast but also Hawaii and to return by the Cape of Good Hope, an impossible agenda for Hull's flagship in light of the turbulent revolutionary scene in South America that preoccupied the American command. However, the new orders to go to Mili (and Hawaii for other business) were feasible for one of the smaller ships in the squadron. Commodore Hull selected the schooner *Dolphin*, described in the biography of Charles Henry Davis, who would serve on the cruise, as a "top-sail schooner, of 180 tons burden and 12 guns, which vessel was tender to the flagship, . . . She was a mere cock-boat alongside of the frigate, and her guns were nothing but six-pounders." On August 14, 1825, writing from the *United States* at Chorrillos, Peru, Hull gave Lieutenant Commandant John Percival his orders:

Sir: Having received instructions from the Hon. Secretary of the Navy, to send one of the small vessels to the Mulgrave range, or group of islands, in search of the mutineers of the American whale ship Globe, (when the services of one of the vessels under my command can be disposed with on this coast without injury to our commercial interests, and as there is not at this time, any immediate call for the services of the Dolphin under your command,) I have to direct that you lose no time in fitting her for sea, and in receiving on board provisions and stores of every kind that she may require for six months, the crew to consist of not more than seventy, including every person on board.

The crew of the Dolphin at this time, consists of more men than she can stow provisions for to last six months; and, it being doubtful whether she can return short of that time, you will cause the crew to be reduced to not exceeding seventy, by transferring all over that number to this ship, . . . As soon as you have received on board your provisions and stores as directed, you will proceed with as little delay as is practicable, with the Dolphin under your command to the Mulgrave range, or group of islands, and use all the means in your power to ascertain whether the mutineers of the Globe are still at the islands and should it appear that they are, you will use such measures as to you may appear best calculated to get them on board your vessel, and to secure them, preferring a mild and friendly course as regards the natives of the islands, to that of using force, to obtain them. If, however, they will not be given up, and you can get into your possession some of the chiefs of the natives and detain them, there cannot be a doubt that their friends will deliver those men to you, on your giving to them a pledge that the chiefs detained by you shall be given up. In that, as well as in all matters relating to the cruise, much must be left to your discretion and good judgment. . . .

You will observe that the men left at the islands had with them two good boats and a quantity of provisions. It is therefore possible that they may have left the island where they first landed, and have gone to some other. In that case, it will be necessary for you to endeavor to ascertain what course they took, and where they probably may be found, and go in search of them, should it appear that your provisions and situation will admit of your doing so.

Should you be so fortunate as to find those men, you will return with them to this station, touching at the Sandwich islands on your way, provided your provisions will allow you to do so. . . .

Should you, during your absence, discover islands or shoals or dangers of any sort, you are to be very particular in ascertaining their precise situation, and of islands whether inhabited or not, and whether they produce wood or any other articles that would offer commercial or any other advantage to our enterprising citizens, should they think proper to visit them.

When word of the mission circulated through the squadron, a number of officers volunteered. Andrew Hull Foote, a midshipman on the *United States* and a cousin of Commodore Hull, wrote to a friend on August 12, "The Dolphin received orders yesterday to prepare herself immediately to proceed to the Mulgrave Islands in order to seize several mutineers of the American Ship Globe. The cruise will be a most delightful one, we are all anxious to join her but the officers still attached to her deserve & will have the preference."

The *Dolphin* was under excellent command. John "Mad Jack" Percival (also known as "Roaring Jack") was a favorite of Commodore Hull's. Percival, born in Barnstable, Massachusetts, in 1779, was at sea by the age of fourteen and had risen to second mate in the merchant service by 1797. While in Portugal that year he was impressed into the Royal Navy and served on the HMS *Victory* and other ships for two months before escaping. In the course of his very brief service in the British navy, Percival became a good friend of Captain Sir Isaac Coffin, the Bostonian with Nantucket roots who chose the loyalist side during the American Revolution and rose to become admiral in the British navy but who never lost his fondness for Nantucket, devoting his fortune to the establishment of the Coffin School, now no longer a school but still a Nantucket landmark. After service on the USS *Delaware* and the gaining of a midshipman's warrant, Percival left the navy in 1801 for the merchant service. Back in the navy in 1809, he served as a sailing master stationed at the Norfolk Navy Yard. He was active in the War of 1812, during which he was credited with several notable successes, one being the capture of a British tender off New York: Percival filled a borrowed fishing boat with produce and livestock, concealed thirty-two men below deck, and surprised and quickly overcame the British ship and towed it into the Battery. He was assigned in 1814 to the USS *Peacock*, part of the Pacific squadron, and later the same year was commissioned a lieutenant. Other assignments including command of the *Porpoise* against West Indian pirates followed, and in 1823 he was appointed first lieutenant on Commodore Hull's flagship, the *United States*.

Some of the legend that built up around Percival is fanciful: for example, he crossed the ocean in a ship manned only by himself and an older seaman and a boy; the two men became sick, and the boy was washed overboard, with the result that no one took the helm, and the ship was abandoned to the sea—only to arrive safely in port as if miraculously navigated.

This kind of story probably added to the appeal Percival had for a writer like Henry A. Wise ("Harry Gringo"), who modeled a figure in his *Tales for the Marines* on Percival.

Percival was a vivid enough figure without myths. He was irascible and blunt but disciplined, responsible, and fair. He was in his late fifties when Nathaniel Hawthorne met him at the Charlestown Navy Yard and left a sketch of him that, projected backward, catches the spirit of the man who, twenty-three years before, had been sent out in search of mutineers in the mid-Pacific. Hawthorne was being dined on board the revenue cutter *Hamilton*, when the captain was informed that Captain Percival was on the deck of a harbor tender tied up beside the cutter, smoking a cigar.

Captain sends him a glass of champagne, and enquires of the
waiter what Percival says to it. "He said, Sir, 'What does he send
me this damned stuff for?'—but drinks nevertheless." The captain characterizes Percival as the roughest old devil that ever was
in his manners, but a kind, good hearted man at bottom. By and
bye comes in the steward—"Captain Percival is coming aboard
of you, Sir;" "Well; ask him to walk down into the cabin"; and
shortly down comes old Captain Percival; a white-haired, thin-
visaged, weather-worn old gentleman, in a blue, quaker-cut-
coat, with tarnished lace and brass buttons; a pair of drab
pantaloons, and brown waistcoat. There was an eccentric
expression in his face, which seemed partly wilful, partly natural. . . . He seems to have moulded and shaped himself to his
own whims; till a sort of rough affectation has become thor-
oughly imbued throughout a kindly nature. . . . He is conscious
of his peculiarities; for when I asked him whether it would be
well to make a naval officer Secretary of the Navy, he said—
"God forbid!" for that an old sailor was always full of prejudices
and stubborn whim-whams &c—instancing himself—whereto I
agreed.

Percival's senior lieutenant on the *Dolphin* was the son of John
Paulding, the captor of Major André, the go-between of Benedict
Arnold and Sir Henry Clinton. Hiram Paulding, when selected by
Hull as senior lieutenant on the *Globe* survivors' rescue voyage, was
in his late twenties and a veteran of naval service from his teenage
years onward. Made a midshipman in 1811, he was active in the War
of 1812, most notably on the *Ticonderoga* in the battle of Lake
Champlain. He served on the *Constellation* and the *Macedonian*
before becoming one of Commodore Hull's officers on the *United
States*.

In 1824, about a month after the *United States* anchored in

Callao, Paulding, who had a "partial" (his term) command of Spanish, was chosen by Hull to carry out a mission to Simon Bolívar in his mountain camp; the main purpose of the mission was to gain Bolívar's support in resolving some tensions that had arisen between the patriot Admiral Guise and the American squadron. On June 4, Paulding sailed north along the coast and two days later landed in the little town of Huacho, from which he was to proceed on horseback to Bolívar's headquarters. (That was the day before the *Globe* arrived in Valparaíso.) Paulding's grueling trip took him over mountain trails on donkeys and often enfeebled horses, through a succession of meetings with local governors in their more often than not squalid houses, and into some colorful encounters, all of which he does justice to in his engaging book, *A Sketch of Bolivar in his Camp*, published ten years later. He describes his welcome by the governor of Supe:

> The Governor . . . introduced me to a party of his young friends who had just assembled for dinner. The *Ollapodrida* and a broiled quarter of lamb were already smoking on the table, and highly to our satisfaction, we were cordially invited to partake. It was a large, roughly made oak table, without cloth or cover, on which our dinner was placed, benches were arranged beside for seats, and with three spoons and as many knives and forks, ten of us dined abundantly without any other inconvenience than that of occasionally conferring and receiving the favor of an exchange of a knife for a spoon, spoon for fork, etc. I know not whether it should be spoken of as an inconvenience, as it seemed at the time to promote the sociability and good understanding of the company. It was particularly pleasing when one of the young ladies proffered the use of her fork or spoon and perhaps requested one's knife in return.

His cordial reception by the Liberator in the town of Huaras was the high point of his three-hundred-mile trek. Impressed by the grace, intelligence, and political vision of his host, and by the striking setting of the mountain headquarters, Paulding, at a dinner with Bolívar and his officers, toasted the revolutionary figure: "Success to the liberating army of Peru and the Washington of the south, may glory attend them."

Paulding is a good writer. His *Sketch of Bolivar in his Camp* was published in 1834, but three years before he had brought out the book that narrated the adventures he had the year after he visited Bolívar, *Journal of a Cruise of the United States Schooner Dolphin Among the Islands of the Pacific Ocean and a Visit to the Mulgrave Islands, in Pursuit of the Mutineers of the Whale Ship Globe.* Hiram Paulding has been compared, fairly enough, with his cousin James Kirke Paulding, who was not only a prolific writer and an associate of Washington Irving but also President Van Buren's secretary of the navy. Both writers are characterized by the fluent presentation of unexaggerated and self-dramatizing detail and imagery.

On August 18, 1825, the *Dolphin* sailed from Chorrillos, Peru, and the rescue mission was under way, but not like an ambulance rushing to an emergency. Percival moved along the coast for almost two weeks, stopping at ports where he could complete the provisioning of the ship. And even the provisioning was not done with a display of urgency; it left time for a bit of recreational seal hunting when the ship anchored off the Lobos Islands: "The noise of our landing gave [the seals] the alarm, and, as we had cut them off from the water, they made the best of their way for the other side of the hill, joining in a terrific growl like so many furious mastiffs. They had reached the top of the hill, and were descending on the opposite side, when we overtook them, and very wantonly killed several."

On August 26, in the port of Paita, Peru, "we filled the deck with pigs, poultry, and vegetables," and the supplies looked complete, but not so complete as not to allow more than a hundred giant tortoises to be taken on in the Galápagos, where the ship arrived two weeks out of Paita.

The ship's stop in the Marquesas, which lasted three weeks, gave Percival and Paulding an impression of the natives that derived from the competition between the Typee and Happah tribes, the conduct of "these wild ladies" (Paulding's term), and the relatively sophisticated character of the people. Paulding's *Journal* anticipates in many ways Herman Melville's *Typee*, which made Nukahiva, the group's main island, the enduring movie model of the tropical paradise.

That was not going to be the case at the next stops, all of them brief, that the *Dolphin* made. Caroline Island was uninhabited and notable only for high surf and shark infestation. The natives of Nukunono ("Duke of Clarence Island") in the Tokelau group north of Samoa were thieves and hostile but easily frightened by pistol shots. On Atafu ("Duke of York Island") nearby the natives were not merely thieves but con men who had found a way to sell the same fishing nets to the white visitors two or three times.

The *Dolphin* was now moving along a route that paralleled the route of the *Globe* after the mutiny, but was considerably to the south. Around the Ellice Islands it turned north, working through bad weather and difficult currents. On November 9 the ship was in the Gilberts, anchoring off Nikunau ("Byron's Island"). Here it contended with a boarding party of arrogant thieves whom the officers were lucky to rid the ship of without serious incident, but a landing party, escaping from the island through almost uncrossable surf, was in serious danger. On nearby Tabiteuea ("Drummond Island") the natives were timid at first, but no less inclined to steal, even if it were only a sailor's hat. Other thefts were more serious. The ship was soon going to need water, and nothing would have been more natural than to send a party ashore to dig wells, but the "enterprising" character of the natives was warning enough not to try that.

The weather was becoming very squally and the currents utterly irregular. The *Dolphin* was within a few hundred miles of its goal, but maintaining course had become very difficult, the ship drifting back during the night as far as it had advanced in the day. Finally, on November 19, 1825, someone called out, "Land-ho!" The unprecedented rescue mission was three months out of Chorrillos.

CHAPTER SEVEN

D O L P H I N

The *Dolphin's* approach to Mili was tentative. The first sighting was late in the day, and for several hours the ship backed and filled and then stood off for the night. The island was almost certainly Jelbon ("the easternmost of the Mulgraves," Lieutenant Paulding wrote), the home of Luckiair, Ludjuan's son-in-law, who a year or so before had brought Lay from Mili Mili for a week's visit.

On the morning of November 20 the *Dolphin* anchored on the lee side, the west, of the island less than two hundred yards off a point where the surf was breaking. At 9:30 Captain Percival took one of the ship's cutters ashore and had his first meeting with the natives. "Very kind and hospitable" Lieutenant Paulding found them, ready to offer the visitors anything they wanted. The first thing they wanted was water for the ship; that was quickly found in several wells.

The real work on Jelbon began the next day, November 21. Some of the crew were assigned to fill and transport the water casks, and others were formed into exploration parties. Socializing with the natives continued, with the ship playing host to some of them, who were eminently well behaved. They were dressed formally as befitted the special occasion, wearing *marmars*, wreaths of flowers, bracelets, and rolls of leaves in their pierced ears. Not only did they not steal anything, but they were politely curious about the ship and anxious to converse, despite the language barrier, "taking pains," Paulding says, "to make themselves understood."

Meanwhile on land the exploring parties struck pay dirt: they found a whaler's lance, pieces of canvas, and other traces of the *Globe*. When the natives who had come on board the ship were shown these objects, their enthusiasm for communication vanished. Perfectly clear questions from the ship's people were met with suddenly blank looks on the faces of the natives, who had up to that point been so chatty. They were masterful at playing dumb.

The *Dolphin*'s officers did not jump to hasty conclusions about the *Globe*'s landing site on the basis of the things the exploring parties had found. And they were right; *Globe* objects would have had no difficulty making their way to the far eastern end of the atoll from the *Globe* camp at the far western end by simple exchange from hand to hand over the months since the camp was plundered.

By November 22, the third day that the visitors were on Jelbon, tension began to replace the initially warm and casual attitude of the natives. It was not merely because of the white men's curiosity about the lance and canvas, but because of the assiduousness of the shore parties combing the island as if they had search warrants. Paulding, who had a keen eye for native reaction, sensed alarm. Some of the

huts that had been occupied the day before were deserted, and most
tellingly, a large canoe that had been on shore in the evening was
gone; it had left overnight.

About the canoe the officers of the *Dolphin* were right to make
special note, for it is highly likely that it carried news about the ship
to the *iroojlaplap* in Mili Mili and also likely that it stopped at
Lukunor, where Hussey was living; it was this stop that brought
Hussey the first word about the ship. In Hussey the startling news
revived the fear and hope provoked by the unknown ship that passed
more than a year before. "The reader can have but a faint idea of my
feelings," he wrote. The men from the canoe reported that the ship
had two masts, had guns on both sides, and carried a hundred men
(quite an overestimate). They themselves, the natives said, had been
on the ship, had been given beads, which they were wearing, and had
found the men on board different looking from Lay and Hussey—
and "very saucy."

Hussey knew at once: it was the navy—it was rescue if the whole
perilous operation worked, and Hussey knew how perilous it was.
Anything could happen. What threatened the rescue was obviously
the hostility of the natives or, more accurately, their unpredictability,
and that was true even of those natives who had been such peaceable
guests on board the ship two days before. If Hussey had been on
hand to witness the reception of the orderly, friendly natives on board
the ship at Jelbon, he would not have been reassured, for he knew
their fickleness. If that was a trait of theirs in ordinary circumstances,
how much more fickle would they be when confronted with this big,
ominous unknown ship? It counted for nothing that the white men
on the ship had been straightforward and friendly—even if saucy,
whatever that meant. They were still a great, new force, and everything that is unknown looks larger than it really is.

Both Lay and Hussey were going to have to marshall their wits to
keep the natives from obstructing the imminent rescue. What they

had to argue against was an ever-varying mixture of superstition, irrational fear, reflexes, sentiment, and caprice. In that forum logic is not
a useful tool. In argument with the natives the styles of the two seamen were not the same: Lay was clever, Hussey was blunt. Now
Hussey was arguing: when the men from the canoe told him that
they would take the ship and kill everyone on board, Hussey's answer
was that they would be shot if they attempted anything against the
ship. It was a warship; that's all there was to it. Their only hope would
be to maintain friendship with the people of the new vessel.

Whether the advice was even noted for delivery, the canoe continued on to Mili Mili. Early the next morning, November 23, it
arrived, and word spread to everyone including Lay that there was a
ship off one of the eastern islands. The chiefs immediately performed
a ceremony invoking the counsel of Anit. (Lay knew what the ceremony was about, but he was not allowed to attend.) The question
posed to the god was, should they board the vessel, a few at a time,
until there were two hundred of them on it and then kill all the white
men? Anit approved. Luttuon ordered a hundred men, divided
between two canoes, to sail.

Lay asked to accompany them and was refused until he managed
to fabricate an effective argument: he convinced the chiefs that the
vessel could not belong to his nation since it had only two masts, and
no American ships had only two masts, and furthermore the people
on the ship being from some unknown place would not be able to
speak Lay's language. The chiefs finally agreed to take him. They
knew he could be the source of some intelligence for them at the
same time that he was a risk—he could tip off the people on the ship
about the massacre, if he managed to have contact with them. The
two canoes sailed and did not arrive in Lukunor before nightfall. In
the morning these two canoes were joined by others, bringing the
total number of men to two hundred.

Although the sources of the *Dolphin*'s adventures at Mili do not agree altogether on chronology, the sequence of the events of the next week is fairly clear. The picture that emerges is one of a pair of seamen hanging between hope and despair, a band of methodical and casually brave rescuers, and a horde of frantic, unresourceful, and confused natives.

The *Dolphin* meanwhile prepared to weigh anchor and leave Jelbon. From the masthead the lookouts could see islands strung out to the south, those would have been part of the Knox spur, and to the west. The crew had finished stowing the casks of water and making some minor repairs on the ship; Lieutenant Paulding made notes on the island's flora and fauna—the rats were very tame and had tufts of hair on their tails. Captain Percival ordered a course toward the western islands. The first one that the ship approached was, from best evidence, Lukunor, so the *Dolphin* happened to be tailing the canoe, moving along on the ocean side of the island chain while the natives were sailing on the lagoon side.

The *Dolphin* had passed a dozen or so islets west of Jelbon that were so small they could be observed adequately from the ship. In contrast, Lukunor, less than five miles west of Jelbon, called for a landing just because of the look of the place, not because of the drama developing there, for the captain did not know that Lukunor was Hussey's address nor that the high chief was assembling a force of warriors there to meet him and, incidentally, bringing the only other *Globe* survivor with him.

A few people from the island met the captain when he landed on the east end of Lukunor, but most of those ran away rather than come close to him. The few that remained were timid and about as far removed as possible from the sociability of their counterparts on Jelbon. The officers were mystified by this—the islanders seemed to be from another nation.

What Percival did not realize was that the situation was now very different from what it was a day ago. The whole population was alarmed by the arrival of the *iroojlaplap* and his warlike posture and his reading of the meaning of the ship. Percival had come upon a nation preparing for war. An exceptional figure in the midst of this tension was the lone native described by Paulding who came out from shore in his canoe, boarded the ship, looked around, and after a short while left. He gave the impression of being simply curious, but in fact he was officially curious—he was a spy sent by Luttuon, and it was his count of the size of the crew that was carried back to the *iroojlaplap* to be entered in his strategic calculation. He was not the last of the spies, as Paulding was to learn from Lay a few days later: the natives took every opportunity to come aboard as if for a social visit and returned with detailed descriptions not only of things but also of individuals on the ship.

After a short time on the island, the captain reentered the boat in which he had gone ashore and moved westward along the coast of Lukunor, with the ship following him. When he reached the west end of the island he found himself at Lukunor Passage, one of the two most important entries into the lagoon. Captain Percival guided the boat through the passage into the "inland sea of great extent," and found it calm and laced with coral shoals. He could see several large canoes approaching from a distance but did not try to contact them, fearing that if he came up to them, he would make them turn back. Instead he turned about and went out the passage, then went ashore at the west end of the island. Here he found four large beached canoes and soon others in the process of landing; these were the ones that he had seen but not approached in the lagoon. He did not know that Luttuon, the high chief, was in one of the canoes and had come with his entourage to observe him and the ship.

The observation was mutual: when Captain Percival walked among the canoes, he found on the platforms of some of them lids from chests of *Globe* sailors as well as ash spars and pieces of cloth. The natives were becoming edgy watching Percival pry. They pretended a cool indifference but lapsed into excited conversation among themselves. When someone from the captain's group pointed questioningly at the chest lids, the native response was a blank stare and a few incomprehensible words.

While some of the *Dolphin* party examined the canoes, others walked through the grove of coconut and breadfruit trees at the back of the beach and mingled comfortably with the natives. Amid the trees were a number of tidy and attractive huts, which drew the attention of the men from the boat. Around one of them a large number of natives had gathered; it was about ten feet high and had a garret area at the top, the view of which was blocked by the raised floor woven of sticks and leaves. For some reason, the *Dolphin* men did not look as closely at this hut as at some of the others. There was no reason for ignoring it, but when they later learned what the garret held, they were glad they had not asked to see it. On the raised floor, guarded by a large band of women, was William Lay; the high chief had confined him there and ordered him to remain in perfect silence while the boat crew was nearby and to make no effort to reveal his hiding place. The women had been ordered to kill him if he disobeyed.

Escape was that close. The anguish of Lay went on for several hours. He could hear what was being said by the sailors near the huts and learned from their conversation what kind of a ship they were from and what they were there for—him.

At night, after the navy people had returned on board, Luttuon sent for Lay and put him through intense questioning about the ship. On his arrival at the island, Luttuon had already gone to Hussey and questioned him. Neither Lay nor Hussey speak of being allowed to see each other at this time, but Lay later told Lieutenant Paulding that both he and Hussey knew that the ship was in search of them— the phrasing of Paulding's account suggests that the two men had been together and able to talk during Lay's time on Lukunor. Hussey told Luttuon that, not having seen the vessel, he could not say much about it, but beyond that what he did tell the chief was spoken with his characteristic directness, not Lay's inventive rhetoric.

Luttuon was hearing very different stories from the two. The ship, Hussey told him, must have come for himself and Lay and was going to do everything necessary to succeed. Luttuon said that in that case he had better kill both of them, for then there would be no one to tell that the natives had killed the others. Hussey replied that the people from the ship already knew that they were alive, so that if they were killed, the natives should expect the naval force to avenge their deaths by killing everyone on the island. This argument worked as well as anything that Lay could have come up with, and Luttuon went off perplexed. Lay and Hussey, as Paulding reports, filled the natives with apprehension "by declaring, repeatedly, that we were invincible, and that there was scarcely any thing we could not accomplish with our six-pounders; they even made them believe, trifling as our armament was, that we could sink the islands with our cannon; so ready is the human mind to receive for truth what it cannot comprehend, if recommended by superior intelligence, though it may be at variance with every thing in nature or reason."

What caused the most anxiety for the natives in the canoes was the remarkable boldness of the visitors. The men from the ship had not displayed any force yet, but their freedom of approach to the island and its people was unsettling. There was no telling what they would do next. The chief's decision was to leave the island and move as far away from the ship as possible and to do so as soon as possible. That meant sailing out into the lagoon at midnight, taking Lay with them. Lay does not name the island he was carried to, but it was probably Tokewa across the lagoon to the north.

In the morning Captain Percival made an attempt to take the ship itself, not a boat, through Lukunor Passage. The technique, towing the ship from a kedge, did not work, and the effort was abandoned— fortunately, for although access to the lagoon would have sped the search, the coral shoals would have been almost impossible to navigate safely. The captain's main strategy was to move in a counterclockwise direction around the atoll until the whole group of islands, if necessary, was covered. That plan would have been hard to carry out if the search had extended very far on the north side of the atoll, where the islands were not a perfect string but a cluster, but the search would not go that far.

The captain assigned Lieutenant Homer to lead a party of a dozen men to explore the islands on foot, beginning on the west side of Lukunor Passage and moving west. It was not known at this point how many submerged reefs the party would run into on its trek, so a boat was sent to follow offshore and pull in to ferry the men between islands where needed. Another boat, sent out in the evening to stay in touch with the land party, returned without catching up to them, as Lieutenant Homer's group had covered a lot of ground, probably reaching at least the western end of the long island of Enajet. The next morning another boat, sent with supplies, did overtake them, Paulding reports, ten miles west of their starting point at Lukunor. The party had been well treated by the natives they had encountered and had been given coconuts without any exchange of gifts. At one point on the island Lieutenant Homer had come upon a mitten with the initials "R. C." When the mitten was taken back to the ship, the initials were compared with the *Globe*'s crew list and identified as those of Rowland Coffin, the young seaman who was suspected of having knowledge of the impending mutiny and of whom his uncle, Gorham Coffin, back on Nantucket was mounting such an exercised defense.

While the ship was following the land party, Lieutenant Paulding went ashore and found deserted huts but a few friendly natives. He had brought his musket and used it to shoot some sand snipe he had found on the beach, much to the delight of the natives, who were impressed by seeing what the musket could do. But Paulding also shot a small white crane and "afterwards regretted it very much" when he learned that the cranes were domesticated birds, treasured by the natives.

The next day, November 26, the ship caught up with the land party, who by this time must have reached the long, boomerang-shaped island of Arbar. The ship delivered supplies and moved on in advance of the party. By 3 P.M. the *Dolphin* was even with the widest piece of land they had yet seen in the atoll. They had reached Mili Mili and were about to anchor near where the *Globe* had anchored. The numerous huts scattered through the forest of coconut and breadfruit trees struck Paulding as "forming a peaceful and romantic scene." The landing was easy. Once it became clear, as it soon would, that this was the landing place of the *Globe*, the *Dolphin's* company could see that the *Globe* had picked the best location on the whole atoll for coming ashore and setting up camp.

There was something mournfully well timed about the ship's arrival at the "capital" of Mili Atoll: the *Dolphin* needed a burial ground. Surgeon Benjamin Wells, who had been unwell from the date of sailing from Peru—disease of the liver was his self-diagnosis—died at 4:45 P.M. on November 27. He had been taking care of the health of the ship's company up until two days before his death, which was no small duty since on a typical day between ten and fifteen men would be on sick report. Wells had greatly endeared himself, Lieutenant Paulding said, to the ship's company, who knew how much he was suffering while caring for them. On the next morning, November 28, a grave was dug at the foot of a breadfruit tree. As big a burial party as could be spared from the ship went ashore, and the surgeon was consigned to the earth with naval honors. Around the mourners a number of natives had assembled quietly, fascinated by what was going on, but when the muskets were fired over the grave, they burst out in howls and laughter. The people at the grave turned on the natives and threateningly ordered them to stand a good distance away, which they did in silence. At the head and foot of the grave were planted orange, lemon, and chermoya seeds, and on the trunk of the breadfruit tree Surgeon Wells's name and rank and the name of the *Dolphin* were carved. This information was duplicated, along with his age and the day of his death, on a brass plate, which was nailed to the tree. It was an odd coincidence that the surgeon was buried so near the *Globe* burials; the *Dolphin* people did not yet know where the *Globe* burials were.

The exploring party, working its way across Arbar and intervening islands, caught up with the ship and crossed into Mili Mili the day of the funeral. At the east end of the triangular island they found the ground littered with cloth, canvas, spears, rigging, a thimble, and the staves from smashed barrels of beef and pork. Farther on they found under a light covering of sand a skeleton "supposed to be the remains of Comstock the chief Mutineer," the *Dolphin*'s log noted, and a box with some Spanish dollars inside it. At this point the natives who had been walking behind the exploring party or in company with them suddenly disappeared or crept, almost out of sight, through the undergrowth. Since night was coming on, the party went only a short distance farther and camped in a deserted hut they had found. In the morning of the next day, November 29, they began to march on—they were almost as far west as possible and would have to turn north to continue—when they saw that natives holding spears and stones had assembled in groups a short distance away. The natives easily outnumbered the exploring party. The total armament of the members of the party was a pistol apiece, and when they checked their ammunition, they found it wet and useless. Lieutenant Homer ordered his men to turn back and go to the hut where they had spent the night, but when they arrived at that place, the hut had been taken down and carried away. Also missing was a large canoe that had been beached near the hut the night before. No native was to be seen anywhere. Homer ordered his group to stay at that point and sent two messengers back to the ship.

The officers on the ship learned from the messengers not only what the present threatened state of the party was, but also what the party had discovered the day before. This was the first word that Captain Percival and the other officers had about the shattered barrels and litter. The discovery removed all question about where the *Globe* settlement had been, but it did not shed any light on where the *Globe* people were now. As far as Captain Percival's information went, there were still nine of them to be found on the atoll.

The sudden bellicose behavior of the natives was worrisome and mystifying. Paulding speculated—and his thinking seems to have reflected that of the other officers—that the natives, if they wanted to kill the people from the ship, had had many opportunities to do so but had acted friendly instead. Why were they preparing to make war now? The conclusion that the officers reached was that the mutineers were living among the natives, were in league with them, and had persuaded them to attack the visitors.

The messengers from the exploring party had come aboard the ship a little after noon on November 29; by 4 o'clock the captain had ordered a launch prepared to back up the party on shore. It sailed with two officers and eleven men as well as the messengers from the party. That deployment left a few more than forty men on the ship, the absolute minimum that the captain wanted to have in readiness if the natives attacked.

The launch, commanded by Lieutenant Paulding, was stocked with five days' provisions as well as supplies for Lieutenant Homer's exploring party. It crossed a reef into the lagoon and approached the exploring party's encampment from that side of the island. Paulding's boat crew went ashore and had supper with the exploring party. On reembarking, Paulding discovered that the exploring party had taken not only the arms and ammunition that he had brought them but also those that he had equipped his own boat with. Nothing would do but to land again, go back to the exploring party, and actually search the men for the swiped arms, looking even in the bushes where they could have hidden some. Winds were very unfavorable to Paulding's boat, and he and one of the midshipmen ended up rowing through part of the night; the normally smooth lagoon had become rough and nasty. It was an exhausting preparation for a day of action, and action was more and more the expectation.

The logical next move on the part of the exploring party would have been to continue north on Mili Mili, cross the small passage between Mili Mili and Malka, and keep heading north until arriving at Naalo. That would have been the route for the launch to take as well, if the original strategy, circling the atoll, was still the plan. But for some reason, which he does not explain at all in his *Journal* account, Lieutenant Paulding headed northeast across the lagoon. All he says about his route was that the wind veered, permitting him to head for an island appearing on the horizon eight or ten miles away, where he could stop and give his boat crew breakfast. It was the morning of November 30.

They had gone a little more than halfway to the island when they noticed that they were not the only ones traveling that course; two canoes had pulled out of islands that they were passing, shot ahead of them and landed where they were planning to land. At the same time, they saw two canoes leaving the island and heading for them. Paulding was distracted by the difficult management of the launch around some especially treacherous reefs—one of the reasons for believing that the island in question was Tokewa, for the reefs south of it extend far out into the lagoon and are notoriously dangerous. The intercepting canoes seemed to be a native coast guard; they held twenty natives carrying the now familiar spears and stones. As they passed, Paulding came alongside them to look them over, a move that led to the natives giving the people in the launch "a great many cross looks." Paulding watched them when they turned back toward the island; what he now saw on the island was a collection of twenty canoes—*walaps*, the largest kind, that would hold from twenty to forty men each. This was the fleet that Luttuon had led away from Lukunor when the officers and men from the *Dolphin* had arrived there and begun to prowl around. And, of course, it was the fleet that carried Lay away to his new place of detention.

When Paulding was sailing close to the two canoes that had come out from shore, he saw clearly that they could move three times as fast as his boat. It was hopeless, he concluded, to overtake anyone from the *Globe* on the water; the natives' canoes could outrun him every time. What strategy could he devise to neutralize the advantage of those twenty canoes? "I determined, therefore, to take possession of all that were now assembled, even though I should be opposed by the natives, and reduced to the necessity of measuring our strength with them." Battle, plain and simple: thirteen with guns versus two hundred with spears and stones. The crowd that he was looking at, Paulding realized, was much too large to be made up of inhabitants of the island; they had to have come from other islands for some special reason. So Paulding kept determining: "I determined to land and search their huts, and look around, before I made so wide a breach with them, as must necessarily result from the seizure of their canoes." For understated nervy resolves, Paulding was hard to beat. The men examining the native huts would have been vulnerable at every moment, but chances had to be taken. The situation became graver when the natives began sending the women and children away from the shore and to the huts. With continued understatement, verging on drollery, Paulding observes that "that indicated a want of confidence in us on their part." The boat headed in through the surf.

The two hundred native men facing Paulding's party were situated fairly far back on the beach, about seventy yards from the shore. All of them were seated. Then a dark-skinned figure in native clothing with his long hair tied in a knot on the top of his head detached himself from the assembled warriors and advanced to a point halfway between them and the boat. Everyone in the boat studied him; the confrontation looked almost ceremonial.

Then the figure spoke: "The Indians are going to kill you; don't come on shore unless you are prepared to fight." Paulding's astonishment was, to use his word, indescribable. This had to be, he thought, one of the *Globe* people, but he looked like a native—his skin was as dark as theirs, he was covered with coconut oil, and he was wearing the familiar woven mat garment.

He repeated his warning several times and described what the natives were planning. The men from the boat would be invited ashore and asked to sit down among the natives, who at a signal would rise up and kill them all with stones. That was not hard for Paulding to believe, but the puzzle created by the whole scene gave him pause. Was this one of the mutineers or an innocent crew member? Among the nine people Paulding had been advised were on the atoll, he knew that at least two were mutineers. Why had not the search turned up this man before, and if he was innocent, why did he not run to the boat for the protection of his rescuers?

What is your name? Paulding asked. William Lay, he replied, of the *Globe*. The *Dolphin* had been given descriptions as well as names of those expected to be on the islands, and Lay fitted at least in stature and youth the description that Paulding knew. Paulding told him to come to the boat. He could not do it, Lay explained, because the natives had ordered him to go no nearer the boat than he was now. Run, and we will protect you, Paulding told him. If he tried that, Lay said, the natives would stone him to death before he could reach the boat.

The whole scene up to this point had been scripted by Lay himself. When the *iroojlaplap* had been planning the slaughter of the men in the boat, Lay had taken on his role as advisor and told Luttuon that the best possible plan would be for the natives to hold back and let him lure the men out of the boat by extending an invitation to come and sit among the natives, at which point it would be easy to kill them. Luttuon liked the idea but had to submit it to Anit for approval. The technique of testing the god's favor is to fold and bind together a lot of straws and then attempt to pull them out of the clump unentangled. If that works, the god approves; if not, the ritual can be tried another day, but until then the god denies permission. On this crucial occasion the god approved, and Luttuon anointed Lay with coconut oil and sent him forward to carry out the trickery.

Paulding and his party were still in the boat while the exchange with Lay had been going on. Everything now would depend on what Paulding wanted to do with Lay's information. His first move was to order his men to fire their pistols for psychological effect and quickly reload from their cartridge boxes. Then they leapt from the boat and walked through the warm green water to shore. Paulding, still uncertain whether he was dealing with a mutineer or not, and unwilling to let him get away if he was a mutineer, went up to Lay, grabbed him with his left hand, and held a cocked pistol to his chest. Paulding was sensitive to the pain such an approach would cause, but figured that if Lay were innocent, he would quickly get over the shock and hurt, and in any event he could not risk losing him.

"Who are you?" Paulding asked again.

"I am your man," Lay replied and burst into tears.

Paulding told Lay to tell the natives that if any one of them stood up or threw a stone, the boat party would kill them all. Lay tried, but he was, as Paulding put it, "delirious with joy," and what came out was a collection of words and half-sentences in a mixture of Marshallese and English, most of it incomprehensible to Paulding and probably to the natives. When Lay burst out with, "They are going to kill me, they are going to kill me," Paulding ordered him to stop and asked him what he meant by saying they were going to kill him. Lay apologized, saying that he did not know what he was saying.

The whole drama was mystifying and worrisome to the natives, two or three of whom stood up and started coming forward. Paulding pointed his pistol at them and told Lay to warn them once again that they would be killed if they stood up or threw stones. The aggressive ones retreated, but one old man, unarmed, kept coming forward. Lay told Paulding to let him approach. The old man took Lay's hand in both of his and asked what the people in the boat were going to do to him. When Lay explained to him, the old man was deeply moved. The old man was the one who had saved Lay's life almost two years before on the day of the massacre. Lay was as emotional as his protector and put his arms around him and promised that he would see him again before he left the islands; Lay was weeping as he spoke.

Paulding understood the extraordinary feeling of the moment but worried about what moves the natives would make as soon as their puzzlement at the scene unfolding in front of them wore off. If they compared numbers, Paulding thought, they would easily see that they could overcome the white men. One shot from their pistols is all the men could deliver; they would not have time to reload before the natives were on them. Paulding interrupted the conversation of Lay and the old man and hurried him off to the boat. Midshipman Charles Davis, a member of Paulding's boat crew and later a rear admiral, called the rescue the boldest act he had ever witnessed.

Lay was weeping with joy. His excitement led him to ask questions repeatedly even after they had been answered. Were his friends well? Nobody knew them. From East Saybrook, Connecticut—does anyone know that part of the country? No, sorry.

As he calmed down, he answered questions about the state of the *Globe* people; all were dead except Cyrus Hussey. This was the first report of the massacre to the outside world. Hussey, Lay said, was on an island to windward of them—would they rescue him as well? He was overjoyed to hear that they would.

As they sailed on, Lay was able to clear up for Lieutenant Paulding the reasons for some of the puzzling aspects of the natives' behavior toward them. The main reason was that the natives had been taking very seriously the advice that Lay and Hussey had been giving them. The two young men had made a good case for the white men being impossible to overcome; the instructions that the two gave to the natives were to let the white men go wherever they wanted, give them what they asked for, and conciliate them in every way possible. These instructions were obeyed the way the regulations of colonial powers are obeyed: the authority of the lawgiver was acknowledged, but there was no trust in the reality of what he is saying. At the same time that they abided by Lay's and Hussey's peacekeeping proposals, they were approaching their two advisors with proposals like (a) cutting a hole in the bottom of the ship, sinking it, and killing all those who did not drown, or (b) making a massive raid by night on the ship. Lay and Hussey had to argue strenuously against these plans.

Tokewa was quickly depopulated: Luttuon headed with his entourage for his home at Mili Mili (where the *Dolphin* was anchored), and Paulding's rescue boat headed for Hussey's island. Paulding knew how the boat crew was feeling; the tension that had sustained them through the rescue had abruptly relaxed, and they were famished and physically and nervously exhausted. Paulding spotted a dry reef in the middle of the lagoon and ordered the boat to tie up there for a meal. The stop, which was a virtual necessity for the crew, was agony for Lay. In his mind every minute lost was putting his own rescue in jeopardy and was giving Luttuon a chance to frustrate the rescue of Hussey. Paulding understood this; it was, in his words, "painful" to observe Lay's anxiety. The meal was a hasty one, and the boat sailed on.

It was a relief for all in the boat, as they approached Lukunor, to see only one canoe on the beach and no sign of a crowd, in fact, no sign of anyone for a few minutes until Lugoma and some old women walked down to the beach. They had come to see what the strange boat was doing; when they saw Lay, they were flabbergasted. He was still wearing the native clothes he was rescued in and to Lugoma had his everyday look. The old women shouted questions at Lay as the boat pulled up: What was he doing with the white men in the boat? And what did the white men want? Paulding did not give Lay a chance to answer but jumped from the boat, grabbed Lugoma, pointed a pistol at him, and ordered Lay to tell him that unless Hussey was produced at once, he would shoot. Lugoma begged not to be hurt and assured Paulding that Hussey would be brought out. Hussey was in the woods and heard the clamoring women calling out his name; he came out, as Paulding describes him, "with his fine yellow hair hanging in ringlets about his shoulders, and his person quite naked, with the exception of a piece of blanket, tied around his loins."

"Well, young man, do you wish to return to your country?" Paulding asked him.

"Yes, sir; I know of nothing that I have done for which I should be afraid to go home," Hussey replied, his eyes welling with tears.

Paulding turned the gun away from Lugoma, who immediately begged Paulding not to hurt Hussey. When he was assured that Hussey would not be hurt, he then asked that Hussey not be taken away from him. The old women joined their entreaties with Lugoma's. Paulding saw the poignancy of the moment; describing it, he capsulized Hussey's whole "family" life on the island:

The scene was an interesting one, and we found a picturesque group assembled on a beautiful lawn, in front of a number of huts, surrounded by cocoa-nut and bread-fruit trees. Huzzy [*sic* throughout Paulding—for good reason since the name was pronounced with a z, not an s, sound] owed his life to the native chief; he had been in the condition of a slave to him for two years. To him he was indebted for many acts of kindness, some of which he had requited by his industry in his service, and some had been cancelled by harsh treatment; yet still he stood in a delicate situation towards the chief. The saving of his life alone, conferred an obligation upon him, which could scarcely be repaid by long and faithful services. The chief evidently appeared to regard him as his son, and when the moment of our departure arrived, and he saw we were determined to take our countryman with us, he joined tears to entreaties, saying he would weep long and bitterly for him. He told Huzzy that he must come back again, and asked me if I would bring him. As the only way in which I could get clear of so strange a petition, urged with so much feeling, I promised to bring him back if his mother consented to his return.

That satisfied Lugoma, who then took Hussey aside to point out to him how hard it would be for him to get his work done without Hussey's help. When he did return, Lugoma told him, he should bring "axes, guns, and cloths, such as his countrymen wore." The request is interesting, for it was the first recorded suggestion by any Mili native that he had even a slight interest in dressing the way the white men dress. Throughout Oceania around this time accounts emerge of the native chief, given a cast-off uniform, wearing it ostentatiously at one time or another but quickly returning to comfortable native clothing. Lugoma may have been the bellwether of new island fashions. Paulding, on the occasion, was the bestower and the recipient of several gifts—for the women rings and beads and for Lugoma a superb gift, a jackknife. Only an axe could have pleased Lugoma more.

Hussey had no packing to do for the trip back to the schooner except for a musket without powder and his Bible. Lugoma had wanted Hussey to have the musket as a weapon *in terrorem* against potential enemies, even though it could not be fired; the Bible continued to be a mystery to the natives, but Hussey, unlike Lay, had held on to his by counteracting their argument that the Bible would bring bad spirits around the house with his argument that if any harm were done to the book, the Great Spirit would avenge it by killing them.

An unexpected proposal of Lugoma's was accepted: he would like to go with them and bring his son for the voyage back to Mili Mili. It was late in the day when the boat carrying *Irooj* Lugoma, his son, and the whole remaining company of the whaleship *Globe* pulled away from the island. It was headed ultimately for Mili Mili and the schooner, but the first stop was at an island where it encountered Lieutenant Homer's land party, who were delighted at the news that the *Globe* survivors had been found and rescued but disappointed that they, after all their trekking, were not the ones to have made the discovery.

Paulding's boat did not have to take the land party aboard because it had its own boat, the one that had been following it to help in the crossing of drowned reefs between islands. At what island the land party was met, Paulding does not say, but given the amount of time elapsed, it could have been Naalo in the northwest corner of the atoll or a small island west of Naalo. The land party's boat was ready to return across the lagoon to Mili Mili and the schooner, and was going to make the trip in company with Paulding's boat, which meant adapting to Paulding's plans, which were not for a direct return.

Reading the thinking of Paulding is an adventure in itself. He learned fast, and Lay and Hussey were good teachers, so he understood the volatility and illogic of the natives' reactions and intentions. Decisions that he made now were not made in the dark. He was indifferent to hazard, a supportive enough trait when one faces two hundred natives with a single shot in one's pistol, but hazard had become a habit for Paulding; he found it a natural circumstance even when it could have been avoided. Instead of sailing back to Mili Mili, which, with favorable winds, he could have reached in an hour and a half, he had to make a stop at Tokewa—for what? To pick up Lay's musket, which he had left behind in the haste of their departure. Paulding found, beached on the shore at Tokewa, the same canoes that he had intended to capture earlier in the day. But they were not there for long: the natives, on seeing Paulding's boat, launched all the canoes and sailed off. A relief? No. Paulding ordered pursuit of the canoes (on the assumption that the useless musket was in one of them?), and when he saw that once again they were outdistancing him, he fired over their heads. That did not achieve the intended purpose of bringing them to, but only made them more alarmed to get away.

The most alarmed person of all when the musket shots rang out was Lugoma. To him the ill-advised firing meant that Paulding wanted to kill all the chiefs, including himself. Lay and Hussey tried in vain to calm him and convince him that Lieutenant Paulding was his friend. Several times he was at the point of taking his son and jumping from the stern of the boat, where they were seated, but he was prevented from doing so. He kept repeating to Paulding that he was his friend and begging not to be killed. Paulding tried to tell him as clearly and emphatically as possible that he in turn was Lugoma's friend and would not hurt him, but Lugoma seemed not to hear what was being said and kept repeating his plea not to be killed.

Night had come on, and Paulding ordered the boat to put in at the same spot north of Mili Mili where they had rendezvoused with the land party the day before. As the boat approached the beach, Lugoma begged passionately to be allowed to leave with his son. He was now almost twenty miles from home. Paulding was afraid that if Lugoma did leave, he would find some other natives, advise them where the white men were camped, and attack them; Lugoma was not allowed to leave. Spreading the sails like an awning against the rain, the group tried to sleep, but Paulding found that he had to put up with

Lugoma, who insisted on sleeping next to him and, every ten minutes, woke Paulding up by running his hand over his face and saying
"*hitera*," perhaps an obsolete form of *jera*—friend—which Paulding
was obliged to repeat to Lugoma if he wanted to be given even a few
minutes' rest.

In the morning, December 1, the boat was set to leave the lagoon
and rejoin the schooner a couple of miles away, but the kedge serving as anchor had become snagged on coral and resisted every effort
to free it. When Lugoma saw the problem, he told his son to jump
in and go down to the anchor to loose it. The boy jumped in the
eighteen-foot-deep water, freed the one-hundred-pound kedge, and
came up signaling to haul away. That task was as run-of-the-mill for
the boy as untying from a coral projection the line on the family's
korkor.

Before the boat could start for the passage at the north end of Mili
Mili, though, Lugoma made it clear that he was still afraid that
Paulding was going to kill him and that he wanted to leave the boat
at that point. This time Paulding agreed. It was time for another parting with Hussey and for a little additional gift giving on Paulding's
part. This time the gift was a variety of seeds, accompanied by
instructions translated by either Lay or Hussey, probably the latter,
on how to plant them and on what kind of fruit they would produce.
Lugoma and son were left to their own devices to make their way
back to Lukunor.

By 8 A.M. the boat with Lay and Hussey as well as the boat that
had been following Lieutenant Homer's land party had come alongside the schooner. Everyone on board the *Dolphin* welcomed the rescued and the rescuers enthusiastically. The job was done. Lay and
Hussey would get haircuts and shaves and American clothes and sit
down to navy food. In Paulding's mind, "We had now accomplished
the object of our visit, and the islands were altogether so void of
interest, except for their novel formation, and the singular habits of

the natives, that we were well content to leave them and return to some other place more congenial to the feelings of civilized men." That was not exactly the thinking of Captain Percival, though, for he was in no more haste to leave the atoll than he had been to leave the coast of Peru at the start of his mission; a week would go by before the *Dolphin* sailed.

The first order of business in the captain's mind was assembling the chiefs of the atoll for a conclusive conference about the whole business of the *Globe* from start to the present. On the morning of December 1, shortly after the return of the rescued men to the schooner, the captain sent word via Luttuon's mother that her son should come, in company with the other chiefs, to meet him. The captain apparently entrusted the delivery of his summons to Paulding and Lay, the latter just hours free from his two-year detention; presumably his barbering and reclothing had been completed before he set foot on the island, presenting a startling new look to those who had known him so long as one of them.

The two men went across the triangular island to the lagoon side, where at the inside of the elbow formed by Mili Mili stood the chief's village. Lay knew it well, but Paulding had not seen it before. Paulding's description of it could be, without a change, applied to the same place today: "It was not extensive, but a beautiful and romantic spot; the grove of cocoa-nut and bread-fruit trees, through which were scattered the huts of the natives, ran about a hundred yards back from the inland sea to a wild thicket that passes through the centre of the islet, in length two or three hundred yards." In population, layout, buildings, and aspects of culture (except for native attire), the modern village is so close to the *iroojlaplap*'s that one stands there today in nineteenth-century Mili Mili.

Luttuon was not in the village; other than a few women and children Paulding and Lay encountered no one. Luttuon's son, Ladro, showed them around the village, pointing out ancestral graves, which the visitors were advised to take care not to walk on. Paulding commented on a small, bantam-like fowl, and Ladro immediately gave it to him; the natives, Paulding was told, never eat them for "they are not cleanly in their food."

In their stroll around the village Lay showed Paulding where he had once buried a Spanish dollar. He was able to dig it up, a souvenir. They ran into a native whom Lay knew well enough to engage in a charade with: Lay did an imitation of a native engaged in battle, which Paulding was a bit nervous watching; he found it "a mixture of the frightful and ludicrous" and was afraid it might be insulting to the native. Lay knew what he was doing, though, and the native was highly amused. By the end of the day there was no sign of Luttuon or the other chiefs.

The next morning, December 2, the captain went ashore and called on the high chief's mother, who could only make excuses for the chiefs' absence and assure him that they would definitely be there in the evening. Percival told her to send for them again and say that if they were not there the next day, he would go after them and might make them pay for not appearing. The mother was frightened now and guaranteed that her son would be on hand the next day. The threat worked, and on the morning of December 3, all the chiefs presented themselves on shore, on the ocean side near the schooner's anchorage.

The summit meeting convened, with Lay and Hussey as translators, and treated a major agenda. The captain identified himself as the representative of the high chief of his country, who had sent him to find the men of the *Globe*. As to the killings that they were responsible for, Percival told them that they would not be punished since those constituted a first offense committed out of ignorance. But in the future any killing or injury of a white man from any ship would call for grave revenge by a naval force that would kill everyone on the islands, as well as destroy all their produce and property. They should

not fear white men who come to their islands in the future; if they treated them well, they would be rewarded. Stealing, lying, and other immoral acts were wrong and, in the white men's country, were punished; murder was punished by death. The natives were asked to return a whaleboat and a swivel gun from the *Globe* and Lay's musket, which they readily agreed to do. Luttuon declared the surgeon's grave a sacred spot and guaranteed that it would receive the same reverential treatment as the marked graves of the natives' ancestors. The captain, explaining that he was rewarding them for the care they had bestowed on Lay and Hussey, gave gifts, which included the familiar axes, cloths, beads, and seeds, but also two pigs, which they were admonished to use for breeding, not kill for food. The pigs were a hit with the natives, who carried them around like puppies, even though the squealing, kicking animals were scratching the bodies of their doting masters. The conference ended, and the visitors retired to the *Dolphin*. The two translators had been given a workout.

This had been the first time that the officers of the *Dolphin* had met with Luttuon, except for the encounter when Lay was rescued, which was not exactly a meeting. Paulding noted his reputation as the atoll's greatest warrior in years, a reputation that seems to have been conveyed to him by Luttuon himself. Luttuon described to the officers his adventures during one war, in which he was forced to leave Mili in a canoe, was at sea for fourteen days ("I think," says Paulding), and finally arrived at Arno, where he was received and sheltered. After visiting thirteen islands, which probably included some of the islands of Majuro as well as Arno, he returned home to Mili with forces from Arno, conquered his enemies, and became a tributary to the chief of Arno, whose daughter (or granddaughter, Paulding says) he married. The relationship of tribute from Mili to Arno was thus begun. It was planned, Paulding says, to take the *Globe*'s boat and swivel gun to Arno and to send Lay and Hussey along—for how long is not clear. Also not clear is whose plans precisely those were; Hussey had spoken of an aborted plan by Lugoma and others to send him and Lay to Arno, a plan that would have meant trouble for its originators.

What struck Paulding most about Luttuon was how much he looked like Simon Bolívar, whom he had met a year and a half before. "His face bore the same marks of care and serious thought, when his attention was not awakened to any particular thing; and, when animated by conversation, the same vivid expression beamed from his fine features, and sparkling black eyes." If the two of them were side by side and dressed the same way, Paulding thought, it would be hard to tell which one commanded South American patriots and which one South Seas "Indians."

After dinner on the ship Paulding asked Lay to accompany him in the ship's launch for some topographical exploration of the island. Around four o'clock they started to sail to some points on the lagoon but encountered rough seas and adverse winds, and finally around midnight anchored for the night, in the course of which Lay caught cold. In the morning, December 4, they found themselves near the *Globe* camp, went ashore, and disinterred Comstock's remains; Lay carried Comstock's skull and cutlass on board the *Dolphin*.

For four or five days the officers and men were occupied with investigating the topography, flora and fauna, and people of the islands; that had, after all, been part of their orders on this mission. It was also a good time for attending to ship maintenance, for cutting and bringing aboard wood, and for such odds and ends as lending the services of the ship's carpenter to the chiefs for the repair of a canoe. The canoe work was such a success that the natives begged that the carpenter be left with them; failing to win that favor, they asked that at least he leave his tools as a gift.

The exploration of the islands was carried on in separate parties by the captain and Paulding. On the same afternoon, December 4, as the recovery of Comstock's skull and cutlass, the captain took Lay, despite his cold, for a trip to the northwestern island of Naalo. The natives there were extremely friendly and curious. During the two hours the captain and Lay spent there they had a substantial talk, although Lay does not say about what, with two of the *lerooj*, women chiefs, of the island. This is the only place accounts of the two survivors mention contact with the *lerooj*, whose importance and power in the islands were, and still are, considerable. No gifts of food were offered to the visitors, as custom would normally require, for Naalo was suffering from a famine. Important for Lay was his chance meeting at Naalo with the old couple who had been father and mother to him, presumably the ones who saved his life the day of the massacre. Lay does not refer to his parting from the old man at the climactic moment of the rescue a few days before, but he explained to the captain who the old people were, and the captain rewarded them with beads and a handkerchief, thanking them for their kindness to Lay, and urging comparable friendliness to any other whites they should meet, probably in their case an unnecessary instruction.

Paulding relates that at one meeting with the chiefs, the captain asked Lay or Hussey who a particular old man was, for, he said sternly, he did not like his face, that is, he looked like a bad man. When the old man saw that he was being talked about, he asked the translator what the captain was saying about him. When he was told, his face took on an expression of "utmost dismay." Within two days he died. Every native who heard the story believed that Captain Percival's dislike had brought about the old man's death, a conclusion as supportable by modern psychology as by superstition, a rare window on the range and power of mind and affect. In primitives only? No, not in primitives only.

How powerful the captain was assumed to be can be gathered not from the common reaction of the natives to him, but from a conversation he had with Luttuon, probably in the course of Luttuon's visit on board the ship. What did Luttuon think of God? the captain wanted to know. Although none of his questions brought clear answers, Percival kept trying and thought he had the right one in, who do you think makes it thunder? Luttuon paused a moment and said, "I suppose you can make it thunder."

While the captain and Lay were in Naalo, Paulding was setting out for a trip to Lukunor and its area to do some exploring of his own, taking Hussey along partly to have a translator and partly to please both Hussey and Lugoma. (Paulding's chronology, which is followed here, is not completely in accord with Lay's; see note.) On December 4 Paulding, Hussey, and a boat crew headed out. Paulding does not explain what obstacles he met en route, but the boat did not arrive at Lukunor until two days later, December 6—the passage should have taken a few hours. The reaction on the island as the boat drew up was joyous. Lugoma waded out toward them until he was waist deep, holding freshly roasted fish in his extended arms. The old women rushed to throw their arms around Hussey's neck and would hardly let him go.

Lugoma was proud to show Paulding the results of his planting of the seeds that he had given him six days before: the ground had been carefully prepared, and the watermelon seeds were already sprouting. He also demonstrated a native fishing technique that Paulding had been anxious to learn about: trapping fish in a corral made of dried coconut leaves hanging from a line; the fish surprisingly will not swim underneath the hanging leaves, even though there is several feet of room for them to do so, and they can be scooped up with nets once confined.

Lugoma offered to put the whole party from the boat up for the night; he had plenty of room in his huts and plenty of fish. Paulding accepted, but with some anxiety; he was concerned for the safety of his group. The tables were turned from five days before, when Lugoma wanted to jump out of Paulding's boat to save himself and his son from being murdered by the white men. Now, in the home of an apparent friend, the white men were afraid of "surprise or treachery," as Paulding put it. From a distance the playing out of fear and anxiety on both sides seems on the face of things irrational, but there is reason beyond reason in it. The officers and men of the *Dolphin* from the start had exposed themselves almost blithely to circumstances about which they were in the dark and which were, even in the dark, pretty ominous. They moved, insufficiently armed or unarmed, among outnumbering crowds of obviously hostile natives who were communicating in language incomprehensible and suspicious. The land party, circling the atoll, did not know how one island's people were going to differ from the last. But Percival and company did not flee the atoll once they had accomplished their mission. And they made moves that could have easily exposed Lay and Hussey to recapture. Captain Percival's decision to assemble the chiefs for a meeting that looked like an affair of state was wise and effective, but he was under no obligation to call the meeting, especially when it was clear that the chiefs were trying to evade it; safety was not the priority.

Even though Paulding's visit to Lugoma, now a week after the rescue, was relaxed and sociable, he was insecure. His problem was how to take standard protective measures without letting on to Lugoma that he was doing so. He sent three of the men to sleep in the boat and ordered Lugoma not to let anyone near it. Those ashore took their arms from the boat, and a system of rotating night watches was set up. When Lugoma saw the man who was standing sentry, he asked if there was not enough room for him to lie down. The answer was evasive; they were trying to avoid impugning Lugoma's hospitality. When Lugoma finally found out why one man was standing watch, he was seriously offended: no one would dare come to his island to hurt his visitors. The visitors protested—Hussey had to find the right words to phrase the protests—that they had every confidence in Lugoma and trusted his friendship implicitly, but that it was the custom among the white men always to have someone standing watch. When all lay down on their mats, Lugoma stretched out with his wife and daughter on one side and Paulding on the other.

Lugoma was a study, and Paulding clearly sensed it. "Lugoma," he writes, "was about thirty years of age, of moderate stature, square built, with low forehead, and flat nose; having an expression of countenace that indicated intelligence and enterprize. Huzzy gave him the character of being very passionate, inveterate in his enmities, fierce and determined in his hostility, but firmly attached to his friends and possessing a benevolent heart." Hussey told Paulding that Lugoma would often become extremely angry with him and even threaten to kill him, but when his anger abated would sincerely regret what he had said and would assure Hussey that he would not hurt him. On one occasion, however, when they were working together in a canoe, something that Hussey did bothered him, and he struck Hussey with a paddle. Hussey exploded with rage and was about to hit Lugoma, when the master apologized to the slave and promised never again to raise his hand against him. If he ever did, Hussey told him, he would kill him.

Paulding was taken by the story and said that it added plausibility to another one that Hussey had told him. Lugoma's son told Hussey that the natives were fascinated by a mulatto boy who was part of the schooner's crew—they may have seen him when spying on the ship, or the boy may have gone ashore. Lay and Hussey already knew the attraction to the boy, for they had heard the chiefs debating who would get the mulatto boy if they took over the ship and killed everyone except the boy. The boy would be a pet. Lugoma was one of the chiefs contending for the boy, Lugoma's son said, and it was his plan to save the life of the boy and raise him until he grew up, and then kill him. When too big he would not have the same appeal.

Paulding and boat crew had a safe night under Lugoma's roof and were bothered only by a heavy rain, but in the morning, December 7, the sky had cleared. Paulding took the boat off for a brief exploration of an island that he describes only as being a few miles beyond that of Lugoma's. It was of little interest, notable only for a dense growth of hard red wood. There were large shellfish on the island, Lugoma told Paulding, and offered to go and dive for them, but Paulding felt Lugoma would have been an inconvenience this time. The large shellfish and the wood suggest that he was near an island like Bue on the north side of the lagoon, but the boat was not out long enough to go that far. Paulding found the island totally uninteresting.

Back at Lugoma's Paulding saw a drum like the *aje* that Lay and Hussey had heard played at the big ceremony a few days after the massacre of the crew. It reminded him of drums he had seen on Nukahiva, but was smaller. When Paulding inquired about it, Lugoma obliged with a recital: his daughter beat the drum while he sang a song that called for operatic acting out—one arm thrust out and the other clutched to his breast. When Paulding asked, through Hussey as translator, what it was about, Lugoma replied that it was a song of the massacre of the white men, "—a rudeness, I did not expect,—even from the untutored Lugoma." That was enough music, Paulding told him.

As Paulding and the others were preparing to enter the boat, Lugoma unfurled his arguments for allowing Hussey to stay: no one can assist me as Hussey can; I have no defense against my enemies without his musket; I may as well cut my throat. When he found all these unavailing, he said that when they did come back they should bring him clothes like theirs—now there was no question: Lugoma wanted to dress like the white men, whether or not anyone else on the atoll did. Paulding should also bring, he told him, guns and axes; in return, the benefactor would be made joint *irooj* of Lukunor and would, of course, enjoy in abundance all the vegetables and fruit that he had just left the seeds for.

The old women said good-bye once again to Hussey, hugging him warmly. Since the boat was to head back to Mili Mili, Lugoma asked Paulding to take along three women who would be carrying baskets of fish for the *iroojlaplap*. Paulding agreed, put them ashore in the afternoon, and was back at the schooner in the late afternoon.

The next day, December 8, Lugoma and son appeared again, having sailed from Lukunor early in the morning and tied up their canoe on the lagoon side. A boat from the schooner was sent to pick them up and bring them out to the *Dolphin*. They had never been on the ship, and Lugoma was more than dazzled by what he saw; he was intimidated and, in spite of the friendliness of the reception extended to him, was visited by his earlier feeling that he was in danger. It was the equipment on the ship that did it this time, the same way that the musket firing had done it a few days before. The sheer display of power, even in the hands of the friendliest people, was awesome to the point of being frightening—as standing close to heavy machinery would frighten a child. He brightened, though, when given an axe, cotton handkerchiefs, and other things. Remember your promise to return, he said as he left the ship.

Around two o'clock in the afternoon the captain, who had gone ashore to escort the *iroojlaplap* and two others on a visit to the ship, came on board with the dignitary and gave him a formal tour of the ship, which produced a reaction opposite to Lugoma's—Luttuon was not particularly curious about what he saw. Captain Percival put on the amplest show he could, ordering the crew to beat to quarters and finally, asking Luttuon if he wanted to hear one of the cannons fired. Luttuon did not commit himself; he was on the spot, for in spite of his reputation as the greatest warrior on the atoll, he was afraid to hear the cannon. When Paulding said he would fire, Luttuon had to admit that, yes, he was afraid.

For this formal occasion Luttuon and party brought gifts for the *jemmaan,* as they called the captain. The term is apt and just a bit amusing—it has not only the meaning but also the slangy connotation of the English word "boss." In time the visitors let it be known that they were tiring of the ship and wanted to go ashore; the captain obliged them. Before they left, Luttuon's son Ladro, who had come aboard with his father, asked if he could join the ship and leave with them; Paulding writes as if the request were directed to him, not the captain, as a result of Paulding's having been together with the boy a number of times and given him presents. Surprisingly his father gave permission, but Paulding felt it would be cruel to take him, probably permanently, away from his home, where his father's position would guarantee him a good life.

In the evening of the same day, December 8, the *Dolphin* left Mili Mili and sailed east along the coast past Arbar and Enajet. By sunrise Jelbon, where the ship had first anchored, was in sight. The route was now north along the line of small eastern islands, then around the northeastern corner of the atoll and west. By sunset they had come even with Tokewa, the island where, Paulding notes, he had rescued Lay.

Paulding's last week before sailing from Mili had been his most anthropological. Early accounts of the Marshalls contain those fresh observations of places and people that are all the more engaging for being the raw material of anthropology without its methodology. Gilbert in 1788 recorded enough to qualify as a latent scientist; Kotzebue on both his 1815–1818 and 1823–1826 voyages, and Chamisso on the first Kotzebue voyage, qualified even more so. Horatio Hale in 1838–1842, as philologist for the United States Exploring Expedition, was an arrived scientist. In the record of progress from Pacific observations to Pacific study, Paulding's contributions occupy a respectable chapter.

He noted topography (the islands of the atoll are "clumps"), botany (few flowers and plants, and the undergrowth disappears where the coconut or breadfruit trees grow), food (breadfruit is not preserved, *bob* is the food of the poor, fish are seasonal), clothing (men's garments look like horses' tails), and huts (the ground level is covered with small pieces of white coral, the upper floor is entered through a small hole placed in the floor's center to discourage rats). When someone is sick, his friends gather to chant appeasing prayers to the god responsible for the affliction. The dead are laid out and not buried until the smell makes burial imperative. The most curious aspect of the native death rituals is that "in the midst of their most bitter mourning and lamentation, some of the mourners will intentionally say or do something calculated to excite mirth, when they all burst out into immoderate laughter, as if their mourning were the affectation of children." When the laughter has spent itself, they resume their mournful chanting, but comparable behavior takes place in the course of the procession to the grave, when a prankster will provoke laughter that lasts until it fades and mourning resumes. Courtship and marriage are business-like and low on ceremony; fidelity is expected. Paulding attributes to Lay and Hussey the story of a young man, who, on discovering that the girl he married was already pregnant, waited for the baby to be born and then killed it by dashing its brains out on a stone; his trial before a council of chiefs resulted in an acquittal because the girl had so gravely deceived him.

Practically everything that Paulding noted about the people of Mili satisfied his reporter's instincts. It was also ample and accurate enough that in 1831 when the *Journal* was published, it could have been useful to the navy and American vessels in general in the Pacific, on the order of the area handbooks compiled by the Library of Congress for the armed forces today.

Two hours before sunrise on December 9, the *Dolphin* sailed away from Mili, having accomplished the kind of Pacific policing that an American ship had never carried off before; it was precisely what Payne had feared would happen when he saw that the *Globe* had escaped. One can only imagine what would have happened if Payne had not brought on his own death at the hands of the natives and was still around with Oliver and the others when the *Dolphin* anchored at Jelbon. It was all over now, though. The *Dolphin*'s launch would not sail up to Lugoma's beach, and if anyone brought cloth to gratify his craving for American clothes, it would have to have been another ship. And there would soon be plenty of those; Bully Hayes, the overfabled Pacific adventurer—played by Tommy Lee Jones in the movie version of his life—settled briefly on Mili, as did a host of beachcombers, traders, and castaways. The missionaries came, and the German merchants came; Lugoma would have been an old man by that time. But the *jemmaan* who could make it thunder never came, and the mulatto boy never came.

And Hussey never came; maybe he could not get his mother's permission.

THE SHADOW
OF THE *GLOBE*

By ten in the morning, six hours after leaving Mili, the *Dolphin* had covered the sixty-five miles to Arno ("South Pedder's Island" as it was known to the *Dolphin*'s officers) and, looking for a landing place, had reached its northeastern point, the right claw of the crab-shaped atoll.

The *Dolphin* had come to the isles of love. Lightheartedly related by modern Marshallese raconteurs is the enchanting legend that Arno at one time was the site of a university of love-making in which young girls were trained to give pleasure to their men. For all the amusement that the discussion of that pedagogy causes today, anthropologists familiar with Arno have found that the school, whatever it was, was not a myth. Paulding does not name the island of the atoll at which Captain Percival went ashore, but if his description is correct, the island was Lonar, the very one on which the sex school reportedly flourished. Doubtless Percival and Paulding and their translators did not know this, but they did observe that the young women were being kept out of sight on another part of the island for the full time that the *Dolphin* party was ashore, something that could have happened on almost any island, but which may have been the result of a heightened sensitivity on Lonar to what happened when the sexes were together.

Captain Percival's reason for the stop at Arno was not to visit the university but to meet Labuliet, the powerful chief, whose domain covered at least the three most southern atolls of the Ratak chain, Majuro, Arno, and Mili. The *Dolphin* officers had learned about him on Mili and knew that he was Luttuon's father-in-law (or perhaps grandfather-in-law) and that he enforced, with threats of war, his demand for regular tribute. The captain, accompanied by Hussey as translator, landed on the beach in front of a village and was met by a few natives, who led him to the high chief. They found Labuliet seated on a mat in front of his hut. According to Paulding he was very old with a long white beard; according to Lay he was about seventy. He was composed and unexcited by the surprise visit; he was able to distinguish the captain as the main dignitary in the group and addressed his message, delivered mainly by signs, to him. The language of Arno, Hussey knew once he heard it, if he did not already know, was the same as that spoken on Mili. Captain Percival had ordered Hussey not to let on that he spoke the language but to listen to what was being said by Labuliet and those around him and to report. What he heard Labuliet say was, "Don't disturb them yet. Wait until to-morrow, and see what they are going to do. They will look round here to see what they can find, trade a little, and go on board of their vessel, to sleep, and to-morrow they will come again."

The captain then told Hussey to speak in their language. The effect of his words was pure shock; the natives were astonished and rattled at hearing their language come from Hussey—and so was Labuliet. When the chief managed to collect himself, he asked where Hussey had learned the language, and Hussey told him. So you are one of the white men I had heard about, Labuliet said; he was interested in what he had heard and was planning to travel down to Mili to see them. Was the other one on the ship, he wanted to know. He was sorry to see that the two men were back now with their own people, for he had planned to bring them from Mili to his island; he would have treated them well, he said.

The captain had a major gift for Labuliet, a battle-axe, so major a gift that the chief was almost unwilling to accept it because he had nothing of comparable value to give in return. He did, however, give the captain some mats, coconuts, and *bob*. The captain would gladly have acquired more food from the island than the small amount in the chief's gift, but Labuliet explained that food was not abundant on the atoll and that there was just enough for its people. But, he suggested, a few miles to the west was another group of islands where there was plenty of food and a small population; that would have been Majuro, today the capital of the Republic of the Marshall Islands, which was only about twenty miles away but which Percival declined to visit.

When Percival asked Labuliet if he had ever seen white men before, the old man said, yes but long ago; it was a large vessel and the men on it did something memorable, they brought their forge ashore. No device could have been more fascinating to the natives, given their fixation on iron, than the one that actually worked the metal. No wonder that the visit was remembered. That forge, designed to produce heat for the smith, may have also produced some light for the historian: the big ship that Labuliet saw may have been the *Rurik*, commanded by Otto von Kotzebue on his

1815–1818 voyage of exploration, and the atoll where the forge was put ashore may have been Wotje. Adelbert von Chamisso, in his chronicle of Kotzebue's explorations, says that the *Rurik*'s forge was set up on that atoll January 24, 1817, nine years before Percival's meeting with Labuliet on Arno. If Wotje was where Labuliet saw the ship, what was he doing so far from Arno? The answer is suggested later in Chamisso's chronicle: Labuliet, who was already an old man in 1817, was lord of Maloelap Atoll ("the Kaven group" to western explorers), about eighty miles north of Arno, and resided on the atoll's Airik Island. Some time in the nine years between Kotzebue's visit and the *Dolphin*'s Labuliet's realm must have changed from the northern Ratak islands to the southern ones, possibly because of the role of Luttuon during the period of exile that he had told Percival and Paulding about back on Mili. Luttuon's task, Paulding speculates, must have been to move from island to island consolidating the power of the great chief, who needed a unified base of support for any war that he might have to conduct; the forces that could be raised on any one island would not have been adequate for a major battle. Luttuon could have been so effective in subjugating the southern islands for Labuliet that Labuliet transferred his kingdom's center to Arno.

The captain's talk with Labuliet lasted about two hours. The subject closest to the old chief's heart was the welfare of his daughter, who was married to Luttuon and lived on Mili. (Paulding, when talking earlier of Luttuon, suggested that the woman might be Labuliet's granddaughter.) Was she alive and was she well? Labuliet wanted to know; it had been a long time since he had received any news of her. When told that she was indeed alive and well, the old man broke down sobbing.

It was night when the captain and his party left Labuliet's home and went to their boat to push off for the ship. They were already a few yards from shore when some natives ran down to the boat saying that the chief had another mat that he wanted to present to the captain and that the chief wanted Hussey to go back to the village to pick it up. The captain declined the offered gift, the circumstances of which could not help but make him uncomfortable. Shortly three more natives ran down to the shore with the same message—Hussey must come up to pick up the mat—and with the additional message that the chief was returning the battle-axe, for he did not want to put himself under such an obligation to the captain. Percival told them that he never took back something that he had given. This time the messengers were left standing on shore, and the captain's boat headed out through the surf to the ship. Paulding leaves his readers to make sinister inferences about Labuliet's intentions; those intentions were frustrated in any event, and the *Dolphin* was able to sail without rescuing Hussey twice.

On December 12, after leaving Arno and making another fairly brief passage—about seventy miles—the *Dolphin* came to Aur Atoll ("Ibbetson's Island"). The ship was selectively moving up the Ratak chain: Mili is the southernmost; Arno and Majuro, side by side, are the next atolls to the north; then little Aur and large Maloelap. After that come seven sizable atolls, which the *Dolphin* turned away from as it headed east to Hawaii in keeping with its original sailing orders. Since the Ratak chain is not straight north-south but northwest to southeast, the *Dolphin* would have been moving farther and farther west if it had stayed with the chain all the way to Bikar in the north, and its course to Hawaii would have become circuitous.

The neat and pleasant village on Aur where Paulding went ashore might just as well have been in Mili or Arno. But the landing party found no one in sight until, poking through the bushes, they came upon a few old people in hiding. They were very shy of the visitors—they said that they had never seen white people before—but they came forward when offered a few simple gifts, and they reciprocated with the familiar presents of mats, coconuts, and *bob*.

Similar as the people were to those on Mili and Arno, they differed in one way that struck the visitors at once: the population seemed mainly old and not as healthy as their counterparts on the other islands. Paulding had never seen toothless old people among other groups of natives and had never seen natives disabled with crippling disorders. He asked why there were only old people to be seen and got the answer through his translator: the girls had been sent away to another part of the atoll lest any of the visitors try to give them gifts. Where the young men were was not explained.

Captain Percival had put his boat ashore on one of Aur's islands different from the one Paulding had landed on and had the same experience of finding only old people left to meet him while most of the inhabitants had gone into hiding. Percival had a low tolerance for people avoiding meeting him, and as he had done on Mili when the chiefs did not show up for a meeting he had ordered, he commanded the old people to send out word that everyone was to return home or fear his "displeasure." The village was repopulated in short order. By 5 P.M. Percival and Paulding returned to the ship from their respective islands, each in boats laden with fruit.

The passage to Hawaii took a month and included some surveying of the ocean for reefs noted by whaleships—erroneously noted, the *Dolphin* concluded; it also included a delicious Christmas dinner of fat *bob*-fed turtle, which had been with the *Dolphin* for thousands of miles, crawling across the deck. On December 12 Aur lay behind the ship in the west, and so did all of Micronesia. Lay and Hussey disappear from Paulding's *Journal* at this point and become absorbed into the crew. As the *Dolphin's* route curved around to the northeast, it passed into Polynesia; the language of the Marshalls was not spoken here, and the officers could no longer call on the two new crewmen for translating.

A month after leaving Aur, the *Dolphin* reached Nihoa, one of the more western of the Hawaiian islands, then Niihau, Kauai, and finally, on January 12, Oahu. On January 16 it anchored at Honolulu. What Lay and Hussey were seeing was probably more familiar to them than to anyone else on the *Dolphin*; while on the *Globe* they had had a considerable amount of time in Honolulu, but the place was totally new to the navy: the *Dolphin* was the first United States naval vessel to enter the port.

The *Dolphin* announced its arrival by firing guns and, not surprisingly, was greeted by a quickly assembled crowd ashore. Part of the turnout was the American merchants and part was the ragtag mob of natives, several hundred in number, some of them completely naked, some partly clad in tapa, cotton shirts, old trousers, or an old jacket and nothing else. They mobbed the visitors, and the officers who went ashore had to push their way through the crowd. The descriptions of Hawaii as one of the newly and notably civilized parts of the Pacific did not prepare Paulding for the barbaric panorama he was facing. "In appearance," he writes, "a comparison of [the Hawaiian natives] with the natives of the Marquesas or Mulgrave Islands, would have been greatly to their disadvantage."

Fifty years earlier all these islands were unknown—they did not appear on any chart. If the *Dolphin* had come then, it would have been received as Captain Cook's *Resolution* and *Discovery* were, and Captain Percival, if he had wanted the honor, would have been revered as the prophesied god Lono. It was in 1778 that the world learned that the Hawaiian chain existed (and a year later that Captain Cook was killed at Kealakekua on the big island). In 1786 the first Europeans after Cook visited the islands, and in 1789 the first American ship, the *Columbia*, arrived. Twenty years later, in 1819, the first American whalers, the *Equator* and the *Balaena*, reached Hawaii, and a few months after them, in March 1820, so did the missionaries. Hawaii was developing fast and was being changed by forces that would only later—or never—reach Micronesia.

During the *Globe*'s four-month stay in Hawaii the port was

crowded with ships. One of them was the *Lyra*, the very ship that had been sailing in company with the *Globe* on the night of the mutiny. It was still under the command of Captain Reuben Joy and was on its first voyage after the one on which it had been near the mutiny. When Captain Joy arrived back in New Bedford in May 1825, the news of the *Globe* was being talked about everywhere, and the *Globe* itself had been back in Nantucket for six months, so it would not have been hard for him to find out what happened the night that the *Globe* showed a light to tack but disappeared by sunrise. Lay and Hussey could have met Captain Joy, but for all of them renewing memories of that night might have been too sensitive; Captain Worth had been a good friend of Captain Joy.

Also in port was the *Winslow*, the captain of which, Owen Chase, had been first mate on the *Essex* in 1820 when it became the first ship sunk by a whale; his *Narrative* of the wreck of the *Essex*, published in 1821, was to spread that unprecedented story far and wide. There is a coincidence suitable for framing in the coming together in the same port of the author whose *Narrative* of disaster and survival made the *Essex* story a classic with the authors whose *Narrative* of disaster and survival made the *Globe* story a classic.

One person that Lay and Hussey met in Honolulu was the Reverend Hiram Bingham, the head of the Hawaiian mission. Mr. Bingham wanted instruction in the language of the Marshalls, with a view toward extending his mission into Micronesia, and the two rescued seamen were probably the first potential instructors to have come his way. The results of this meeting are described in Appendix C.

The islands were being changed by forces from within, and before it left Honolulu, the *Dolphin* would have become a player in these changes. In 1819, with the death of Kamehameha, the elaborate system of *kapu* or taboo (which included such bans as that on men and women eating in the same room) was dismantled, leaving a bewildering moral void in the lives of the people. The void began to be filled a year later by the arrival of Hiram Bingham and his missionary establishment. By 1823, with the conversion to Christianity of Kaahumanu, the most powerful woman in the islands, a new and rigorous moral code, as coercive as *kapu*, was installed.

The Hawaii that the *Dolphin* had arrived in was Kaahumanu's new moral creation, and the *Dolphin* was soon in conflict with it. The issue was *hookamakama*, prostitution. Sexual morality was a part of the moral package that Kaahumanu had imposed, but interpretation and enforcement were loose and inconsistent. The weeks around the *Dolphin's* arrival were times of reexamination of the degree to which the civil authority should be an overseer of private morality. It seems that the pleasures of women were available easily enough to seamen ashore on liberty and most easily to officers housed onshore. What was turned into the issue of the day, though, was the long-standing tradition of visitation of local girls on board ships in the harbor. This was suddenly banned.

Percival got an earful from his men about the denial of the services of the mermaids who had been frequent visitors to the ship. It did not take long for the captain to become the advocate of his men. The *hookamakama* crackdown in Percival's eyes was denying his men one of the necessities of life. How he first communicated this view to the Hawaiian authorities and the missionaries is unclear, but on February 21, Elisha Loomis, a member of the mission, recorded the following in his journal:

> It is with feelings of shame and regret that we have witnessed the conduct of Capt. P. since his arrival at these islands. Nothing that I know of has ever happened here, which will have such a tendency to degrade the American name in the eyes of this government. Soon after the arrival of Capt. P. we learned that he was exceedingly displeased with the chiefs for prohibiting females from visiting the ships and . . . called upon [Governor] Boki, Kaikioewa,

and others and inquired who gave the orders to prevent females from visiting ships. He was told, the King and his guardian, Kaahumanu. He declaimed with great violence against the Missionaries—said they trade upon Kaahumanu but he would come and tear down their houses. This evening was appointed to have a talk with the Government. Boki said it was the desire of the chiefs to have their public business transacted in writing—but Capt. P. swore he would not—he would come and talk with them and if they did not come to his measures and remove the prevailing restrictions, he would open a fire upon them. His vessel was small but it was like fire. If Mr. Bingham should come to the talk he would shoot him. If he should see a native attempt to take a native [girl] from one of his men he would shoot him" etc etc. Some of the chiefs were very much alarmed for our safety.

Of the two *fires* in the passage, the one attributed to Percival as meaning that his ship was on fire with lust was too good not to be popularized, as it was in several accounts.

The meeting scheduled for that night was canceled because of a heavy rainstorm and rescheduled for the next day, the twenty-second, at noon. More than one account of this meeting exists; Loomis says that Percival "appeared unusually pleasant" and talked reasonably about interfering with females serving the ships or punishing them. One of the arguments that Percival favored—and that the missionaries were intent on refuting—was that a year before when Lord Byron (cousin of the poet) brought the *Blonde* to Honolulu, his ship was allowed to take females on board. Another account of Percival's meeting with the chiefs is that recorded by Bingham (whom Percival excluded from attending) as taken down from Kaahumanu's report to him of what had been said. From the various accounts historian Linda McKee, an authority on Percival and the missionaries, has reconstructed the essence of the most heated part of the argument:

Percival: "Who governs the Islands?"

Kaahumanu: "The young king."

Percival: "And who governs him?"

Kaahumanu: "I do."

Percival: "And who governs you?"

Kaahumanu (piously): "My God."

Percival (pointing a finger scornfully): "You lie, you damned old
   bitch! Mr. Bingham governs you!"

Four days later, Sunday, February 26, the usual number of sailors
from the *Dolphin*, according to Paulding (Bingham said twice the
usual number), were given shore leave. Some of the *Dolphin* men met
crewmen from whalers, probably in taverns, and in time the
expanded group headed toward the house of Kalanimoku where
Sunday services, led by Bingham and attended by Kaahumanu,
Governor Boki, and others, were about to begin. The sailors called
out threateningly for a lifting of the prostitution ban, and some of
them began to smash windows in the house. Bingham, solicitous for
his family, he said, ran to his own nearby house and found that his
wife, aware of the disturbance, had locked the door to keep out the
demonstrators and in so doing had locked her husband out. He tried
to make his way back to the house where his congregation had been
meeting and was grabbed, narrowly escaping a beating. Seeing some
of his native converts nearby, Bingham called out to them, "*Aole anei
oukou malama mia ia'u?*"—Aren't you going to take care of me? They
did and attacked the sailors so violently that one was almost killed.
The riot ended quickly when Percival, who had been summoned at
its outbreak, waded into the crowd with his cane, beating and arresting the demonstrators from his ship.

Percival apologized to Bingham, promised repair to the damaged
houses (Bingham's windows had been broken like those in

Kalanimoku's house), brought Bingham on board to identify the miscreants, and sent a letter to other captains in the harbor suggesting that they reduce the number of men released for shore leave.

Percival had been the advocate of his men seeking shipboard prostitutes and was to remain so—but he was a disciplinarian too, and the riotous conduct was nothing in his mind but a disgrace to the United States. The *Dolphin*'s log for the next day read:

Punished for Misconduct on Shore the following Men viz. Wm P. Smith, 19 Lashes with the Cat o nine Tails. Wm Miller 30 Lashes—Phineas Blodget—30 Lashes. . . .

Weeks later, in an April 8 entry in his journal, Elisha Loomis recounted, secondhand, reports he had heard of Percival's words to some of the chiefs:

At a dinner given by Capt. P. a few days since to the chiefs, the former informed them that there was no one but himself here that understood what was right. Listen to me says he. He then took a bible and read something concerning David and Solomon—and observed that David was a bad man—he murdered many people etc. but Solomon was a good man—he had a thousand wives— that was right—there was no harm in having many wives—and why did the chiefs speak of marriage? Solomon was not married etc. Hannah Holmes said to me a short time since, that Capt. P. endeavored to get her sister to live with him. He said he was married to a wife in America, but when he took a journey inland he had another wife there—when he went to France, he had another there, and it would be good to have another, even herself there.

The day after the riot Governor Boki lifted the ban on the girls' visits. A few days later Levi Chamberlain, who like Loomis was a member of the mission, wrote in his journal, "Cap. P. it is said is now *maha*," a word meaning "relieved"—it would express the feeling one has on having an obstacle taken out of his path. "Rejoice not over me O mine enemy, when I fall I shall rise again. The Lord grant that the enemies of the Lord may be defeated by their own success—so that what they call *their* gain may prove the gain of virtue & religion & the *loss* of *satans* cause."

What were William Lay and Cyrus Hussey doing in the midst of all this turmoil? Probably just watching. The total impression of character left by their story to date suggests that they were not among the petitioners for *hookamakama*. A modern native of Mili Atoll has asked if there is any evidence that Lay or Hussey fathered children while on the atoll—for there are blue-eyed Milians. The safest bet is no. And as for blue eyes, the atoll has been, since the time of the *Globe*, host to plenty of visitors with that trait. The missionaries relate that despite the conflict with the *Dolphin*'s captain and men, a number of the ship's officers and men attended Sunday services. There, if one is illustrating the story, is the most comfortable place to sketch in Lay and Hussey.

Percival had attended to a variety of business included in his orders—more official and important than prostitution—including acting for American commercial interests that were owed a considerable amount of money in the islands. He had seen to the ship's repair, and on May 11, 1826, the *Dolphin* sailed from Honolulu heading directly south until it reached the Austral Islands and the island of Rapa, where it made substantial visits, being well received by natives and collecting a sizable amount of provisions for the last leg of the trip, the long passage to South America. On June 14, as it approached Tubuai, the *Dolphin* encountered the Nantucket whaleship *Loper* and passed on the news that it had the *Globe* survivors, Lay and Hussey, on board. The *Loper* carried this report back to Edgartown, where it arrived October 19, 1826. Two days later, the *Inquirer* reported:

THURSDAY, [October] 19. *Ar.* a lighter from Edgartown—reports the arrival there this day of ship Loper, Starbuck, of and for this port, 4½ months from Otaheite, with a full cargo of sperm oil to Levi & Jos. Starbuck. The Loper left at Otaheite, in June, ship Lima, Swain of this port, with 1500 bbls oil. The Lima reported . . . Globe, Swain, 350. . . . The U.S. schoonor [*sic*] Dolphin was at Otaheite when the Loper left, having on board two of the surviving crew of the Globe.

Although the story erred in placing the *Dolphin* at Tahiti, which it skirted far to the south and did not touch at all, it contained the last bit of news that Nantucket was waiting for about the fate of the *Globe* people. For Lay and Hussey the most striking news picked up from the meeting with the *Loper* was probably the report that the *Globe* was sailing in the same seas that they were. One can only guess how a sight of their old ship would have affected them—or what they would have felt if they realized that so much time had passed since their adventures on the fateful whaler that the *Globe* was now out for a full year on this subsequent voyage.

On July 23 the *Dolphin* arrived at Valparaíso, mission accomplished. Paulding, who has not even alluded to the *Globe* in his narrative of the preceding half-year, ends his journal, "[Our cruise's] beneficial effects will long be felt by our countrymen, who are engaged in the whale-fishery; and, although we suffered many hardships, privations, and dangers, we were happy in being the instruments, in the hands of Providence and our government, of proving that crime cannot go unpunished in the remotest part of the earth, and that no situation is so perilous as to justify despair." A bit abstract, as resounding as a hymn, but unassailable.

The *Dolphin's* log for August 29, 1826, notes that those of the crew who wanted to be transferred to the frigate *United States* were asked to give their names; thirty-nine did, William Lay and Cyrus Hussey among them. The log of the *United States* for September 2 lists thirty-four men transferred, again Lay and Hussey among them. Nothing in either ship's records after the rescue on Mili distinguishes the two men from all the other crewmen aboard both ships. The *United States*, to Commodore Hull's vexation, was delayed for months in its departure for home because its replacement, the *Brandywine*, had not arrived. Finally, on December 16, 1826, the *United States* sailed from Callao and reached Valparaíso January 6, 1827. On January 23 it sailed from Valparaíso and on April 22 was off Sandy Hook. It anchored in the Hudson River, began discharging and paying off the crew, and on April 30 was towed to the Navy Yard. Lay and Hussey had been out four years and four months.

The two men were still subject to some examination. There is no suggestion of suspicion of either one, and the process has the air of a technicality. Even while the *United States* was still tied up in the Hudson and before it was towed to the Navy Yard, Francis Macy, a family friend of the Husseys, had called on Commodore Hull to offer any assistance that he could to the two seamen; he reported the following in an April 27, 1827, letter to Hussey's father:

> I requested the Commodore to allow Cyrus to go on shore with me but owing to the peculiar situation of the two young men he would not comply, not having at that time been on shore himself since his arrival, but evinced a disposition to assist them all in his power. We this morning called upon the United States District Judge for the purpose of having Cyrus removed from the Ship by writ of Habeas Corpus, the judge informed us that it would be necessary to have the affidavit of Hussey before he could grant it, but that there would be no dificulty [*sic*] after procuring that document. We then took a Companion with us and proceeded on board the Frigate, where we fortunately found the Commodore,

who without any hesitation allowed us to take Cyrus on shore with us upon our personal responsibility. He is now at our house, & I hope in a day or two to be able to procure his complete release. It is the opinion of Commodore Hull that nothing will be done by the U S & that he will receive orders from the Navy Department to release them both immediately, until that takes place Cyrus will remain with us & I can assure you it gives pleasure both to Mrs Macy and myself to be able to assist him at this time. Commodore Hull & Lieut Percival of the United States speak in praise of both Cyrus & Lay, & I am persuaded will derive as much satisfaction in restoring those two young men to their parents & friends as we do in assisting them at this time. Should you deem it necessary to give any particular instructions in regard to Cyrus you may rely upon the ready consideration of both my brother & myself as far as is in our power to assist you. Cyrus has been seventeen months in the service of the U. States & during that time has conducted himself with perfect propriety, which must be a great satisfaction to his friends for by this he has gained the good will & esteem of all the officers of the ship.

Commodore Hull wrote to Secretary of the Navy Southard on May 14 that he had permitted Hussey to go to Nantucket and Lay to Saybrook pending their appearance at an examination at the end of May. On May 10, almost as soon as he had reached Saybrook, Lay wrote to Hussey:

Dear friend or as I might in one sense call Brother I now take pen in hand to rite to you to let you know that I have arrived in Say Brook and found my friends all well I wish you to assertain whether there is any thing coming to me from the Oil that came home in the Globe I wish you to see the owners and do the same you would for yourself and if there is any thing belonging to me to bring it on to New York to me Yourself when you come. I have no news to rite but beg a most affectionate remembrance hoping we shall never forget the perils and dangers we have been carried through and that we are now among friends and in a christian land in haste Yours respectfully

There seems to be no record indicating whether Lay or Hussey received their shares of the profit on the oil returned, but the lays on 372 barrels would not have been worth walking down to the wharf to inquire about. The letter's value is that it is a unique authentic expression of the survivor's feeling for his companion, unmediated by a ghost writer—and, it may be noted, strikingly close in tone and diction to the text of the ghost writer, who must have been a good listener when he put the *Narrative* together.

On May 20 Commodore Hull wrote to Cyrus Hussey himself:

I have been directed by the Secretary of the Navy Since you left the Ship to deliver you over to the Civil Authority; I should therefore recommend your taking some friend with you and state your case to Judge Thompson and take his opinion, or be examined by him should he think proper to examine you. Was I in your Situation I should wish a discharge from the proper authority that nothing could be said hereafter. I hope you found your friends well and that you will remember the advice I have so often given you. Your friends are respectable and you should look forward to a Situation above a Common Sailor.

When you see your father inform him that I have received his letter, and thank him for his good wishes toward me.

If the little I have done in restoring you to your family & friends has been a service of comfort to them I am more than compensated in having been so fortunate as to gain their good wishes.

The letter, interestingly, is addressed to Hussey care of Nathan Comstock at 191 Front Street, the Comstocks' business address. Hussey, after a brief visit to his family on Nantucket, had returned to New York for the judicial hearing at the end of May and may have been a guest of the Comstocks instead of returning to stay with Francis Macy. If so, what did they all talk about? It was a teeming household: Including the children of Nathan's second wife, Anne, there were at least eight young Comstocks in residence. If William was living with the family, that would have been one more. George was on hand—he was going to be working for his father's business, handling accounts and correspondence from 191 Front Street for at least two years. It was a *Globe* family, and the most vivid presence was the one who was not present at all, Samuel. Hussey was willing to talk about the *Globe*—his and Lay's book would be out in a year. Did the Comstock family want to hear from him? In fact, did the family want to hear from George? George was willing to talk and to write too. And if Nathan did not want to hear from them, would the children, whose curiosity must have been passionate, have held their questions in? Did one of the sisters ask how he *looked*?

As the *Globe* adventure concluded, the participants went their various ways; George eventually settled in California, Lay and Hussey stayed briefly in touch. Lieutenants Percival and Paulding returned to sea, the *Globe* sailed again, and William came out of the wings for his time on stage.

George worked for a couple of years as his father's amanuensis and accountant before handing those duties over to his younger brother Thomas. George was married twice, the first time to his cousin Lucy Comstock; two children born to them died as infants. After the marriage ended, Lucy remarried. George's second marriage, to Mary Hollins of Newcastle, England, took place in New Orleans; the fact that their first child was born in Louisiana in 1847 and the second (of three) was born in San Francisco in 1853 suggests that George (like so many Nantucketers) was drawn west by gold fever. He died in 1855, leaving three children, the oldest being eight.

Money, which Owen Chase said was one of his motives for writing the narrative of the shipwreck of the *Essex*, may have been a major motive of the two *Globe* survivors—probably because they needed it. Lay was the moving force behind the publication of his and Hussey's *Narrative*. His letter to Hussey dated September 24, 1827, about the publication of the book shows him as effective in business as he was in arguing with Luttuon:

> I now take my pen to let you know how I get a long and what arrangements I have made with the printer. Wm. Bolles of New London will print and bind a book with 150 pages duodecimo on good paper and lettered for 18 cents the first 3000 copies and all over for one shilling and those in boards for 12½ cents and will take part pay in books and wait a suitable time for the remainder. I have no doubt in my mind but we shall sel 3000 if not 5 with great proffit if not at our subscription price. Do get the work revised and come on here with it as soon as possible and dont delay I want to get through with it this fall and get the books distributed. I shall expect to see you ou[t] here with the narrative as soon as the 15th of October if not before if Cyrus M has gone to sea I shall expect his father to come on just the same and we shall proceed the same and get the work done. I want to know your feelings about the printing [fragment breaks off].

One wishes the ghostwriter's name had been mentioned; it seems clear that the writing was being done on Nantucket even though four-fifths of the book is told as Lay's account. On some occasion during the summer Lay and the writer must have worked together on the text. Lay's request that Hussey Senior take over the work of the book "if Cyrus M has gone to sea" is pertinent, for Cyrus had in fact gone to sea when this letter arrived.

Hussey sailed September 13, 1827, on the Nantucket whaleship *Alexander*, Captain Samuel Bunker. He had been home from his adventures on the *Globe* less than four months; everything that he was going to contribute to his and Lay's *Narrative* had to have been recorded by the writer in that time. Five days after Hussey sailed, his sister Margaret and his father wrote him warm, newsy letters (news of the last five days!), in which the keenness with which they miss him is evident. Letters to whalemen out for two or three years are often touching, but the need to say "I miss you" after five days shows pretty strong feeling. Margaret's letter is utterly charming. She apologizes, "I am not use to writing much but perhaps I shall improve in writing to thee. I suppose the[e] loves to see straight lines but thee wont see them here if thee does"—all of which is written in exquisitely straight lines. "I suppose," she continues, "thee would a great deal rather have a letter from a grown person than from me because they could write things of more consequence." No, Margaret.

At some point Hussey changed ships; the Nantucket whaler *Congress* had been out a year longer than the *Alexander* and would be assumed to return sooner. It did, arriving back in Nantucket on May 2, 1829, with 2,507 barrels and some very sad news; on a page of a copy of the Lay and Hussey *Narrative*, Nantucket historian Fred Sanford wrote, "Mr Hussey died off Cape Horn on his way home from another voyage he had been upon in Ship 'Congress' of Nantucket in the Year 1829 24 years of age." If the story of the *Globe* did not contain one final absurdity, it would not be complete. The young man who was inexplicably spared from an island massacre and who escaped execution at the hands of the votaries of Anit and who talked the *iroojlaplap* out of killing him dies a death at sea—a profoundly sad but also banal fate.

Gilbert Smith, according to reports on Martha's Vineyard, "lived and died in France," having been enlisted there to build up the French whaling fleet. Another Vineyarder, one of the lost *Globe* seamen, Rowland Jones, is commemorated by a carved stone in the West Side Cemetery in Edgartown with the concluding lines,

> *Far, far from home from Friends and kindred dear*
> *By Savage hands this lovely youth was slain.*
> *No Fathers pity or no Mothers tear,*
> *Soothed the sad scene or eas'd the hour of pain.*

Lieutenant "Mad Jack" Percival was promoted to commander in 1831 and captain in 1841; he commanded the *Erie* off Brazil, the *Cyane* in the Mediterranean, and the *Constitution* on a cruise around the world. He died in 1862. Lieutenant Paulding rose through the ranks to rear admiral at the end of his career. He sailed on the *Constellation* and other ships, commanded the frigate *St. Lawrence*, headed the Washington Navy Yard, and was active in Civil War assignments. He died in 1878.

The *Globe* sailed again, under Captain Reuben Swain II, about seven months after its return to Nantucket, leaving port June 13, 1825, for the Pacific. That was two months before the *Dolphin* sailed on its rescue mission, so the *Globe* was traveling in the wake of the rescue ship, and if Captain Swain had wanted adventure, he could have overtaken the *Dolphin* at the moment of the rescue. It is not likely that Captain Swain wanted adventure. The *Globe* returned in May 1828 with 2,105 barrels, the kind of result that it had been achieving on every voyage except one.

On the ship's return, Captain George Macy, who specialized in converting and selling old whalers, bought an interest in it, loaded it with a cargo of lumber from Belfast, Maine, and took it to Madeira or Cape Verdes (Captain Macy's son's recollection) and exchanged the lumber for other cargo to sell in South American ports including

Buenos Aires and Montevideo. The first mate on this voyage was Stephen Kidder, one of the escapees on the *Globe*'s flight from Mili Atoll. Off the coast of South America the *Globe* was boarded by pirates, who took some money and small objects. In 1830, at the end of a two-year voyage, the *Globe* was sold, condemned, and broken up in the port of Santos, Brazil. Maybe a sentimental moment—for whom?

And William. The complete oeuvre of William Comstock has, almost certainly, not yet been found. Variously described as a reporter living in Brooklyn and "an obscure writer whose contributions figure in some of the periodicals of the 'fifties" (even though identified titles of his come mainly from other decades), he is taken seriously as one of Melville's sources, and he is a hilarious satirist. Maybe he is the same William Comstock who wrote temperance tales. One literary history gives him a bit of attention in the course of a more extensive treatment of his son Augustus, who wrote under the pen name of Roger Starbuck and specialized in sea stories (Augustus had reportedly gone on more than one whaling voyage) and westerns.

Son Augustus followed to some extent in William's footsteps, but Augustus accommodated the popular market more than his father— not that William would have disparaged the popular market, but he had too many different things to say to fit a pattern.

William's 1838 book, *A Voyage to the Pacific, Descriptive of the Customs, Usages, and Sufferings on Board of Nantucket Whale-Ships*, grew out of a series of eight 1835 articles on whaling in *The Boston Pearl and Literary Gazette*. Apart from the critical attention that has been paid to it as one of Melville's white whale sources, it is a vivid representation of the human drama of whaling and is far above the level of "popular" writing; it is engrossing and suggestive—anything but naive.

His Artemus Ward take-off, *Betsey Jane Ward . . . Hur Book of Goaks*, is inspired hilarity, and its chapter titled, "The Travelling Show," is perhaps the funniest treatment ever of Nantucket in literature. There are plenty of barbs at Nantucket in *The Terrible Whaleman*, but they have grown to luxuriant profusion in *Betsey Jane Ward*.

To an extent, William's versatility is daunting to the reader who would like to understand what precisely is being said in *The Terrible Whaleman*. William is not just telling a story for the sake of a good sequel to *A Voyage to the Pacific*. Nor is he, as has been charged, mounting a misguided defense of his brother out of loyalty. The first light that William sheds on what he is doing in the life of brother Samuel is in his two-paragraph preface to the book:

> The author of this work fell in with William Lay, in Providence, several years ago. Having given the young man an invitation to his boarding-house, he was obliged by a visit from him in the evening. Mr. Lay signified that he was not well pleased with the edition of the Globe Narrative, which he was at that time selling. He said that neither he nor Hussey wrote a syllable of it; but having laid the facts before a writer belonging to Nantucket, the whole had been put into its present shape, for the *trifling* consideration of fifty dollars—said writer being, in many ways, leagued with those who had suffered by the mutiny, and dependent upon them for his support. A gloss had therefore been given to the "plain unvarnished tale" of the youths, and many of the facts had been ingeniously *twisted* to fay in, and lay up with the strands of prejudice and partiality. He therefore offered the author of this work, another fifty dollars to correct the errors, and supply the defects of the writer, intending to get out a second edition as soon as he had disposed of the first. As the author left the country a few weeks after this conversation, he had not an opportunity to carry the plan of Mr. Lay into effect; but hopes that in the following pages he has given the public a more faithful account of the mutiny than any that has yet met their view.

Although, "no place can murther sanctuarize," yet the foulest deeds may be extenuated. It probably adds to the interest of a tale of horror, to load the actors in its scenes, with every imaginary failing which ingenuity can invent, and the historian usually considers a murderer a fair object for him to exercise his eloquence upon, a proper target for the sharpest arrows in his quiver; but while his just indignation is aroused by the depravity of his subject, let him entertain a little regard for poor human nature, and not serve up from the hurly-burly pot of his rancid imagination, such a dish of ill-sorted and contradictory vices, as shall make his species appear much baser than the devil ever intended them to be. When a reckless and intrepid villain is [branded] with cowardice, and a sagacious plotter is styled an ignoramus, the common sense of the reader is liable to partake of the shock which the writer intends only for his sensibilities. The description of the chief mutineer in Lay & Hussey's Narrative, is a mere effigy, and the account of him in the Criminal Calendar, is a clumsy portrait of it.

Here William prints an eight-stanza version of the text of Henry Glover's poem, "The Young Mutineer," including the stanza that was too sensitive to print when the poem appeared in the Nantucket *Inquirer*. (See Appendix E for text and discussion of the poem.) One may judge what the approving use of that stanza is a token of—certainly not a simple-minded defense nor the opposite, a simple-minded indictment. The stanza reads:

> *He lies on the beach—with a heart-rending yell,*
> *Horrid and despairing, he sunk down to Hell,*
> *His glazed eyes in horror were turned up to Heaven,*
> *His last yell to the skies, in wild echo was given—*
> *In vain it ascended, no mercy was there,*
> *To cheer the dark dying of the Young Mutineer.*

In between his account of Samuel's early life and his going to Nantucket to join the *Globe*, William interrupts his narrative with the omen that stands as the epigraph to Chapter Three and with a discussion that almost looks like a passage that has wandered in from another book. It may puzzle, all the more since it brings the building action to a halt and leaves Samuel standing on the verge of signing on a whaleship that the reader knows is going to be *that* whaleship. This is what William writes at the most heightened moment yet in his story:

Are we not sensible that there are feelings in our souls which have never yet been fledged, which are cramped in our terrestial bodies, and cry, like General Burgoyne, for elbow room? The pensive or sublime emotions raised by some peculiar kinds of music, lead the mind to the very gate of Paradise—but no farther! It seems, as if a spirit spoke to us; but we cannot understand his words—we taste but are not filled. Like Tantalus we inhale the steam of the viands, but cannot reach the substance. At the sound of the Aeolian harp, an ocean of ideas rolls towards us; but breaks at our feet, and we step not in. We travel back to a thousand years in one moment; but memory fails and we recognise nothing. The gates of a mighty city seem to be opened—we look in; but all is dark, and we see neither pallace nor tower. The belief in the supernatural is the effect of our determination to give these indescribable sensations, form and substance—to make that tangible which is shapeless and immaterial.

Yet in searching for the marvellous, it is not well to neglect that portion of it which is actually within our reach, and, every day, falls under our observation, albeit, unheeded and unimproved. Do you ask for apparitions? What more wonderful and mysterious apparitions can you desire than the creation itself presents? We are suddenly, and unexpectedly thrown into a world teeming with every thing that is beautiful and grand. What matters it whether the apparition comes to you, or you go to the apparition? It is an apparition still. Suppose that with ripened faculties and cultivated mind, you have existed for some fifty years, alone, in some spot where the universe was not; beyond the attraction of any planet, sustained independent by your own gravity—You had never seen matter, save that of which your own person is composed. Suddenly, this world comes rolling up to your astonished eyes from the depths of ether, clad in the fur of her million clouds. Rocks, trees, rolling oceans, and thundering cataracts burst upon your view—the chorus of a myriad of singing birds breaks in your ears—the most gaudy flowers and delicate blossoms adorn the valley and the hill—the twisted vine upholds her lucious grapes—and all you see betokens luxury and grace. Would not that be apparation enough for you? Would you desire something more marvellous still? Yet we are amongst all these wonders; we are sent to see them—but so gradually does the mind unfold itself, and so much interwoven with every thought of our minds are these amazing apparitions, that we tacitly declare they are a part of ourselves—of our own manufacture—and forget that one grain of sand is really as much of a wonder and a miracles as the "thousand ghosts" of Osian when they "shriek at once on the hallow wind."

The very next sentence begins, "To return to our hero—" but in fact we had not left him. Samuel is a bit like the figure standing with his own gravity in some spot where the universe was not—almost the apotheosis of the narcissist. What if the world had come rolling up to his astonished eyes? What if he had been favored with that supreme apparition, worthy of a mystic, and had been able to see what is? And what if we can? Is the world that appears to us less wonderful with the sorry figure of the person lost in himself standing amid the myriad of birds and flowers? The important thing is what is real. The mutineer is unfathomable and aberrant, but he is real. And therefore wonderful—a thing of wonder. That, for the terrible whaleman's brother, is what the terrible whaleman was.

The old whaling logs had a formula for closing every day's entries: "So ends." The two words descend like a curtain on the brutal, thrilling, tedious, satisfying, unsatisfying, perilous, tragic, unpredictable days of the whaleship. On one ship the curtain comes down on deeds of blood and a mind sailing by itself—things of wonder. So ends.

THE CREW OF THE
GLOBE

The manifest of the *Globe* lists the officers and crew at the time of sailing from Martha's Vineyard. As noted in chapter 3, the name "Pray" (in other documents "Prass") given for the seaman from Fayal is probably a misunderstanding of his actual name, Braz, which is common in Portugal. The last column was clearly not on the document at the time of issue; it attempts to update the condition of the crew as it was known some time between the *Globe*'s arrival in South America under the command of Gilbert Smith and the receipt of the news carried by the *Dolphin* that there were only two survivors on the island. Thus, it lists Samuel Comstock as dead, but Rowland Coffin and Columbus Worth as still on the island. Naturally the manifest does not contain the names of the replacements recruited in Honolulu. "Do" is an abbreviation for *ditto*.

LIST of Persons, composing the Crew of the Ship Globe of Nantucket whereof is Master Thomas Worth bound for the Pacific Ocean

Names	Places of Birth	Places of Residence	Of what Country	Age	Height	Complexion	Hair	
William Beetle	Edgartown	Edgartown	United States	26	5' 7 ¾	Dark	Brown.	Dead killed January 26 1824
John Lumbert	Nantucket	Chilmark	"	25	5' 11 ¾	Fair	Brown.	Do Do
Nathaniel Fisher	Edgartown	Edgartown	"	20	5' 8	Light	Brown.	Do Do
Samuel B. Comstock	Nantucket	New York	"	20	5' 6	Dark	Dark.	Dead killed Feby 17 1824
Gilbert Smith	Edgartown	Edgartown	"	20	5' 6	Light	Sandy.	Returned
Nahum Mahurin*	Bridgewater	Bridgewater	"	23	5' 9 ½	Dark	Dark.	Did not sail from this port on said ship
Rowland Coffin	Nantucket	Nantucket	"	17	5' 1 ½	Light	Sandy.	On Mulgrave Islands
Cyrus M. Hussey	"	" "	"	17	5' 4 ½	Dark	Brown.	Do Do Do
Stephen Kidder	Edgartown	Edgartown	"	18	5' 8	Dark	Dark.	Returned
Peter C. Kidder	Nantucket	" "	"	21	5' 9	Dark	Brown.	Returned
George Comstock	"	New York	"	15	5' 4 ½	Dark	Black.	Returned
Columbus Worth	Tisbury	Edgartown	"	15	5' 4	Dark	Black.	On Mulgrave Islands
Rowland Jones	Edgartown	Edgartown	"	16	5' 4	Light	Brown.	Do Do
Holden Henman	Canton	Canton	"	23	5' 9	Light	Light.	Deserted at Sandwich Islands
William Lay	Saybrook	Saybrook	"	17	5' 9	Dark	Dark.	On Mulgrave Islands
Jeremiah Ingham	"	" "	"	17	5' 8 ½	Light	Sandy.	Deserted at Sandwich Islands
John Cleveland	Tisbury	Tisbury	"	21	5' 6 ½	Light	Light.	Discharged at Sandwich Islands
Daniel Cook	Boston	Boston	"	22	5' 7	Mulatto	Black.	Deserted Sandwich Islands
John Ignt. Pray	Fayal	Nantucket	Portugal	14	5' 1	Dark	Black.	Do Do Do
Paul Jarrett	Barnstable	Barnstable	"	24	5' 6	Mulatto	Black.	Do Do Do
Constant Lewis	Tisbury	Tisbury	U. States	19	5' 10 ¾	Fair	Black.	Do Do Do

I Thomas Worth do solemnly, sincerely, and truly swer that the within List contains the Names of the Crew of the Ship Globe together with the Places of their Birth and Residence, as far as I can ascertain the same. Sworn this thirteenth day of December 1822 Before me, Thomas Cooke J Collector.   Thomas Worth

District & Port of Edgartown Decm 18th 1822

These may certify that Nahun [sic] Mahurin mentioned in the within list was taken out of the within named ship by order of Law Previous to his leaving this Port and Constant Lewis is in[ ]led in his stead

Thomas Cooke J. Collector

APPENDIX B

GEORGE COMSTOCK,
"NARRATIVE"

George Comstock's account of the mutiny, published here in full for the first time, covers the period from the sailing of the *Globe* to its arrival at Mili Atoll. It is the most authoritative account of the mutiny and is the source, for the period covered, of the account in Lay and Hussey's *A Narrative of the Mutiny, on Board the Ship Globe, of Nantucket*, which at many points merely paraphrases George's narrative.

A striking feature of George's narrative is the precise notation of latitude and longitude of the *Globe* after the officers were killed. This is the kind of information recorded in logs and journals, suggesting that George was keeping the record himself or copied the information from someone who was. If Samuel was the only person on the ship familiar with navigation—as has been assumed, although Gilbert Smith obviously knew something about navigation—then George may have been taking down the ship's position daily from his brother, possibly even on his brother's orders. It is certainly clear, though, that George's narrative was not written with the knowledge or permission of Samuel; the narrative could have been written during the return home and the latitudes and longitudes inserted then.

The following transcript of George Comstock's "Narrative of the Mutiny capture and transactions on board of the Ship Globe of Nantucket after Sailing from Edgartown" was made by Thomas Heffernan in the library of the Nantucket Historical Association (NHA) and later compared with the 1882 transcript made by Isaac Sherwood Coffin, which, like the original Comstock manuscript, is in the possession of the NHA. This Coffin text is in a typescript made by Coffin's daughter, Helen Coffin Buchanan, from her father's transcript.

Some words or parts of words in the manuscript are lost where fragments, typically a quarter inch by a quarter inch, have crumbled from the margins. The following signs are used in the text:

↑transactions↓	arrows around word indicate that it is an insertion made by George Comstock
< >	angle brackets indicate cancellation of illegible text by George Comstock
<wood>	angle brackets around word indicate cancellation of legible text by George Comstock
[ ]	brackets around space indicate lost word
[ ]ad	brackets around part of word indicate lost letters that cannot be inferred
[watch]	brackets around words indicate word inferred from parts of letters and/or context
[*flax*]	brackets around italic words indicate Heffernan's addition for clarification
da—d	a dash between letters indicates letters suppressed by George Comstock
——___====	series of dashes, double lines, or underscoring reproduce George Comstock's markings in the manuscript

No words that are missing in their entirety have been inferred. Superscript letters in the original manuscript are almost always underscored by a line and two short vertical strokes, markings that are omitted here.

Leaf 1 recto (1 verso is blank)

PREFACE

[Spiral pen strokes]

Before I enter upon my Narration I will give the reader some few things respecting the same as to the truth or impossibility of such an undertaking as is here Narrated —— It is < > the impression of ↑my↓ mind to set down and note every accident exactly as it happened and not err on either side from the just or unjust part of the work as well and far as my knowledge would let me go in this case as it is well known that such things as these (viz. Murdering the officers of a ship taking the vessell and going to a foreighn land and beginning to discharge the cargo on the beach) will not at all do in a country governed by such [la]ws and worthy heads as America is no but the full effect [o]f the constitutional laws should be here put in force.   - If not sea captains and officers lives would be very much in danger [of] Open insult and murder. But with an aggreeable sensation I can say that such cases are very unfrequent if ever before being done by a United States vessel (belonging to the US) as ever I heard of for such ↑transactions↓ should never be ↑suffered↓ but it seems in a fatal hour as if the Devil possessed these individuals to do so base an act and as for the boatsteerer he was used much better by the Capᵗ and offiers than either of the rest of their own community he could not rest easy the fatal act was plotted performed and he put to death in less than 1 months time. It appears as though he ↑had↓ been given up to his own sins to do as he thought best and see how soon he could work his own destruction which soon followed after having imbued his heart in innocence's blood and bathing himself in wickedness and perdition. —— —— —— —— —— —— ——

We will now turn to the Narrative but let our reader first Pray for the wellfare of America and the Independence of the United States. Long live her laws. Narrative

2 recto

Narrative of the Mutiny
capture and transactions on board of the Ship
Globe of Nantucket
after Sailing from Edgartown

The Ship Globe of Nantucket (the ship in which the mutiny was executed belonged to Messrs Michele & Son Merchts, and others in the above mentioned place.

We sailed from Edgartown Dec 15th ↑1822↓ but carried away our crossjack yard and was obliged to put back for another ↑one↓ whilst we lay in the harbour at anchor one of our men Naham Mahurin left us and Constant Lewis shipped in his place. on the 19th we hove up [o]ur anchor and brought too again at Holmes Hole here we lay till mor[n]ing and then made sail about 9 oclock AM. Discharged [o]ur pilot in the sound and proceeded to sea on the 1st of Jan we had a very heavy gale of wind but having a good ship to send and the wind fair we kept her along under a close reefed Main topsail and Foresail it lasted us 48 hours during which time we were in emminent danger of being boarded by the sea but by very good management at the helm we run it out. On the 9th of Jan we made the Cape ↑de↓ Verds bearing SW dist 25 miles. On the 17th of Jan we crossed the Equinoctial line had very fine weather on the 29th we saw sperm whales gave chase caught one which made 75 barrells. After trying him out made sail having kept under short sail whilst trying. 23 Feb. Saw the Falkland Islands had it very calm for 1 day on the 1st of March saw the ship Lyra of New Bedford and spoke her she being out 72 days we 71. 5th of March cleared Cape Horn and stood to the North Saw Whales but once until we reached the Sandwich Islands which we made the 1st of May 1823 early in the morning came up with Owyhee about 4PM The man at the mast ↑head↓ gave the notice there were black fish off the lee bow but after looking with a glass we found they were canoes we were then about 10 miles from the land it being calm we stood along under easy sail the canoes came up with us towards night bringing Potatoes sugar cane yams cocoanuts bannanas and fish which we bought with a few small pieces of iron hoop After measuring the ship by fathoms they left us at night we were off karakakoon [there] were Capt Cook was killed —— —— —— —— ——

2 verso

We stood off the shore at night till 12 oclock then stood in for the land. we lay off and on the Island till night then stood off in the same manner ↑as↓ before After getting a recruit of Pumpkins, Hogs, Potatoes, Melons, Plantains, Bannanas, And cocoanuts we set sail for Woahoo which we made the next day We stood off and on the harbour till night and then stood off for the coast of Japan in company with the ships Palladium of Boston and Pocahontus of Falmouth which we parted company with in 2 days after having chased ↑a↓ sperm Whale together. When we arrived on Japan we see but very few whales and so it continued for the season. Whilst here we got 550 barrells and saw the following ships. Sea Lion, George Porter, Marcus, Enterprise, Paragon, Phoenix, Princess Mary of London, and the Lyra of New Bedford, all the ships excepting the Marcus, belonged to Nantucket. After falling in with the Lyra we mated together or hove in our chances to divide the oil we should get together after that time After cruising a short time we left the coast for the Sandwich Islands where we recruited our <wood> Water, vegitables &c. Whilst lying here 6 of our men left us in the night 2 of them were caught and put in irons but one of this [ ] having very slender hands slipped his irons and let the other out after shipping. Silas Paine, John Oliver, Thomas Linneston, Anthony Hanson an indian, and a Woahoo Indian, William Humphrey a bla[ck] stewart. After getting all things in readiness we left the Island for the la[st] time to some who little thought what was to happen so soon but there is but one eye that see the hearts of the wretches who put so fatal a deed into execution. We run down to the Southward of the Equinoctial in about 2 South Latitude cruised a short time for whales then shaped our course to the Northward being bound to Fanny's [*Fanning*] Island. whilst cruising off this Island expecting to make it the next day an occurrence took place perhaps more inhuman, cruel, and Murderous than ↑was↓ ever before put into print It was Sunday the Sun rose Proud and Magnificent and spead her warm rays over the unhappy mortals it should never behold on earth again ——

About 7oclock we were told to get breakfast we retired to the forecastle and the officers to the cabin. before I go further I will give a few lines respecting the time food and usage on board the ship before this by the officers given to the men. When we were 5 days out we were cut short of meat which shortness was very irregular sometimes having enough for 2 crews at others not half enough for one but this could not be put upon our captain for he meant for us to have 3 barrells of meat in a month which is generally allowed in a whaleman but the stewart by making an unequal division caused the blame to be on our captain which some of the crew being quick to grumble and find fault made a noise about but nothing was done till we arrived to the Sandwich Islands [from] [on] the coast of Japan from that time till the mutiny we had a [large]

3 recto

supply of provisions of [all kinds] < > were on board of the ship but there is one thing to mention when we went down to meals we would scarcely have the victuals brought down before the 2nd mate would come with this cry Where are you there forward, come out of that or I will be among you [th]en if we did not start immediately the Mate or Capt would come with [ ] and oaths threaten of breaking our backs &c if we did not come up [ ] instant after we were called thus it went on the part of the crew [ ]ad shipped in Woahoo were except one a rough set of cruel beings which were neither fit to die or live this was very much against us all as they were continually murmering about the food usage &c.

—— —— —— ——

—— Thus one day our capt came and ordered us out of the forecastle with his usual oaths and threats. When we came up he ordered us to take a pull on the fore brace whilst doing this he spoke to one of the men somewhat in this manner I will knock you to h-ll if you don't come out of that forecastle in little more haste next time (I donot know these were exactly the words used but they were to that purpose) The man told him he would pay for it if he did —— [   ] captain then struck at him with his fist but the man flinching escaped his blow and run forward the mate followed him and took him aft to the Capt who seising a 2½ inch rope commenced whipping him after taking him [by the] throat we all assembled aft some were for speaking to the captain [not] to whip the man so unmercifully but none had the heart to speak. One of the boatsteerers came and told us to revenge it that he would see us out. < > But we did not want to do anything to produce a quarrell with the officers so when he had whipt the man till he had bruised his back in a shocking manner he sent him forward Several of us then said if we went in to Fanny's Island we would ↑leave the ship↓ amongst these was myself. I had been very well used by the cap^t and had nothing to complain of but foreseeing that there would be some noise yet between the crew and the officers I was determined to leave the ship to get clear of so much turbulence and dissention. The talk now was to take a boat in the boatsteerers watch who perpetrated this vile act and go ashore in to the woods there stay till the ship sailed if we were not discovered but this was stopped by something of more consequence. Night came; the Sun set; perhaps the last for some Ah! fleeting indeed are the moments of poor mortal man. I say the sun set not willing to behold the bloody conflict. Undiscovered unbetrayed these murderous treacherous deceiving and unfeeling wretches began their work according to their own story after the fatal act. One of the boatsteerers splicing the spritsail brace the other came to him and told him there was once a conflict between the English and french the english informed the french they had seen the sun set but one of them would not see it rise he aft—

3 verso

terwards informed him he meant him but he got mistaken for the boatsteerer was afterwards saved as I shall hereafter relate the manner in its due place We were now in company with the ship Lyra of New Bedford the cap^t of which had been on board of us most all of the day but in the evening returned on board of his own ship after making an aggreement with the cap^t of our ship to set a light at 12 oclock and tack ship. At 10 oclock (Smith whos ha[   ] came of the < > boats crew) called us (the waist boats crew) it be[ing] our watch. I may here inform the reader of the manner in which whalemen keep watches during the night &c. —— —— —— —— —— ——

A whaleman generally carries 3 boats (though some carry 4-5 and 6 and some only 2 we were of the class carrying 3 boats The Capt, Mate, & 2nd mate generally stand no watch when there is no oil on board that is blubber to be tried out as they boil night and day when a chance offers.

There are generally 6 men to a boat. and 3 to stay on board of the ship whilst the rest are in pursuit of the whales. The manner in which the whales are discovered is this. There is allways 1 man at each top gallant mast head (if they have them up) excepting the mizen and sometimes there these men look around the ship in every quarter till they see something look like a white smoke rise above the water and blow away very quick they know this to be a whale and give notice in this [ ] over there she blows continuing to halloo every time he sees her blow. The ship is immediately headed for her if the whale is not to windward in which case the boats are let < > down into the water and they commence ↑rowing↓ where she was seen last. When the boats are up with where they see the whale last the boatsteerer who strikes the whale stands up and looks out for her when they see the whale they pull ahead for her and strike her if she does not perceive them in which case she goes down and it is very uncertain whether they get the whale or not. but if he strikes her the boat backs out of her way till she lies still if she lashes her tail very much when struck. They then pull up to her and lance her if there is any whales handy and swimming pretty fast they sometimes heave a < > harpoon made fast to a < > drug into her which stops her from running.

[*Diagrams of whales and of implements of the hunt*]

4 recto

another boat pulls up and strikes the whale &c —— —— —— —— —— ——

The whales are then brought along side the ship and there made fast till cut in (i e the blubber) which is done as soon as possible it is then bailed till all the oil is out and then hove overboard or burned —— ——

Now having hinted a little respecting whaleing to give the reader an insight to some parts of this mutiny I proceed on with this melancholly tale. These boatsteerers before mentioned divide the watches between ↑them↓ then each one taking the 3ᵈ of the night to stay on deck with his boats crew. Smith it appears had the first watch and then called us that is the waist boats crew I being one of the number stayed on board the ship when the boats was off did not belong to any boat but stood a watch with the boatsteerer of the waiste boat whose name was Comstock The other boatsteerer's (or third mates) name was Fisher (who was killed) who had that part of the night from 2A.M. till 6. It being my relief at the helm I took it to stand from 10 till 12 P.M. The boatsteerer came to me when I first took the helm and told me to keep the ship a good full which it was my duty to obey without asking any reasons as I knew not wether the capᵗ had told him too or not —— he came to me several times and cursed me because I had the ship up in the wind but I took no notice of this till my helm was up and I took up the rattle to shake it for relief from the stand but I had scarcely began to shake it when Comstock came to me and said if I made the least D——d bit of noise he would send me to h—l this was very sudden and alarming to me his suspecting nothing I began to rattle but was thus suddenly checked from a brother in flesh but not in heart for if he had been he would have put away this wicked design < > ↑thinking↓ it would ruin me forever for little did he think I would ever get home to tell the fatal news. he then came and lighted a lamp and went into the steerage. this conduct was very alarming to me and I stood thinking what was ↑it↓ best to do in this situation when I took hold of the rattle the second time to shake it in hopes of rousing up some body by the noise but the boatsteerer comeing on deck I dare not rattle he came and laid something heavy < > on the work bench which was along side of the cabin gangway =====

4 verso

which I afterwards found to be a boarding knife (a long knife about 2 feet in length and 2 inches wide sharp both back and edge also sharp pointed used to cut the blubber off when heaving it in as there is generally 4 or 5 peices ↑made↓ to a whale sometimes 6 or 7 and more ——

The knife is in this shape [*diagram of knife*]) he then went in the waist I beleive for I see nothing more of him untill he had committed the murder so I shall give the account as I heard him relate it and also which I heard myself —— —— —— —— ——

It seems he went down in the cabin followed by Silas Paine of Sag Harbour, John Oliver of Shields Eng. Wm Humphries ↑(stewart)↓ of Philadelphia and Thomas Linmeston [*Lilliston*] who came as far as the gangway (< >) and then ran forward and turned in not willing to have any thing to do with killing the officers and according to his own story he did not think they would put it into execution so to be as brave as any of them (as he termed it) he aggreed to go but finding them bent on their work he retreated and I believe he had not the least notion of going into the cabin at any time. accompanied by these villains Saml Comstock went into the cabin so still as not to be perceived by me at the helm. The first that I knew of their having begun their work was an axe which I distinctly heard on deck and was afterwards informed was Comstock when he struck the capt who lay in a hammock in the cabin his stateroom being too warm to lie in. At the first stroke he cut the top of his head very near off he repeated his stroke and then run to Paine who it seems was stationed with a boarding knife to stick the mate as soon as he struck the capt which was immediately done but he [boned] the knife which awoke the mate who begun thus (being awoke so sudden) what; what; what; what; what is this; Oh Paine; oh Comstock dont kill me have I not allways, here Comstock interrupted him yes you have allways been a d——d rascal you tell lies about me out of the ship will you; its a da——d good time to beg now you are too late the mate then clinched him by the throat knocked out the light and Comstock lost his hatchet but [singing] out faintly for a hatchet being choaked very hard by Beedle the mate Paine felt for one and accidentally put his hand upon one which Comstock took and hit

5 recto

Beedle over the head with and broke his skull he fell down in the pantry and there lay groaning till Comstock dispatched him The stewart held the light all this time and Oliver was cruising round putting in a blow when it came handy the 2nd mate and 3rd lay all this time listening but spoke not a word in hopes their lives would be saved—after killing the mate Comstock (leaving a watch at the 2nd mates door) came up to light a lamp to the binnacle. I then spoke to him and asked him if he was going to hurt Smith the other boatsteerer he said yes he should kill him and asked me where he was I told him I had not seen him (although he had been aft talking with me) for fear if I told the truth he would kill him or go in pursuit of him. he perceiving me shed tears asked me what I was crying about I informed him I was afraid they were going to hurt me he told me he would if I talked that way this rather silenced me ↑from fear of myself↓ as I then thought he had most done his wicked deeds he then left me took his light into the cabin and got ready to attack the 2nd and 3d mates after loading 2 guns he took one and fired through the door in the direction he thought they were and shot Mr Fisher through the mouth he then asked them if either of them was shot < > Fisher answered yes he was shot in the mouth Mr Lumber asked Comstock if he was going to kill him (previous to his shooting Fisher) he answered him in a joking manner oh no I guess not. They now opened the door and Comstock making a pass at Lumber with his gun missed and fell into the stateroom Lumber collared him but he jerked himself out of their hands at this time Fisher got his gun and put the boyanet at his heart but Comstock told him to put it down he obeyed him in hopes he would spare his life Comstock then took the gun and run Mr Lumber through several times then he told Fisher there was no hope for him he had got to die (also to remember the scrape he had with him in company with the Enterprise of Nantucket which was as follows Comstock came to Fisher to play who being very athletic took Comstock up and handled him very easy this made him ashamed and he got in a passion and struck at Fisher who took him up several times and laid him on deck pretty hard Comstock then told him he would see his hearts blood for this but Fisher thought nothing of this but it was now brought up) and now to die like a man.

5 verso

Fisher turned himself round back too and told him he was ready Comstock then put the muzzle of the gun to his head and fired which killed him immediately Lumber was then begging to spare his life but Comstock told him he was a bloody man he had the bloody hand and would be avenged —— he run him through the body again and he then begged for water but Comstock told him he would give him water and again run him through and left him for dead it appears by their story as if Comstock the boatsteerer murdered the whole or finished them. They then came up and ordered all hands called who were roused up by the noise they were ordered to come up and make sail they then set a light for the Lyra to tack but kept on the same course to get away from her the reefs were shook out and topgallant sails sets flying jib &c. but before I go further I will give some short acct of Smiths (the other boatsteerer who was to have been killed) adventures who after perceiving the noise arose and proceeded on deck thinking there was some scrape between Comstock and the capt but what was his astonishment when arriving at the cabin door he see Comstock with a boarding knife using this dire language. I am the bloody man I have the bloody hand I will have revenge; he then went forward into the forecastle and asked the crew what he should do some advised him to hide in the fore hole some to go aloft but he answered them he would do neither but would go boldly before the murderers and if his life was to be took he would ask for ½ an hour to exercise in religious duties one of the mutineers came to the forecastle gangway and ordered the men up to make sail they knew it was of no use to hang back or they would all be killed if they did nothing went to making sail Comstock called for Smith he immediately answered here am I and came to him who put his arms bloody and murderous around his neck and embraced him and says you are going to be with us are you not he answered oh yes indeed he would do any thing he asked him too. (This he knew to be the best way to get along things being as they were. The mutineers then through the capt & mate overboard. The mate had life when thrown over but the capt had a boarding knife run from his bowels out of his throat and then an axe struck on to the knife besides his head cut in a shocking manner

6 recto

The mutineers then gave orders for Mr Lumber & Fisher be brought up out of the cabin a rope was made fast to Fishers neck and he dragged from the cabin Lumber had a rope fast to his feet but on heaving him overboard he caught hold of the plank shire and hung by his hands and said Comstock you said you would save me but Comstock kicked his fingers so that he fell overboard < > he swam very quick after being in the water a minute we see nothing more of him a boat was ordered to be hoisted to pursue him but thinking the crew would take the boat and go to the Lyra they gave orders not to hoist her out. The Lyra now had her light set for tacking we set our own but kept on the same course and set all sail being but a light breese the journal from here to the mulgraves I will give in due course as matters transpired Jan. 26th 1824 had light breeses from the ESE at 2 oclock AM which continually increased until 2p. This day cleared out the cabin which was a scene of blood and destruction the mates brains were laying in every direction over the cabin deck the blood of the capt likewise was strewed over the table and cabin floor which was cleaned out and every thing brought on deck to be cleaned

Lat. 5°50'N

Lon. 159°13W

[Scrollwork to the right of latitude and longitude figures]

Jan 27th these 24 hours commenced with moderate breeses from the Eastward middle & later part calm employed cleaning the muskets and guns which were 15 in number making cartridge boxes &c.

Lat. 3°34'

Lon. 160°45'W

Jan 28th had fine weather and light breeses from the N by W This day the black stewart was hung for the following crime. I was appointed steward after the ship was took by the mutineers and my business calling me to the cabin I saw as I entered the stewart formerly who was now called purser loading a pistol I asked him what was he loading it for he answered me he heard something very strange and he was going to be ready for it I immediately went to Comstock and informed him what was going on in the cabin he came to Paine who was now made mate and asked him to follow him coming

6 verso

into the Cabin he saw Humphreys still standing with the pistol he inquired of him what he was going to do with it he told him he had heard something that he was afraid of his life Comstock told him if he had anything to tell about such things come and let him know it before he went to loading pistols and demanded what it was he had heard Humphreys answered him very suspiciously but after all gave out that Gilbert Smith (the boatsteerer that was saved) and Peter Kidder (a man very easily scared) were going to take the ship. This was a very unlikely story but Gilbert Smith & Kidder were summoned to attend and asked if any such thing was going on between them they answered in the negative that no such talk had ever been out of their lips. all this happened on the evening. next day morning they were summoned up and a jury called of 4 men. The prisoner sat between 6 men who presented bayonets at his heart to prevent escape Smith & Kidder sat on a chest in the rier. The prisoner was asked a few questions which he answered but low and unlikely —— Comstock then made a speech in the following words. It seems Wm Humphreys has been found guilty in doing an traitorous and base act in loading a pistol or detected in the act of loading it for the purposed act of shooting Paine & myself but being detected he has been tried and now the jury will give in their verdict guilty or not guilty if guilty he should be hanged to a studding sail boom shipped out 8 feet on the fore yard but if not guilty Smith & Kidder should be put to the aforementioned gallows but his death was sealed the night before and kept secret. The jury gave in that he was guilty. Therefore a watch he bought of Capt Worth was took from his pocket and a cap put on his head and he lead to the bow where he was ordered to rest on the rail and the cap drawn over his eyes every man was ordered to take hold of the execution rope and when Comstock struck on the bell we were to run aft with the rope and sling him to the fore yard. he was told if he had any thing to say to speak as but 14 seconds were allowed him to [die in] he began in the following manner when I was born I did not think I should ever come

7 recto

to this but the bell struck and he was swung to the fore yard without a kick or a groan he died immediately the rope was then cut away after hanging a few minutes first getting fouled aloft he towed along side when a runner hook (or blubber hook) was got and made fast to him to make him sink he was then cut away his chest was remmembered to allways be locked so it was searched after his death and 16 dollars in specie found in it which he took from the cap^tns trunk Thus ended allready the life of one of the mutineers and thus it is and allways will be with such desperate villains

Lat 3°31

Lon. 161°54

Jan. 29th these 24 hours squally thoughout reefed the topsails the wind to the Northward. carried away the foreward back stay to the main topmast

——— ——— ——— ———

[Large circle before latitude and longitude figures]

Lat. 3°41' N

Lon. 164°30 W

Jan 30th these 24 hours fresh breeses from the N by W steered W by N at 9 oclock having steered to the westward until now

Lat. 3°49'

Lon. 167°16'

Jan 31st this day fair breeses throughout & clear weather employed making boarding [pikes] &c. for defense if we should see a ship as we were obliged to do every thing ordered by our new made Capt The wind N by E ____

———

Lat. 3°37' N *[Scrollwork here]*

Lon. 170°06' W

Feb 1st fine weather wind to the Northward employed this day as before steering West ——

Lat. 3°34' N *[Scrollwork here]*

Lon. 172°44 W

Feb 2ⁿᵈ fine weather and breeses from the Southward

> Lat. 1°5' N
> Lon. 175°54 W

Feb 3ᵈ light breeses from the NE by N steering SW by W

> Lat. 2°7' N
> Lon. 176°32 W

Feb 4ᵗʰ Same weather but the wind to the N steering W by S

> Lat. 1°50' N
> Lon. 178°47' W

Feb 5ᵗʰ squally weather throughout winds all ways

> Lat. 1°35' N
> Lon. 179°10 E

Feb 6ᵗʰ Squally & rainy Run under 3 topsails double reefed during the night toward land which we expected to be near

> Lat. 1°54' N
> Lon. 177°31 E

[Lines of decoration or design at the bottom of the page]

7 verso

Jan [sic] 7ᵗʰ These 24 hours began with thick & squally middle part clean and fine weather luffed by the wind (which was from ENE) at 2 AM at 6 AM made sail and steered W by S 8 ½ AM saw *[one inch space]* one of the Kingsmills Groupe bearing W by S. Stood in and took canoes along side who had nothing but a few beads of their own manufacture. Here was exercise enough for any mind surrounded by Thousands of living creatures ↑with↓ not half <the> understanding or provided half so well for as our common criminals but habit has rendered it heavy and withdrew the luxury of a more polished clime. I will give some small acct of these inhabitants before I go further —— —— —— ——

After coming up with the land we see immeasurable quantities of cocoanut trees and other kinds on a narrow sand beach not over 20 rods wide we run along side of it and soon see a number of inhabitants on the shore and 1 or two dogs. what these natives live on is a species of bread fruit and yellow flower of a sweet taste which they pounded quite fine & small fish about 6 inches long. They tattew themselves and appeared to be quite hostile we run along the shore & at night luffed & endeavoured to beat along ↑off↓ the shore tack & half tack —— —— —— —— ——

Feb 8ᵗʰ squally and fresh breases from the N took a departure from Knogs [*Knox*] Island one of the Kingsmill groupe Lat 1°27'N Long. 175°14'E in the morning run through the channel between Knogs [*Knox*], Marshalls & Gilbert Islands luffed too and sent a boat ashore at Marshalls Isle but did not land as the inhabitants appeared to be hostile & endeavoured to steal from the boat after leaving the shore fired a volley of musketry among the natives and expected to have wounded some then set the sail and chaced a canoe with 2 men in it and fired into it they hove too and the boat came up with theirs when within a short distance perceived one of them was wounded the poor native took up a basket manufactured by themselves from a species of flags [*flax*] familiar to those Islands & a number of beads which he offered to these inhuman cruel brutish Americans and held up his hands to signify there was all they had he would give us that if they would not kill him Oh, how

8 recto

unfeeling must be they hearts of such wretches they cannot be called any thing better no name no tittle is half revengeful enough if the righteous are scarcely saved where have and will these vile inhabitants of the earth go hell itself is not bad enough no nor all the pains imaginable. The blood was seen to crimson the poor mans eyes grew dim alas he layed in the canoes bottom and we expect left this world which was as dear to him as to those who shed his blood—But after the devil gets full hold it puzzells a bright genious to get away let us leave this melancholy scene. The boat then came on board & we set sail for the mulgrave Isles —— —— —— Feb 9ᵗʰ took a departure from the five Islands in Lat. 1°48'N Lon. 175E bearing east dist 4 leagues at 4 P.M. nothing particular this day ——

Feb 10th Commenced with fresh breeses from the ENE & some squally the mutineers felt ugly and malicious as we had a headwind

Lat. 4°40'

Lon. 174°10E

Feb 11th Commences with fresh breeses from the Northward at ½ P.M. made the land bearing NNE dist 4 leagues stood in and took canoes also sent a boat ashore & brought off some of the women or girls and a large quantity of cocoanuts some fish &c. We stood off this night & Feb 12th stood in again took the girls ashore & cruised the shore to find a landing place & reconoitered the country to see if the soil would admit of cultivation but found it very poor the next day the 13th Feb after having stood off all night we run down the coast & at at [*sic*] night came to a low narrow Island & run in determined to anchor if any place could be found. a man was sent in the chains to heave the lead he pronounced 12 fathoms orders were given to have the anchor all ready for droping but the next sound found no bottom we run in till we had regular soundings and let go the anchor within 20 rods of the shore on a coral rock bottom 7 fathoms water the boat was lowered and the kedge took out astern to prevent her from swinging onto the shore. The sails were furled the ship moored and we all retired to rest except an anchor watch but rest as it was not fit for brutes much more for human beings we lay deploring our fate yet glad to get out

8 verso

of the ship (as we expected now soon to remove ashore) the next day 14th Feb. was spent in looking for a landing place a boat set out in the morning & went away to the eastward of where we lay at anchor at noon They came back and informed us they had found a pretty good landing place but there was no shore but what ↑was↓ quite rocky a boat set out after 2 oclock PM. and went to the westward but returned at night without any satisfactory answer it was now fixed upon to land where we now lay which was a very irregular spot

End

LAY AND HUSSEY'S MARSHALLESE VOCABULARY

One of the most remarkable achievements of the two marooned *Globe* survivors was the acquisition of a command of the Milians' language that was so good that the natives themselves commended the two seamen for their fluency. The soundest evidence of their grasp of the language is the vocabulary list they assembled after their rescue—it had to be after the rescue since nothing to write with would have been available on Mili.

Horatio Hale, ethnographer and philologist with the United States Exploring Expedition, 1838–1842, records that "On their [Lay's and Hussey's] arrival at Oahu, the Rev. Mr. Bingham, missionary at Honolulu, took down a vocabulary of such words of the native language as they could remember." Bingham's purpose was to be ready for eventual proselytizing in Micronesia. Hale learned of this study of Marshallese directly from Bingham, who analyzed forms, orthography, and pronunciation of the words in a brief study, which Hale draws on. Hale says that Bingham said of his study, "it is very imperfect," a judgment that Hale immediately qualifies by saying, "but the deficiencies are such as must properly be referred to a limited knowledge of the language on the part of the two men, who could have acquired little more than a smattering of the most common idioms, with such words as were needed in the daily intercourse with the natives." This opinion is intolerable, especially when coming from a philologist, who could see evidence of the two men's fluency in the accounts of easy communication in their *Narrative* and in Paulding's *Journal* (both of which Hale indicates that he was familiar with), and who could also see that the range of vocabulary in the Lay and Hussey list went far beyond everyday common idioms, and who could not fail to realize that the words recorded by Lay and Hussey on the list in their *Narrative* or the ones jotted down by Bingham are only randomly chosen examples out of a much larger active vocabulary.

Bingham's own word list is reprinted in Hale's publication (431–34). It is shorter than Lay and Hussey's list; the two lists overlap only partially. Probably Lay and Hussey could have made their list much longer (and possibly did for Bingham) but wanted to give the readers of their *Narrative* just a sampling of words that would convey an impression of the look and sound of the language. Whether Bingham could have had access to other sources from which to study the Micronesian language study (like the word list in the second volume of Kotzebue's *A Voyage Around the World* [1821]) is unclear. He did not discuss the language with Hale until a decade after meeting with Lay and Hussey; what Hale prints of Bingham's grammar and word list could have come from considerable study since meeting the two seamen, but the two seamen were very likely his first instructors. Lay and Hussey's list has been compared with *The Marshallese-English Dictionary* (Abo in Bibliography) and has been discussed with Alfred Capelle, one of the editors of the dictionary; Lay and Hussey get high marks for accuracy. The list of words sheds light not only on the two men's knowledge of the language in general but also on the subjects that made up the discussions they held with the natives.

The following are excerpts from Lay and Hussey's "A VOCABULARY Of Words and Phrases, used by the natives of the Mulgrave Islands, with their definitions and so spelt and divided in syllables as to give the Reader a very clear understanding of the pronunciation."

166

A long time	Et tow	Musketoe	To cotch up
Yourself	Guay	Fear	Cwurd
Sleepy	Mu tegee	Giving	Iti dir inge
Victuals	Cuck con	A rope	Tow
Scrape	Goo tock	Wind	Gut to
Build	Ae	Rain	Woot
Hold on	Coppy dirty	Lay down	Bah boo
Man	um marn	Get up	Der ry cock
Woman	Civ rah	Not good	Nah uab
Boy	Lod rick	Very good	En no
Girl	Lid rick	Taking	Com el tah te
An infant	Hi d r ry	Fighting	Tarr yin ia
Black	Eg gil ly mit	Kill	Mon ny
White	Em mew it	Smoke	Bout
Red	Em mirt	Sand	Boak
Drink	E rauck	Diving	Doo lock
Fingers	Jan thurt	Digging	Cob e coob
A bird	Paw o	Bury	Col ly boo ny
A knife	Noad rick	Sewing	Thil thil
Begging	Angue ot	Eat	Mong ah
Work	Derry bol	Singing	Al lil
An adze	Jal tosk	Sun	Al
A nail	Mer ry	Moon	Al lung
Grass	Oo j o et	Star	E jew
Leaves	Bel ly bal	Sky	Lid ere lung
Counting	B n ne bun	Sun down	Doo lock Al
One	Jew on	Sun rise	Tuck in Al
Two	Roo ah	To- day	Raun ene
Three	Te lew	Yesterday	In nay
Four	A men	To nign	Boon ene
Five	Ri lim	Tomorrow	Geen a raun
Six	Dil je mo	[on Puking	Mum mit
Seven	D jil je majew	A blanket	Cawd
Eight	Ad je no	[on A costume	Ene
Nine	Ad dil y mo jew	Fuel	Con ny
Ten	Dongue ole	Land	Yin ny

A VOCABULARY Of Words and Phrases, used by the natives of the Mulgrave Islands, with their definitions and so spelt and divided in syllables as to give the Reader a very clear understanding of the pronunciation.

167

A bottle	Buck ah	Bailing	An ain
Cutting	Boo way	Mast	Cod jew
Fastening	Geal ing	A saw	Dir re ban
Stealing	Mid dart	A sword	Jah jav
A rat	Kid dir rick	A handle	Je jew er
Hair	Co coa no bot	Running	Tit hurt
Ear	Lou dil lyg nu	A musket	Boo wat
Eyes	Mid dat	A cannon	Bac ca
Nose	Baw thurt	Powder	Bow on ope
Mouth	Loung ing [ed	Fire	Kid ja ick
Chin	Chim in ny gne	Hewing	Jick e jick
Chief	Tam moon	A house	Imm
Forward	A marn	Fish	Ikk
Egg	Lip	Stone	Buck ah
Drift	Pay lock	Head	Bur run
Paddle	Aun arn	Hand	Bon
I know	E del lah	Foot	Nane
Yes	Ing ah	A shark	Bac co
No	Aub	A spear	Mor ry
Backside	Al by gin	Cocoanuts	Koree
Playing	Cook ke ry	Breadfruit	Mah
Medicine	Oo noe	Go	Wy lum
Whale	Rat	Come	Wy to
A louse	Git	Very large	El lip
Strong	Mad jo jow	Scar or cut	Gin net
Enough	Em mut	Thunder	Daw roort
Thread	Uer	Lightning	Dar rum
Forget	Mer no lock wy	Lizard	Cid re be lin
See	Lal ly		

A canoe, or any vessel	Woa or Wah
Put it down there	Lickitin i genny
Throw it away	Jow lock y
I am thirsty	E mar row
Give me some drink	Letto lim ma dirick
Finger nails	Og guck
Your father	Gim mum

APPENDIX D

THE COMSTOCK FAMILY

The best source of genealogical information on the family is John Adams Comstock's *A History and Genealogy of the Comstock Family in America*, which gives the earliest English history of the family as well as the genealogies of the American Comstocks. Another important source is Cyrus Ballou Comstock's *A Comstock Genealogy: Descendants of William Comstock of New London, Conn. Who Died After 1662*; also pertinent are the Barney Records and Folger Records in the Nantucket Historical Association, census records, and William Wade Hinshaw's *Encyclopedia of American Quaker Genealogy* (Ann Arbor: Edwards Brothers, 1940). As is usual in extensive genealogies, there are gaps and disagreements in these records. Dates in the extracted material below are from John Adams Comstock's book unless otherwise noted.

The line of descent from William Comstock, the first settler, is:

William[1] (c. 1595–c. 1683)

Samuel[2]

Samuel[3]

Samuel[4]

David[5]

Samuel[6]

Nathan[7] (1776–1859)

Nathan married twice; by his first wife, Elizabeth Emmett (1782–1818) he had:

Samuel	Born September 1802 according to the two Comstock genealogies; born October 8, 1802, according to the Nantucket Vital Records
William	April 24, 1804–November 20, 1882, according to all records
George	Born 1808 (Barney Records and census records: January 29, 1808); died October 28, 1855
Thomas	1810–1855
Phebe	1812–1820
Lucy	Born 1805 (Barney Records), 1806 (census records)
Martha	1814–1892
Elizabeth Anne	Died 1860

By his second wife, Anne Merritt, he had:

Nathan
John Merritt
Louisa
Mary
Sarah

To answer an occasionally asked question, Samuel Comstock was the seventh cousin of Henry T. P. Comstock, who gave his name to the Comstock lode, and the sixth cousin once removed of Anthony Comstock, the famed anti-vice crusader.

"THE YOUNG MUTINEER"

"The Young Mutineer" was written by Henry Glover (1804–1825), almost certainly a childhood acquaintance of Samuel Comstock. William Comstock reprints a version of the poem in the preface to his life of Samuel "to show the view which those took of the affair [of the mutiny], who were well acquainted with the subject of these pages, previous to his departure in the Globe." The poem was fresh news, having been written between October 25, 1824, when the story of the *Globe* was first reported in the Nantucket *Inquirer*, and November 29, a month later, when a version of it appeared in the *Inquirer*. Although the poet's point of view may be distinctive and his diction more figurative than the average Nantucketer's, the poem probably captures the reactions of contemporary islanders immediately on hearing the news of the mutiny; it may even draw some phrasing from words heard in the town.

The known versions of the poem vary in length from seven to twelve stanzas and have the dated narrative bounce of anapestic tetrameter (same as "*'Twas the Night Before Christmas*"). Apart from the different number of stanzas, the six versions of the poem located differ only in punctuation and minor matters of phrasing ("yells" for "cries," "beach" for "shore," etc.). Of the versions found, the most authoritative may be one in the Nantucket Historical Association (NHA) with the cover inscription, "Presented me by the Author Henry Glover / Peleg Mitchell Jr." It is eight stanzas in length, as is the version printed by William Comstock in *The Terrible Whaleman*; both contain the sensitive stanza about Samuel's eternal punishment. (William's attribution of the poem to a "Captain Coffin" is inexplicable.) Two manuscript versions, both seven stanzas long, seem to be copied from the November 29, 1824, *Inquirer*. One has the note, "Copied from Mrs. K. Starbuck's copy [of the *Inquirer*] by M. E. S. Nov. 7th 1896." More interesting is the one signed by Margaret Cary and George H. Cary. Margaret is Cyrus Hussey's sister, the one who, as described in the afterword, wrote her brother five days after he sailed on his last voyage. George H. Cary is her son and Cyrus Hussey's nephew. George was born in 1847, twenty-three years after the *Globe* events. There is a suggestion in the signatures of mother and son on the transcript of the poem that Margaret wanted her son to know the *Globe* story and brought the poem to his attention at what she considered a good moment.

The poem below is the twelve-stanza version transcribed and annotated by William C. Folger, who writes, "These lines were Printed in the Pawtucket Chronicle, from which paper I copied them, if I mistake not." It is selected here only because it is the most inclusive. Since the shorter version of the poem appeared in the *Inquirer* so soon after the news of the mutiny was received, it is likely that the twelve-stanza version was a later expansion of the original verses. The first four stanzas below are original to this Folger version, and the tenth stanza is the one (already discussed in the afterword) that the *Inquirer* omitted.

> *O'er the caves of the ocean, the gallant ship sped,*
> *Where the Sea coral shines, like the bright ruby red;*
> *Where the blue sapphire studs the tall arches of green,*
> *Where the wild Naid roves, and the mermaid is seen,*
> *And naught on her track spake of incident drear,*
> *Save the fiend in the breast of the Young Mutineer.*

> *O'er the wild stormy ocean the gallant ship sailed,*
> *Till the far southern islands were joyfully hail'd,*
> *Where they fondly had hoped from the depths of the water,*
> *The leviathan to draw, for a red, cruel slaughter.*
> *Nor dreamed that a horrid death waited them there,*
> *From the arm and the k[n]ife of the young Mutineer.*

But crushed were their hopes, when at midnight's dread hour
A shout and a blow spake the murderers power,
And those who were bedded in safety to sleep,
Chang'd that bed for a grave in the billowy deep.
The sea-moan their requiem, a hammock their bier,
Their bearers, the band of the Young Mutineer.

But short was the hour of that murderous band,
And few were their days in that wild foreign land,
Which is wash'd by the wave of the same briny flood
That drank the red cup of their innocent blood!
And bitter, and short was the cruel career
Of the fiend in the breast of the Young Mutineer.

His sun rose unclouded, and brightly it shone,
In the pride of the morning, and promised a noon
Of glory and gladness—It sunk to the flood
In blackness and blindness, and blasted by blood.
Disown'd and dishonoured, its last gloomy glare
Was shed on the grave of the Young Mutineer.

Tho' beardless his cheek, yet his was a soul
That ne'er knew a master, that brook'd not control.
Tho' beardless his cheek, yet his was a hand
Acquainted with daggers, a voice to command.
An eye that ne'er wept, a heart without fear,
Were the pride and the boast of the young Mutineer.

Yet he lies on the beach of a lone desert isle,
And his dirge the green waves are chaunting the while,
As they in wild tumult roll over his head
And wash the high rock that marks his wet bed,
Where lie, with a heart that ne'er knew a fear
The mangled remains of the young Mutineer.

He lies on the beach the cold waters beside,
And dreadful and dark was the death that he died.
No Mother mourns o'er him; no fond fair one weeps,
Where far from the land of his fathers he sleeps,
But the chill wild winds whistle, the sea birds career
O'er the wet sandy grave of the young Mutineer.

He lies on the beach by a comrade in guilt,
His forehead was cloven, his best blood was spilt.
The cries of his victims had risen to God
And their wailings were quench'd in the murderer's blood.
He fell—yet none mourn'd their leader, none shed a tear,
O'er the mangled remains of the young Mutineer.

He fell on the shore—with a heart rending yell,
Wild and despairing, he sank down to hell;
His glaz'd eyes in horror were turn'd upward to Heav'n,
His last cry to the skies in wild echoes was given—
In vain it ascended, no mercy was there,
To cheer the dark death of the young Mutineer.

He lies on the shore where the weeds & the shells,
Mark the bounds of the sea as in tumult it swells.
They scoop'd out a grave, and there laid him at rest,
And they heap'd the wet sand on his bare, bloody breast,
And they rolled a huge rock, and they planted it there,
To mark the lone grave of the Young Mutineer.

In year[s] that are coming the seamen shall tell
Of the murderer's spectre, and the murderer's yell,
And the tale the lone watches of night will beguile,
As they sail near the shores of that desolate isle;
And their beacon shall be as they thitherward steer,
The black rock on the grave of the Young Mutineer.

William C. Folger adds a note at the end of the text of the poem: "The author, Henry Glover, son of Capt. Benjamin & Judith Bunker Glover, was born 6th of March, 1804, and died 30th of August 1825 at Port au Prince, San Domingo. He was a young man of superior abilities and great promise, and was at the time of his death in his twenty-second year." Glover was, as far as is known, ahead of everyone else in turning the *Globe* story into literature. While Lay and Hussey acted quickly to make literature out of their experiences, Henry Glover was already in print; at the time of Glover's death, Lay and Hussey were still unrescued on Mili Atoll.

The Cary version of the poem is in the NHA library, Collection 74, folder 14. The Mitchell, "M.E.S.," and William C. Folger versions are in the NHA, Collection 43, folder 4. Most of the material on Glover and his poem was discovered by the research of Elizabeth Oldham.

BIBLIOGRAPHY
AND NOTES

Keywords and abbreviations in the notes correspond to those given before bibliographic entries here. Beyond the George Comstock "Narrative" printed in full for the first time in this book (Appendix B), the primary works on the *Globe* are L&H, Comstock T, and Paulding. Among secondary works on the *Globe*, the most studied are those by Edouard Stackpole below; these include his introduction to the Corinth Books edition of L&H.

REPOSITORIES

MVH   Martha's Vineyard Historical Society
NA   National Archives
NHA   Nantucket Historical Association

BIBLIOGRAPHY

Abo   Takaji Abo, Byron W. Bender, Alfred Capelle, and Tony DeBrum, *Marshallese-English Dictionary* (Honolulu: University of Hawaii Press, 1976).

Amory   Thomas Coffin Amory, *The Life of Admiral Sir Isaac Coffin, Baronet* (Boston: Cupples, Upham & Co., 1886).

Anbinder   Tyler Anbinder, *Five Points* (New York: Free Press, 2001).

Anderson   Charles Roberts Anderson, *Melville in the South Seas* (New York: Columbia University Press, 1939; New York: Dover, 1966).

Banks   Charles Edward Banks, *The History of Martha's Vineyard, Dukes County, Massachusetts*, Vol. 3 (Edgartown, Mass.: Dukes County Historical Society, 1966).

Barbour   Hugh Barbour, ed., *Quaker Crosscurrents: Three Hundred Years of Friends in the New York Monthly Meetings* (Syracuse, N.Y.: Syracuse University Press, 1995).

Beachcomb   *Beachcombers, Traders & Castaways in Micronesia.* Web site, accessed January 31, 2002. www.micsem.org/pubs/publications/histwork/bcomber/marshalls.htm

Beaglehole   J. C. Beaglehole, *The Exploration of the Pacific* (Stanford, Calif.: Stanford University Press, 1966).

Beegel   Susan Beegel, " 'Mutiny and Atrocious Butchery': The *Globe* Mutiny as a Source for Pym," in Richard Kopley, ed., *Poe's Pym: Critical Explorations* (Durham, N.C.: Duke University Press, 1992), 7–19, 277–80.

Bellwood M   Peter Bellwood, *Man's Conquest of the Pacific: The Prehistory of Southeast Asia and Oceania* (New York: Oxford University Press, 1979).

Bellwood P   ———, *The Polynesians: Prehistory of an Island People* (London: Thames and Hudson, 1978).

Bingham   Hiram Bingham, *A Residence of Twenty-One Years in the Sandwich Islands* (Rutland, Vt.: Charles E. Tuttle, 1981).

Blackman   William Fremont Blackman, *The Making of Hawaii: A Study in Social Evolution* (New York: Macmillan, 1899).

Booker   Margaret Moore Booker, *The Admiral's Academy* (Nantucket, Mass.: Mill Hill Press, 1998).

Browning   Mary A. Browning, "Traders in the Marshalls," *Micronesian Reporter* 20 (1972), 32–38.

Burrows   Edwin G. Burrows and Mike Wallace, *Gotham: A History of New York City to 1898* (New York: Oxford University Press, 1999).

Bwebwenatoon	Jane Downing, Dirk H. R. Spennemann, and Margaret Bennett, *Bwebwenatoon Etto: A Collection of Marshallese Legends and Traditions* (Majuro: Republic of the Marshall Islands Ministry of Internal Affairs Historic Preservation Office, 1992).
Chamisso	Adelbert von Chamisso, *A Voyage Around the World with the Romanzov Exploring Expedition in the Years 1815–1818 in the Brig Rurik, Captain Otto von Kotzebue.* Trans. and ed. Henry Kratz (Honolulu: University of Hawaii Press, 1986).
Comstock C	Cyrus B. Comstock, ed., *A Comstock Genealogy: Descendants of William Comstock of New London, Conn. Who Died After 1662* (New York: Knickerbocker Press, 1907).
Comstock G	George Comstock, "Narrative of the mutiny capture and transactions on board of the Ship Globe of Nantucket after Sailing from Edgartown," unpublished manuscript, NHA, Collection 15, folder 71. Transcript: Appendix B of the present book.
Comstock J	John Adams Comstock, *A History and Genealogy of the Comstock Family in America* (Los Angeles: Privately printed by Commonwealth Press, 1949).
Comstock N	William Comstock, *Mysteries of New York* (Boston: At the Yankee Office, 1845).
Comstock T	———, *The Life of Samuel Comstock, the Terrible Whaleman* (Boston: James Fisher; New York: Turner and Fisher, 1840).
Comstock V	———, *A Voyage to the Pacific, Descriptive of the Customs, Usages, and Sufferings on Board of Nantucket Whale-Ships* (Boston: Oliver L. Perkins, 1838).
Comstock W	———, Betsey Jane Ward [pseud.], *Betsey Jane Ward, (Better-Half to Artemus) Hur Book of Goaks with a Hull Akkownt of the Coartship and Maridge to A4said Artemus, and Mister Ward's Cutting-Up with the Mormon Fare Secks* (New York: James O'Kane, 1866).
Cromwell	Otelia Cromwell, *Lucretia Mott* (Cambridge: Harvard University Press, 1958).

D&D   Louis B. Davidson and Eddie Doherty, *Captain Marooner.* Introd. William McFee (New York: Crowell, 1952).

Davis   Charles H. Davis [Jr.], *Life of Charles Henry Davis, Rear Admiral, 1807–1877* (New York: Houghton, Mifflin, 1899).

Daws   Gavan Daws, *Shoal of Time: A History of the Hawaiian Islands* (New York: Macmillan, 1968).

Dening   Greg Dening, *Islands and Beaches: Discourse on a Silent Land, Marquesas 1774–1880* (Honolulu: University of Hawaii Press, 1980).

Deposition(s) Depositions before U.S. Consul Michael Hogan, Valparaíso (June 9, 15, 30, 1824) in NA, Record Group 59, M146, roll 1.

Dillon   Peter Dillon, *Narrative and Successful Result of a Voyage in the South Seas: Performed by Order of the Government of British India, to Ascertain the Actual Fate of La Pérouse's Expedition.* 2 vols. (London: Hurst, Chance, 1829).

Ellis   Edward Robb Ellis, *The Epic of New York City* (New York: Coward-McCann, 1966).

Ennaanin Dirk H. R. Spennemann, *Ennaanin Etto: A Collection of Essays on the Marshallese Past* (Majuro: Republic of the Marshall Islands Ministry of Internal Affairs Historic Preservation Office, 1993).

Erdland   August Erdland, *The Marshall Islanders: Life and Customs, Thought and Religion of a South Seas People* (New Haven, Conn.: Human Relations Area Files, 1970).

Fairburn   William Armstrong Fairburn, *Merchant Sail.* 6 vols. (Center Lovell, Maine: Fairburn Marine Educational Foundation, 1945–1955; repr. Gloucester, Mass.: Ten Pound Island Book Co., 1992).

Finney   Ben R. Finney, *Voyage of Rediscovery: A Cultural Odyssey through Polynesia* (Berkeley: University of California Press, 1994).

Frazer   James George Frazer, *The Belief in Immortality and the Worship of the Dead* (London: Dawsons, 1968).

Gast   Ross H. Gast, *Contentious Consul: A Biography of John Coffin Jones* (Los Angeles: Dawson's Book Shop, 1976).

Gilbert   Thomas Gilbert, *Voyage from New South Wales to Canton in the Year 1788* (London: Debrett, 1789; repr. Ridgewood, N.J.: Gregg Press, 1968).

Hale   Horatio Emmons Hale, *Ethnography and Philology.* In series: *United States Exploring Expedition During the Years 1838–1842, under the Command of Charles Wilkes, U.S.N.*, Vol. 6 (Philadelphia: Lea and Blanchard, 1846; repr. Ridgewood, N.J.: Gregg Press, 1968).

Hawthorne   Nathaniel Hawthorne, *The American Notebooks.* Ed. Claude M. Simpson (Columbus: Ohio State University Press, 1972).

Haynes   Douglas Haynes and William L. Wuerch, *Micronesian Religion and Lore: A Guide to Sources, 1526–1990* (Westport, Conn.: Greenwood Press, 1995).

Heflin   Wilson Heflin, "Herman Melville's Whaling Years," dissertation, Vanderbilt University, 1952.

Hezel Fi   Francis X. Hezel, SJ, *The First Taint of Civilization: A History of the Caroline and Marshall Islands in Pre-Colonial Days, 1521–1885* (Honolulu: University of Hawaii Press, 1983).

Hezel Fo   ———, *Foreign Ships in Micronesia: A Compendium of Ship Contacts with the Caroline and Marshall Islands 1521–1885* (Saipan, Mariana Islands: Trust Territory Historic Preservation Office and the U.S. Heritage Conservation and Recreation Service, 1979).

Hoyt   Edwin Palmer Hoyt, *Mutiny on the Globe* (New York: Random House, 1975).

Inquirer   Nantucket *Inquirer.*

Kidder M   Signed account by Stephen Kidder in Journal of Obed Macy, NHA, Collection 96, Journal 4, 34–40.

Klain   Zora Klain, *Educational Activities of New England Quakers* (Philadelphia: Westbrook Publishing, 1928).

Kotzebue V   Otto von Kotzebue, *A Voyage of Discovery, in the South Sea and to Bering's Straits in Search of a North East Passage Undertaken in the Years 1815–1818*. 3 vols. (London: Longman, Hurst, Rees, Orme, and Brown, 1821).

Kotzebue N   ———, *A New Voyage Round the World in the Years 1823, 24, 25, and 26* (London: H. Colburn & R. Bentley, 1830).

Kuykendall   Ralph S. Kuykendall, *The Hawaiian Kingdom*. 3 vols. (Honolulu: University of Hawaii Press, 1938–67).

Kuyk-Day   Ralph S. Kuykendall and A. Grove Day, *Hawaii: A History* (Englewood Cliffs, N.J.: Prentice-Hall, 1961).

Lamb   Martha J. Lamb and Mrs. Burton Harrison, *History of the City of New York: Its Origin, Rise, and Progress*. 3 vols. (New York: A. S. Barnes, 1877).

Langdon   Robert Langdon, *A Gazeteer of Obsolete/Alternative Names of the Pacific Islands with Their Current Equivalents and A Gazeteer of Current Names of the Pacific Islands with Their Obsolete/Alternative Names* (Canberra: Pacific Manuscripts Bureau, 1976; detached from *Pambu* 42 [Jan. Mar. 1976]).

Langsdorff   George H. von Langsdorff, *Voyages and Travels in Various Parts of the World during the years 1803, 1804, 1805, 1806 and 1807*. 2 vols. (London: Henry Colburn, 1813–14).

Lankevich   George J. Lankevich, *American Metropolis: A History of New York City* (New York: New York University Press, 1998).

L&H   William Lay and Cyrus M. Hussey, *A Narrative of the Mutiny, on Board the Ship Globe, of Nantucket* (New London: Publ. by authors, 1828); repr. *A Narrative of the Mutiny on Board the Whaleship Globe*. Ed. E. Stackpole (New York: Corinth Books, 1963). References in this book are to the Corinth House edition.

Leach   Robert J. Leach, *Quaker Nantucket* (Nantucket, Mass.: Mill Hill Press, 1997).

Lewis   David Lewis, *We, the Navigators: The Ancient Art of Landfinding in the Pacific* (Honolulu: University of Hawaii Press, 1994).

Log   Log of the US Schooner *Dolphin* (1824–27), Vol. 1. NA, Record Group 24.

Long   David F. Long, *"Mad Jack": The Biography of Captain John Percival, U.S.N., 1779–1862* (Westport, Conn.: Greenwood Press, 1993).

Longworth   David Longworth et al., *Longworth's American Almanack, New York Register, and City Directory: for the . . . Year of American Independence* (New York; Publ. by David Longworth, 1797–1843).

Loomis   Albertine Loomis, *Grapes of Canaan: Hawaii 1820* (New York: Dodd, Mead, 1951; Woodbridge, Conn.: Ox Bow Press, 1998).

MVV   *Vital Records of Edgartown, Massachusetts, to the Year 1850* (Boston: New England Historic Genealogy Society, 1906).

Macy   Silvanus J. Macy, *Bibliography of the Macy Family 1635–1868* (Albany, N.Y.: Joel Munsell, 1868).

Maloney   Linda [McKee] Maloney, *The Captain from Connecticut* (Boston: Northeastern University Press, 1986).

Maloney U   Linda M. Maloney, "The U.S. Navy's Pacific Squadron, 1824–1827," in Robert William Love, Jr., ed., *Changing Interpretations and New Sources in Naval History* (New York: Garland, 1980), 180–91.

Maria   Journal of 1822 voyage of the *Maria* kept by George Washington Gardner, Jr., NHA, Collection 335, folder 956.

McKee   Linda McKee, " 'Mad Jack' and the Missionaries," *American Heritage*, 22 (April 1971), 30–37, 85–87.

Meade   Rebecca Paulding Meade, *The Life of Hiram Paulding, Rear-Admiral, U.S.N.* (New York: Baker and Taylor, 1910). *Dictionary of American Biography.*

Melville   Herman Melville, *Redburn: His First Voyage* (Evanston and Chicago: Northwestern University Press and the Newberry Library, 1969).

Mercein   William A. Mercein, *Mercein's City Directory, New-York Register, and Almanac, for the Forty-Fifth Year of American Independence* (New York: W. A. Mercein, 1820).

Mitchill   Samuel L. Mitchill, *The Picture of New-York, or, The Traveller's Guide Through the Commercial Metropolis of the United States* (New York: I. Riley, 1807).

Monaghan L   Charles Monaghan, "Lindley Murray, American," in Ingrid Tieken-Boon van Ostade, ed., *Two Hundred Years of Lindley Murray* (Münster: Nodus Publikationen, 1996), 27–43.

Monaghan M   Charles Monaghan, "The Murrays of Murray Hill: A New York Quaker Family Before, During and After the Revolution," *Quaker History* 87, 1 (1998), 35–56.

Morrell   Benjamin Morrell, Jr., *A Narrative of Four Voyages, to the South Sea, North and South Pacific Ocean, Chinese Sea, Ethiopic and Southern Atlantic Ocean, Indian and Antarctic Ocean* (New York: J. & J. Harper, 1832).

Olson   James S. Olson, ed., *Historical Dictionary of the Spanish Empire, 1402–1975* (Westport, Conn.: Greenwood Press, 1992).

Paulding   Hiram Paulding, *Journal of a Cruise of the United States Schooner Dolphin Among the Islands of the Pacific Ocean and a Visit to the Mulgrave Islands, In Pursuit of the Mutineers of the Whale Ship Globe*. Introd. A. Grove Day (Honolulu: University of Hawaii Press, 1970).

Phillip   Arthur Phillip, *The Voyage of Governor Phillip to Botany Bay with Contributions by Other Officers of the First Fleet and Observations on Affairs of the Time by Lord Auckland*. Introd. James J. Auchmuty (London: Angus and Robertson, 1970).

Philbrick   Nathaniel Philbrick, *In the Heart of the Sea* (New York:

Viking, 2000).

Pigafetta   Antonio Pigafetta, *Magellan's Voyage: A Narrative Account of the First Circumnavigation*. 2 vols. Trans. and ed. R. A. Skelton (New Haven: Yale University Press, 1969).

Pratt   Fletcher Pratt, *The Navy, a History* (Garden City, New York: Garden City Publishing, 1941).

Reynolds   *Report of J. N. Reynolds of Facts Obtained at Nantucket of South Seas and Pacific Ocean*, NA, Record Group 45.

Reynolds L   Larry Reynolds, *James Kirke Paulding* (Boston: Twayne, 1984).

Sharp A   Andrew Sharp, *Ancient Voyagers in Polynesia* (Berkeley: University of California Press, 1964).

Sharp D   ———, *The Discovery of the Pacific Islands* (Westport, Conn.: Greenwood Press, 1985).

Stackpole L   Edouard Stackpole, "Introduction," in William Lay and Cyrus M. Hussey, *A Narrative of the Mutiny on Board the Whaleship Globe* (New York: Corinth Books, 1963), v–xxvi.

Stackpole M   ———, *Mutiny at Midnight: The Adventures of Cyrus Hussey of Nantucket Aboard the Whaleship Globe in the South Pacific from 1822 to 1826* (New York: William Morrow, 1939).

Stackpole S   ———, *The Sea-Hunters* (Westport, Conn.: Greenwood, 1972)

Stackpole W   ———, *The Mutiny on the Whaleship Globe: A True Story of the Sea* (n.p., 1981).

Starbuck   Alexander Starbuck, *History of the American Whale Fishery From Its Earliest Inception to the Year 1876*. 2 vols. (Privately issued by the author, 1878; repr. New York: Argosy Antiquarian Ltd., 1964).

Still   Bayrd Still, *Mirror for Gotham: New York as Seen by Contemporaries from Dutch Days to the Present* (New York: New York University Press, 1956; Westport, Conn.: Greenwood, 1980).

Tabrah   Ruth Tabrah, *Hawaii: A Bicentennial History* (New York: W. W. Norton, 1980).

Tobin   Jack Tobin, *Stories from the Marshall Islands* (Honolulu: University of Hawaii Press, 2001).

Trayser   Donald G. Trayser, *Barnstable: Three Centuries of a Cape Cod Town* (Hyannis: F. B. and F. P. Goss, 1939).

Webb   Nancy and Jean Francis Webb, *The Hawaiian Islands: From Monarchy to Democracy* (New York: Viking Press, 1958).

Westcott   Allan Westcott, "Captain 'Mad Jack' Percival," *United States Naval Institute Proceedings* 61, 3 (March 1935), 313–19.

NOTE ON THE SPELLING OF MARSHALLESE WORDS

The spelling of Marshallese common nouns used in this book follows that in Abo. So does the spelling of place names except where widespread usage favors another form, most notably Lukunor instead of Lukwon-wod. Many Marshallese place names on maps are from the islands' Japanese period (1914–1943), when Jelbon was Chirubon and Malka was Madekai. Other variant forms are noted in the text or notes as they occur. Mili has appeared over the years in variant spellings, including, today, the scholarly precise form Mile, which is occasionally seen but which has been judged not to have acceded yet to popular acceptance.

NOTES

Introduction

xvi **Nako and the afterlife:** Tobin, 195, note 1. Nadikdik, or Knox, is the spur of islands southeast of the main Mili Atoll; Nako is its almost southernmost island.

Chapter One: Brothers

3 **The Comstock family moved** to New York in 1811; it is a good guess that they moved May 1, which was *the* moving day in New York, since it was the day leases expired. The children's precise ages at the time of the move would depend on the day of the move.

4 **Early Nantucket whaling:** Starbuck, 12–36.

5 **Ship records:** Starbuck, vol. 1, passim.

6 **Wearing green leaves:** Anderson, 73; Langsdorff, I, 92–95.

7 **Samuel's early life:** Unless otherwise attributed, details and anecdotes are from Comstock T.

11 **Comstock genealogy:** Treated in Appendix D.

12 **Quaker Monthly Meeting school:** Klain, 122, on Nathan. Klain, 10, quotes a letter c. 1780 of Moses Brown, a campaigner for setting up a Nantucket Quaker school: "I have never had an idea that Friends especially here in New England have a desire or appreciation for high learning; for, indeed we are an illiterate set of people compared with others. Very few, I think only five or six in our Yearly Meeting are acquainted with any tongue but their own, and many cannot write even their names."

13 **Great Mary ancestor of Samuel:** Mary Coffin Starbuck was mother of Jethro Starbuck, who was father of Mary Starbuck, who was mother of E. Mitchell, who was mother of Elizabeth Emmett, who was mother of Samuel.

Quaker dominance: Leach, 97.

15 **Barker:** *Appleton's Cyclopedia of American Biography* (New York: D. Appleton and Co., 1888), I, 165. Nantucket genealogist Dwight

Beman has traced the relationship of Barker and the Comstocks: Elizabeth Emmett's maternal grandmother, Hepzibah Barnard, was a first cousin of Sarah Folger, Jacob Barker's mother.

16   **Lambert:** Still, 74–75.

Beaver: Fairburn, I, 504–505.

17   **Nine Partners:** Barbour, 150–51

Curriculum; Lucretia Mott: Cromwell, 15–21.

18   **The city:** The main sources for the description of the city are Burrows, Ellis, Lamb, Lankevich, and Still.

19   **Five Points:** Anbinder, 13–20 and passim.

20   **Greenwich Village:** The Comstocks' move during the epidemic is referred to in Comstock T, 65.

Addresses: Longworth; Mercein.

Whale products: *New York City Mercantile and Manufacturers' Business Directory for the Year Ending May 1, 1857* (New York: West, Lee, and Bartlett, 1857), 220–21.

26   **Liverpool:** Still, 63–64.

Melville: Melville, 186, 191.

27   **Josiah Macy:** Macy, 171–85.

28   **Morrell:** Morrell, xix.

29   **Beaver:** Fairburn, IV, 2161–62.

30   **George:** Log in New Bedford Historical Society, International Marine Archives, and microfilm in NHA. On a couple of occasions as the *George* worked its way along the Chilean coast, it gammed the whaleship *Essex*, out on its last voyage before its final and celebrated one in the course of which it became the first ship sunk by a whale. On board the *Essex* were George Pollard Jr. and Owen Chase, who were to be captain and first mate on the ship's fatal voyage and whose three-month survival at sea was recounted first by Chase in his *Narrative of the Most Extraordinary and Distressing Shipwreck of the Whale-Ship Essex*. The recorded gams between the *George* and the *Essex* took place weeks before Samuel Comstock joined the *George*, so he would not have had a chance to see the two soon-to-be-famous mariners.

32   **Brown and Murray:** Barbour, 150, 154, 162; Monaghan M 35–56.

Chapter Two: Port Life and a Sinking Star

37 **Cotton and Lincoln:** Had they been senseless enough to join Samuel in his scheme against the mate, they probably would have aborted rewarding careers: John Cotton went on to become captain of the Nantucket whaler *Loper* in 1830, and John Lincoln became captain of the *Japan* in 1829. An honor came Lincoln's way while he was still first mate of the *Japan* in 1827, when his captain named an island after him—Lincoln Island is today Onotoa in the Gilberts. There is obvious irony in this in view of Samuel Comstock's longing to have an island of his own. On Lincoln: Stackpole S, 344–45, but noting that Lincoln Island is Onotoa, not the nearby Tamana.

38 **Easter Island:** The *Inquirer* (April 18, 1822) reports the welcome that the *Foster* received on Easter Island; it may have made the place especially plausible to Samuel as a site for his planned kingdom: "The Ship Foster, Capt. Chase, sailed from Esther [*sic*] Island 10th of January.— While there, he was treated with great civility by the Natives, who were 3 or 6000 in number.—They were divided into two parties, which were frequently at war with each other, and when this happened they generally massacred all the prisoners.—They furnished him with potatoes, fruit &c. the produce of the Island, for whatever he was disposed to give them.—He presented them with some seeds of different kinds, and taught them, as far as possible, the use of them, at which they appeared to express a sense of gratitude."

44 ***Foster* spoke the *Globe*:** 1820–1822 log of the *Globe*, NHA, Collection 220, log 273. The two ships at that moment were considerably northwest of Henderson Island, where the survivors of the whaleship *Essex*, sunk by a whale, had arrived by chance after a month in their open boats. The ships were in no position to know of the men on the island, but there is a chance that the *Globe* had one tenuous tie to the *Essex*. The *Globe*'s log for September 12, 1821, when it was 37°58' N/173°30' W, records: "Saw a large spar 60—or 70 feet long 4 feet square and banded together and some copper on it. we took it along side but it was too heavy for us to hoist in we let it go and steard to the westward." In the ten months since the whale attack, the winds

and currents could have carried what would have been the only structural relic of the *Essex* to the point northwest of Hawaii where the *Globe* tried hauling the huge spar in.

44 **Struck a whale:** That is, Samuel's boat *could have*—and, by all odds, must have—struck a whale; he doubtless would have claimed it had in any event.

46 **Burrows:** Sometimes, as in William Comstock's *Terrible Whaleman*, spelled Burroughs. See Pratt, 173.

"Patriot frigate": I am grateful to Robert Scheina, Industrial College of the Armed Forces, for information on the sale of American warships to the navies of the new South American nations.

47 **William at sea:** William does not mention the name of his ship, but there is reason to believe it was the newly built *Maria*, the captain of which was George Washington Gardner, former captain of the *Globe*. The *Maria* was brought down from Higganum, Connecticut, where it was built, some time in the late summer or early fall of 1822 (*Maria*, 1–2). William says (Comstock T, 61), "The time soon arrived for me to go to Nantucket, as the ship in which I was about to embark for the Pacific Ocean, had reached that place." The phrase suggests delivery of the ship rather than return from a voyage. The abstract card for Seaman's Protection Papers in NA lists a William Comstock, age eighteen, port of Nantucket, and is dated July 18, 1822. Referring to the way he learned that Samuel had gone out in a whaler, William writes (Comstock T, 63), "When I was told in the Pacific by Captain George Washington Gardner that he had sailed in the ship Globe, I was struck with amazement." The obvious inference is that Captain Gardner was his captain and that he was therefore on the *Maria*. The *Maria* sailed March 17, 1822, and the *Globe* a month later. There would have been opportunities in gams or in Hawaii for Captain Gardner to have picked up news about his old ship, the *Globe*, including names of the crew. It seems, though, that both ships were in Hawaii in the winter months; it would seem natural that the two brothers would have met there, and that William would have noted that. The *Maria* was in the Line Islands, not too far from the *Globe* at the time of the mutiny.

Chapter Three: I Have the Bloody Hand

49 ***Globe*:** From the register of the *Globe* in NHA, Collection 67: "... the said Ship or Vessel was built at Scituate in the State aforesaid, ... as appears by the certificate of [ ] Foster of said Scituate—master carpenter under whose superintendence said vessel was built. And Charles Russell appointed to measure said vessel having certified that the said Ship or Vessel has two decks and three masts and that her length is [ninety] four feet her breadth [twenty-six] feet nine inches her depth thirteen feet four and a half inches and that she measures two hundred ninety three & 42/95 tons that she is Ship rigged has a squared stern no galleries and no figurehead." (Brackets enclose partly obscured words.)

***Globe*'s dates and oil records:** Starbuck.

***Maria*:** Account of George Washington Gardner, Jr., in NHA, Collection 335, folder 956.

51 **Martha's Vineyard genealogy:** MVV, Banks, and records on file at MVH. Both the captain and First Mate Beetle were newlyweds. Worth had married Hannah Mayhew in July, and Beetle had married Eliza Pease in September. The two couples would have a home life only until December. In a little over a year both wives were to be widowed; Hannah Worth's widowhood would end, after five years, in a leviratical marriage when Captain Worth's brother John became her second husband.

Primary sources: The firsthand accounts of the mutiny are Comstock G, L&H, Kidder M, Deposition, and statements made to Lieutenant John Percival by William Lay and Cyrus M. Hussey, December 5 and 7, respectively, 1825. The depositions were given before Consul Hogan on June 9, 1824 (Stephen Kidder and George Comstock), June 15 (Peter C. Kidder and Gilbert Smith), and June 30 (Anthony Hanson and Joseph Thomas).

52 ***Globe* sails:** On December 15 the *Globe* had finished loading supplies and sailed, but almost at once had to turn back with a damaged crossjack yard, the lowest yard on the mizzenmast. The repair took only four days, and the *Globe* moved for one night to Holmes Hole (today Vineyard Haven) and sailed again on December 20.

52 **Cold water:** William Comstock is the source of the anecdote about Samuel throwing cold water on anyone asleep on watch. If William was serving on the *Maria* (as suggested in chapter 2 note to page 48), he may have transplanted something that he observed on his own ship to Samuel's: The boatsteerers would "go forward and throw a bucket of water on to a man or boy asleep on the windlass as a warning to keep awake on their watch on deck" (*Maria*, 3).

53 **"Differing with Comstock":** S. Kidder, Deposition.
Cook drunk: G. Comstock, Deposition.
Route of the *Globe*: Comstock G.

54 **Off Hawaii:** William describes an overnight amour of Samuel's with a native woman smuggled aboard in defiance of the captain's orders (but with the captain's tolerance once he discovered that Comstock was the offender). The needle of plausibility moves to the minus end of William's dial with this episode, in which "Lady Comstock," in reward for her visit, comes on deck in the morning with rose blankets and a Scotch cap, transported, of course, in Samuel's commodious chest for just such an occasion.
Iron: Hezel Fi, 39. Browning, 32, speculates that the first iron may have come to islanders in the form of spikes in driftwood timbers from wrecked Spanish ships.

55 **Ships encountered:** Comstock G. Other ships met put the *Globe* in Oahu in May 1823, barrels unknown (reported by the *Iris*, in *Inquirer*, February 16, 1824); off Japan June 1823, 250 barrels (reported by the *George Porter*, in *Inquirer*, August 30, 1824); and in Oahu in October, 600 barrels (reported by the *Ganges*, in *Inquirer*, April 5, 1824). The barrels on board in Oahu in May may have been "unknown" because Captain Worth did not want to report having only seventy-five.

56 **Lumbert:** Letter printed courtesy of the Martha's Vineyard Historical Society.

57 **Payne and Humphreys:** Spellings of the names vary; the forms adopted here are those used in most sources.

58 **Places of origin of recruits:** Most accounts follow George Comstock in giving Sag Harbor as for Payne, but Gilbert Smith (Deposition)

gives Rhode Island. Smith and Stephen Kidder give Philadelphia for Humphreys, but Thomas (Deposition) gives New Jersey. Smith gives Barnstable for Hanson, but Hanson himself (Deposition) gives Falmouth.

58 **Thomas:** Thomas was shipped as steward but replaced by Humphreys (Thomas, Deposition). In their depositions Stephen Kidder, Peter C. Kidder, and George Comstock express their suspicions of Thomas.

59 **Hogan:** Letter, August 11, 1824, in NA, Record Group 59, M146, roll 1.

60 **Comstock to Lay:** Comstock T, 76.

Thomas: In his deposition Thomas reports Comstock's words on an earlier mutiny attempt. Thomas says that he was whipped three or four days before the mutiny, which is at odds with all other accounts.

63 **Rowland Coffin:** Suspicions about Rowland Coffin were voiced by Peter C. Kidder, George Comstock, and Gilbert Smith in their depositions. Smith said, "Rowland Coffin knew of it, because he told me about two Days after the Murders that if Comstock had come into the forecastle [ ] to talk about it he would let [ ] know of it. Said Coffin continued to be very much with the Murderers after it had happened, and carried to them all the information that passed forward." Coffin was later (see chapter 6) vigorously defended by his uncle Gorham Coffin.

" **'How many that watch . . .' ":** Recorded by George Comstock; repeated in various phrasings in other accounts.

66 **"I suppose you think . . .":** Comstock T, 95.

Columbus Worth: Smith, Deposition.

67 **Attack on the captain:** Comstock T, 82.

68 **Had George seen Smith?:** A possible discrepancy in succession of events. George said that he lied to his brother about not knowing where Smith was, for he *had* seen him. The suggestion is that Smith had come upon George at the helm the *first* time he came on deck, although he does not mention encountering George until the second time he came up.

Where Smith bunked: Smith (Deposition) says that he lived aft before the mutiny and in the forecastle after it; "aft" may mean that he originally lived in steerage (like Hanson, the cook)—it obviously does not mean he lived in the cabin.

68 **Grievance against Beetle:** Smith, Deposition.

75 **New officers:** Stephen Kidder, Smith, and Thomas give Humphreys as second mate and purser (Depositions). Smith (Deposition) gives George as steward (as does George himself [Deposition]).

76 **Signing laws and color of the seals:** Smith, Deposition.

77 **Date of Humphreys's hanging:** Hanson says Humphreys was seized one day after the mutiny, and Thomas says two days (Depositions); Kidder M says four or five days.

    Comstock investigation: Kidder M, 34.

    "Would choose such judges": Smith, Deposition.

    Shook hands: George Comstock, Deposition.

    Number of jurors: The Smith and Stephen Kidder statements are from Depositions. Kidder M gives the number four but does not name them. L&H and Comstock T give two, almost certainly because the writers misread the 4 in George's "Narrative" for a 2—which indeed it does resemble. The Lay account reconstructed by Paulding (144) gives two jurors, Rowland Coffin and Payne, but several details in this nine-page summary of the mutiny story are imprecise.

78 **Humphreys's execution:** The fullest firsthand account is in Kidder M.

    Sandglass: The choice of 14 seconds was not a caprice; the glass was part of the equipment used in taking log and line measurements. The normal sandglass for the purpose would be the 28-second size, which would be used to time the release of line in the water to determine how far the ship had traveled in 28 seconds, thus permitting a calculation of the ship's speed. A 14-second glass would simply be inverted once to equal the 28-second variety.

    Hung fifteen minutes: Kidder M.

79 **Body dragged:** Comstock T, 92.

    P. Kidder: Deposition.

80 **Gear thrown overboard:** Kidder M; Thomas and Smith Depositions.

    Black paint: Kidder M, 35; Comstock V, 59–62. William includes in

The Terrible Whaleman at this point a clownish episode in which Comstock forces two angry crewmen to fight a duel with guns that he has loaded, unknown to them, with blanks. Written for comic effect, the account is hard to credit, but it avoids jarring against its tragic setting only because it would fit, in other contexts, the whims of Samuel.

80 **Naval exercises:** Comstock G.

81 **Hanson:** Deposition.

"**Adrift":** Hanson, Deposition.

Sailed west: The fact that the ship crossed today's international date line February 5, 1824, does not affect the dating in any records dealing with the *Globe*, for in the early nineteenth century, travelers from west and from east stayed with their home calendars no matter where they were, even though the principle behind the date line was well known. Sometimes in places like the Philippines, where east and west met, the one-day discrepancy would be noted.

82 **Numerous sperm whales:** Kidder M.

Marshall's Island: Gilbert, 32: "The southernmost island of the chain, I left first for Captain Marshall to name, which he thought proper to name Gilbert's Island; the middle, I named Marshall's Island." See chapter 4 for the role of Marshall and Gilbert.

83 **Northern reaches of the Gilberts:** George's precise record of latitude and longitude at this point contradicts the statement attributed to Lay by Paulding (143) that the ship sailed directly from Tabiteuea ("Drummond Island") to Mili; George has it moving farther north in the Gilberts before heading for Mili.

84 **Men and women:** S. Kidder, Deposition

85 **Point of anchorage:** Comstock G.

Chapter Four: No Lasting City

89 ***Rolla:*** Hezel Fo, 115.

90 ***Awashonks:*** Heflin, 210–18.

Island discovery: Sharp D, Hezel Fi, Beaglehole. One of the best indications of what an American whaleman in 1824 would know and not know about the ocean is the "Report of J. N. Reynolds of Facts

Obtained at Nantucket of South Seas and Pacific Ocean," which was written four years after the *Globe* mutiny from interviews with Nantucket captains who had precise details to recount about a surprising number of islands and nothing to say about hundreds of yet unexplored ones.

90 **Spanish and Portuguese:** Hezel Fi, 14–17. Alonso de Salazar was the first European in the Marshalls when, in 1526, his *Santa Maria de la Victoria* sighted what was probably Taongi. In 1529 Saavedra stopped at islands whose descriptions suggest Eniwetok or Bikini, and in the next forty years islands that were—or probably were—Wotje, Kwajelein, Ujelang, Lib, Mejit, Likiep, Ailuk, Jemo, and Wotho were sighted or visited by Spanish ships sailing in the northern part of the Marshalls.

Naming Mulgrave Islands: Phillip, 171, 364–65.

91 **"First Fleet":** Phillip, Gilbert.

"Outer Passage": Hezel Fi, 65, 82.

First settlement of islands: Bellwood M and P.

92 **Encountering Milians:** Gilbert, 35–39. One native is described in Phillip (171), but not in the ampler and more authoritative Gilbert account, as wearing a cross; the cross is not evidence of earlier contact between the Milians and Europeans. It could have come from one of the early Spanish contacts with northern Micronesia two centuries before and made its way through many hands to Mili at the southern tip of the Ratak chain.

93 **Typhoons:** Ennaanin, 173–80.

Mili place names: Rupekoj, Bokbar, and Bokdikdik appear on maps made during the Japanese era as Rubegeshi, Bukubaru, and Bokurigirikki. Even today Bokdikdik is considered an extension of Mili Mili and from references in the *Globe* sources, appears to have been regarded as, in effect, part of Mili Mili. Mili Mili's name is formed on the model of New York, New York. All the islands in the atoll could append Mili to their names, but normally this would be done to distinguish, as in the case of Mili, a village from the atoll of the same name or to distinguish a village on the atoll from a village of the same name on another atoll—if there were a Naalo on Jaluit, one could speak of Naalo Mili and Naalo Jaluit. The triangular village of Mili Mili is the widest point in the atoll; it is sizable enough to have held a three-runway landing field, which the Japanese carved out of taro patches. Today only vestiges of the airfield remain.

94 **Building pigpen:** Gorham Coffin to Daniel Webster (December 22, 1824) in NHA, Collection 74, folder 11.

95 **Burn ship:** Kidder M, 36.

97 **Sword:** Kidder M, 37.

98 **Map:** In NHA Collection 15, folder 71.

102 **Anchor:** Around 1992 an anchor was found at a point off the coast a bit north of Mili Mili, and speculation arose that it was the *Globe's* anchor. Ramsey Reimers, whose firm, Robert Reimers Enterprises, was conducting diving site surveys in the area, reports that the anchor was described as having a line attached. Since the *Globe's* cables were apparently hemp, not chain, it is unlikely that the undecayed cable would still be intact. On the *Globe's* cable see Worth Papers, NHA, Collection 129, Book 8, pages 2–3.

Chapter Five: Etto Amro Pad Ioon Aneo

110 **Ludjuan:** Lieutenant Paulding in his *Journal* (149) quotes Lay as saying, "I was taken to live with the old man who had saved [my life]. He was so very poor that I scarcely ever got enough to eat of the coarsest native food. . . . At last, the high chief took compassion upon me, and made me live with him; after which I always had plenty to eat, and was at liberty to work or not, as I pleased." This is one of several points of disagreement between L&H and Paulding; the authority of L&H in this matter is considerably greater, and Ludjuan is treated as Lay's master throughout. It is possible that Lay's relationship with particular natives was more complex than any account shows. The assignment of Hussey to Lugoma has been challenged by Dadashi Lometo, currently the senator from Mili in the Nitijela, the Marshallese parliament, and assistant to the president of the Marshall Islands. Lometo, who traces his lineage from Longerene, who figures in the "war" at Naalo reported

in L&H, explains that a family tradition holds that Hussey was a ward of Longerene, not Lugoma. The claim cannot be dismissed out of hand. Considering the range of various spellings of Marshallese names by European and American visitors, it is not far-fetched to imagine that the two names are the same. Even the association of Longerene with Naalo in the war account in L&H is not decisive. Erwin Bollong, who is the present-day *iroojlaplap* of Mili Atoll, said in an interview on July 21, 2001, that Longerene lived in Arbar and Lukunor. If he did live in Lukunor, which is treated as Lugoma's island in L&H, there is additional reason to speculate that Longerene and Lugoma are the same person. The problem that remains is that L&H, in one of the two chapters attributed to Hussey, treats Longerene as a different person newly introduced into the narrative at the point of the Naalo war. Paulding's testimony on the subject is unequivocal; after referring to Lugoma, he says, "that was the name of Huzzy's chief." The decision to treat Lugoma as Hussey's master is made with these considerations in mind.

117 **Cooking:** Pit cooking is common in the Pacific; for a description of the technique on Hawaii, see Paulding, 208–209.

118 **Lukunor:** Properly, Lukwon-wod, but the Anglicized form is used here because of its common use by many Marshallese.

Jelbon: On some charts and records Chirubon; Lay called it Dillybun and Hussey Dilabu.

Jekaka and bob: In L&H and elsewhere: *cha-ka-ka* and *bup*.

119 **Canoes:** This information is mainly from Alson Kelen, director of Waan Aelon in Majel (Canoes of the Marshall Islands), an organization in Majuro devoted to building classic Marshallese canoes and teaching the craft.

121 **Micronesian religion:** Haynes is an ideal introduction to the subject.

Hale: Hale (87–90) and Frazer (83) cite Lay and Paulding. Drawing on Chamisso, Frazer presents a comparable picture of the island's worship: "The inhabitants of Radack adore an invisible God, in heaven, and offer him a simple tribute of fruits, without temples and without priests. In their language *Iageach* signifies god: the name of the god is

Anis. When war or any other important affair is to be undertaken, solemn offerings are made, always in the open air. One of the assembly, not the chief, consecrates the fruits to the god, by holding them up, and invocation; the form is *Gieien Anis mne jeo*, the assembled people repeat the last word. There are, on several islands, holy trees, coco-palms, into the crown of which *Anis* descends. Round the foot of such a tree four beams are laid in a square. There does not appear to be any prohibition to enter the space enclosed, and the fruits of the tree are eaten by the people."

121 **Generic divinity:** Frazer (83) agrees with Erdland: "[T]he word *anij* applies to evil spectres or phantoms which do harm to man, or at all events inspire him with terror; in a wider sense the word designates all terrible beings, such as sea monsters and poisonous fish." But for less threatening beings, see Frazer, 93, on minor spirits and myths. Tobin is a most ample and readable introduction to the subject. The island pantheon would not be complete without the *noniep*—the friendly, almost neighborly little beings, somewhat comparable to the Hawaiian *menehune*. Tobin collects Marshallese legends and tales, many of them suggestive of Ovid's *Metamorphoses*, and some of them recounting the interplay of humans and spirits. See also Bwebwenatoon.

123 ***Riab:*** *Reab* in L&H.

125 **Fish poisoning:** Ciguatera fish poisoning is caused by a toxin from a dinoflagellate plankton eaten by reef fish or fish that eat reef fish. A given fish may be toxic at one time but not at another or in one area but not in another, depending on consumption of the plankton. Symptoms appear within hours after the fish is eaten, and are varied, but vomiting and diarrhea are common. Scombroid poisoning (from fish like tuna, bonito, mackerel, albacore, and others) results from a combining of marine bacteria with chemicals in spoiled fish. The symptoms include headache, dizziness, abdominal distress, difficulty swallowing, and sometimes swelling. The duration of the disorder is usually measurable in hours. Causes other than fish poisoning (such as malnutrition and kidney disorders) can be considered; contact dermatitis in particular can produce facial swelling as extreme as that

described by Lay and Hussey, but usually does not extend to the extremities. I'm grateful to Dr. Scott Norton for this information.

126 **High chief:** Chamisso (152), speaking of a predecessor of Labuliet, Lathethe, defines his territory as taking in the southern part of the Ratak chain, namely Majuro, Arno, and Mili; that would have been Labuliet's realm as well.

128 ***Coquille:*** Hezel Fo, 116. In 1824 an American whaleship, the *Boston*, Captain George Joy, visited Ebon, southwest of Mili, and another, the *Maro*, Captain Richard Macy, visited Ujae considerably west of Mili. There is no indication that either was the ship seen off Mili. The Lay (L&H, 57–58) and Hussey (L&H, 93) accounts of the sighting of the ship are not in complete agreement.

133 **Etiquette:** In 1999 the author attended a garden party on Majuro Atoll at which about eighty people assembled in the fashion Lay described, enjoyed a lavish meal, and at the end carried off, one and all, Styrofoam boxes containing all they had been served but had not consumed. It went without saying that it would have been grossly impolite not to carry off the uneaten food.

Murder: Paulding (172) relates that Lay witnessed an execution of a man charged with some offense; he defied his killers and fought and cursed them to the last.

Chapter Six: The News

136 **Route of the *Globe*:** Dillon, vol. 2, 104–106.

112 days: If one counts both the day of departure and of arrival; Smith's count in his deposition is imprecise.

Chilean ship: Smith, Deposition.

137 **Arrival in Valparaíso:** Smith, Deposition; Dillon, vol. 2, 104–106.

Hull and Pacific squadron: Maloney, 364–96.

***Globe* leaves Valparaíso August 15, 1824:** *El Correo de Arauco* (Viernes 27 de Agosto de 1824), No. 27. Relacion de los buques que han entrado y salido de la bahia de Valparaiso en el presente mes de Agosto. Salidas: Dia 15. La fragata ballenera Globo Norteamericana, con destino a aquellos Estados: su cargamento aceite de ballena

[(Friday, August 27, 1824). No. 27. Notice of boats entering and leaving Valparaíso harbor in the present month of August. Departed on the 15th the North American whaleship *Globe*, headed for the States with a cargo of whale oil].

140 **Joseph Thomas:** Miscellaneous Records of United States Circuit Court, "Prisoners in Boston Jail . . . May June 1825"; United States Circuit Court Docket, vol. 5 (May 1822–October 1833), "Examinations on Criminal Complaints, December 1824"; *Inquirer* (November 22 and 29, December 13, 1824; May 30, 1825).

141 **Gorham Coffin to J. Q. Adams:** NHA, Collection 15, folder 71.
George Comstock statement: Transcribed in letter to Adams.
Coffin to Southard and Hull: NHA, Collection 15, folder 71.

142 **Coffin to Daniel Webster:** NHA, Collection 74, folder 11.

143 **Petition:** NHA, Collection 15, folder 71.
Order to send vessel: Maloney, 397.
Southard orders: Maloney, 372.
***Dolphin*:** Maloney, 397.
Hull orders to Percival: *Report: the Committee on Naval Affairs, to whom was referred the petition of John Percival. . . .* 22nd Congress, 2nd Session. To accompany bill HR 731 (February 9, 1833), 3–5.

145 **Foote:** NA, Area files, M625, roll 282, item 008.
John Percival: Authoritative treatment in forthcoming biography by James H. Ellis. Maloney passim, *Dictionary of American Biography*, Long, Trayser, Westcott.
Isaac Coffin: Amory, Booker.

146 **Wise:** *Tales for the Marines* (Boston: Phillips, Sampson & Co.; New York, J. C. Derby, 1855). Ellis, in the forthcoming biography, suggests as other uses of Percival: Melville's "Mad Jack" in *White-Jacket*, James Michener's Captain Hoxworth in *Hawaii*, and Edwin L. Sabin's "Mad Jack Percy" in *Pirate Waters*.

146 **Hawthorne:** Hawthorne, 71–72.

147 **Paulding:** Meade, *Dictionary of American Biography*.

149 **James Kirke Paulding:** Reynolds.
Seals: Paulding, 14–15.

149 **Marquesas:** Paulding, 29–71; for twentieth-century treatment illuminating Paulding, see Dening.

150 **Smaller islands:** Paulding, 72–103.
Difficult currents: Paulding, 106–107.

Chapter Seven: Dolphin

152 **Easternmost of the Mulgraves:** Jelbon would be farthest to the east of all islands except those in the Knox spur to the southeast, but the Knox group is often treated as a unit by itself, not a part of Mili, and the references in Paulding to islands to the south being visible from the masthead (made when on the point of leaving Jelbon) would have been references to the Knox islands, indicating that the ship was north of them, not anchored at one of them.

Chronology: Paulding's account of the days at Mili, especially his account of the rescue, is the most detailed and most logical in dating. Except as noted, it is followed in this chapter. Some confusion attends the records of events between November 22 and 24. November 22 was the day that the *Dolphin* left Jelbon, arrived at Lukunor, and began exploring the island. Lay indicates that November 23 was the day that news of the ship was brought to Mili Mili, prompting Luttuon's mobilization. If the details, in Paulding, of the solitary spy sent by Luttuon and the four canoes found on the beach at Lukunor were moved from November 22 to 23, they would integrate better with the overall narrative, for they would have been related to Luttuon's arrival at Lukunor. According to Lay, Luttuon and his warriors left Mili Mili the same day they were informed of the ship, November 23, and arrived at their destination (Lukunor) at night. There would have been no time to send out a spy or undertake any of the things assigned to their first day on Lukunor; these are more natural for November 24, when action on the island was at its peak—the native fleet was on hand, relics of the *Globe* were found on the canoes, Lay was secreted in the hut and, at day's end, was taken with Luttuon's canoes to Tokewa. The main preoccupation of the *Dolphin* people from November 24 to 26 was following the progress of Lieutenant Homer's land party. Minor discrepancies, like the finding of Rowland Coffin's mitten on the twenty-fifth according to Paulding and on the twenty-seventh according to the *Dolphin*'s log, probably result simply from the authors' writing final drafts from notes. Paulding's chronology of the days around the rescue is followed in this chapter, with one exception, the statement (118) that the land party arrived at Mili Mili the day after the surgeon's funeral; the surgeon's funeral (according to Paulding and the ship's log) was November 28. The land party would have had to arrive the day *of* the funeral, that is, the twenty-eighth, for they discovered the rubble of the *Globe* camp that day and encamped for the night in a deserted hut before sending two messengers the next day (the twenty-ninth) to the ship for help. The author of the L&H narrative presents, mainly in Lay's segment, an impossible chronology: both Lay and Hussey rescued on November 29 and received on board the *Dolphin* the same day. There is a discrepancy in the *Dolphin* log's recording of the arrival of the launch carrying Lay and Hussey at the ship on November 30; this is irreconcilable with the log's record of the sending out of the launch on November 29—the launch found Lay and Hussey the next day, the thirtieth, and stopped overnight before returning to the ship with them December 1. The log is correct in entering the discovery of the skeleton assumed to be Comstock's under November 29.

156 **Lukunor:** The island is a bit shorter east-west than Paulding indicates. **Hussey's address:** The evidence for Lukunor's being Hussey's residence is an accumulation of geographic references in L&H, including such statements as the one describing Lukunor ("Luj-no-ne-wort") as "the place where Hussey lived" (L&H, 52).

158 **L&H indicates that Lay had a glimpse of the ship** before being confined.

160 **Enajet:** Popular form, more precisely Anejet.

162 **Surgeon's plaque:** Davis (37) reports that the USS *Narragansett* visited Mili in 1872 and found the surgeon's grave respected and still under taboo.

163 **Five days' provisions:** The log (November 29) says five days' provisions for ten men.

167 **Straws:** Paulding (174) describes the ritual and says it was practiced before Lay was allowed to act out his plan to warn the rescuers.

168 **Rescue:** L&H differs from Paulding on a number of points: L&H (1) describes Lay going down to the beach with one hundred of the smartest natives, whom he had instructed not to give a hostile appearance, (2) has Paulding utter the cliché "I'll be among you," (3) has Lay running to Paulding, (4) describes the boat as holding thirteen men and two officers, and (5) says that Paulding aimed his pistol at the old man. **Boldest act:** Davis, 31–32. Midshipman Davis had been, a week before, disciplined for loafing on watch (Log, November 21).

170 **Hussey's island:** Accounts are somewhat vague on Hussey's location the day of the rescue, but the evidence in L&H (65, 102–103) and Paulding (132) suggests strongly that Hussey was kept at Lukunor when Lay was taken away in Luttuon's fleet.

174 *Hitera*: A curious word: it is similar in sound and apparently in usage to *eidara*: "The men, at first only a few, came hesitantly toward us with green branches. We also broke green branches. The peaceful greeting 'Eidara,' already often heard, was called out to us, and we returned it in the same way" (Chamisso, 134). A glossary in Kotzebue V (vol. 2, 419) translates *eidara* as "good." Neither *hitera* nor *eidara* is in use in modern Marshallese. Alfred Capelle and Byron Bender, editors of *Marshallese English Dictionary* (Abo), suggest the present equivalent is the word for friend, *jera* or the honorific *l'ojera*.

176 **Percival's address:** Paulding account supplemented by L&H ampler version.

179 **Old man:** The setting would make it sound as if Percival's traumatic judgment was delivered at the final summit meeting with Luttuon and the other chiefs (because both Lay and Hussey were present to translate), but if that was the occasion, the ship would already have left Mili before the old man's death, and no one would have heard of it.

180 **Not in accord:** Paulding describes sailing with Hussey for Lukunor on December 4 and arriving December 6, staying overnight at Lugoma's, and returning with Hussey on December 7 to Mili Mili. The next morning, December 8, Paulding reports, Lugoma arrived for a last

visit and was taken on board the schooner, and in the afternoon Luttuon was given a formal visit to the schooner. That completed, the ship got under way, leaving Mili. L&H have Hussey still in Mili Mili on December 6, serving as the captain's translator, and date the departure from Mili on December 7, not 8. The log shows the departure date as December 8 (the proof being that the ship loaded casks of water from the island that day before sailing).

185 **Jemmaan:** Paulding spells it "Tamon."

187 **Later ships:** Twenty years after the *Globe* arrived at Mili, the "French whaleship *Angelina* of Havre, Capt Edouard Hyenne, put in at Mili on Dec 12 [1844]. Three canoes came out and the natives presented gifts to officers and crew. Convinced that the islanders were friendly, the captain and mate went ashore with two boat crews, but these men were never seen again and were presumed to have been massacred. After laying off for eight days while its boats coasted the island in search of the missing men, *Angelina* returned to Honolulu" (Hezel Fo, 119).

Bully Hayes: Hayes's ships, *Leonora*, which he was captain of, and *Neva*, which he owned, made a number of trading stops at Mili in 1871 (Hezel Fo, 129).

Movie: *Nate and Hayes* (1983).

Beachcombers, traders, and castaways: Beachcomb.

Afterword: The Shadow of the Globe

189 **Details of the voyage from Mili to Hawaii** are from Paulding, except where as noted, from the *Dolphin* log or other sources.

University of love: Leonard Mason, at the time an associate professor of anthropology at the University of Hawaii, visited Arno in the summer of 1950 on a research project concerning the economic and social situation on that atoll. He was accompanied by a graduate student from Hawaii. He was told about the unique institution by two women on one of the islands at the east end of Arno Atoll, and promised not to reveal any details of the meeting. "It was quite an experience," Mason said fifty-one years later, "but I have kept the secret as requested."

191 **Forge:** Chamisso, 141.

Labuliet: Chamisso, 152.

195 **Cook and general Hawaiian history:** A good introductory history is Tabrah. The classic is Kuykendall. Also Kuyk-Day, Daws, Webb, and Loomis.

Equator and *Balaena:* Starbuck, I, 225; Blackman, 188.

Missionaries: Bingham, 283–304.

196 **Whalers:** U.S. Consular Despatches, Honolulu, cited in Gast, 96.

Bingham and Lay and Hussey: Hale, 87, 431–34.

197 **Conflict with missionaries:** McKee offers the most thorough treatment not written by a participant in the events.

Loomis: Elisha Loomis Journal in collection of Hawaiian Mission Children's Society Library, entry for February 21, 1826. By permission of the Hawaiian Mission Children's Society Library (HMCSL).

200 **Loomis:** Elisha Loomis Journal, entry for April 8, 1826. By permission of HMCSL.

201 **Chamberlain:** Levi Chamberlain Journal in collection of Hawaiian Mission Children's Society Library, entry for February 28, 1826. By permission of HMCSL.

Commercial interests: Gast, 77–94.

203 **Francis Macy:** NHA, Collection 74, folder 11.

204 **Hull to Southard:** NA, Record Group 45; NHA, Collection 74, folder 11.

Lay to Hussey: NHA, Collection 74, folder 10.

205 **Hull to Hussey:** New-York Historical Society, Hull Collection, reel 1.

206 **George working for his father:** Business correspondence 1828–29 signed per George Comstock, NHA, Collection 334.

207 **Lay to Hussey:** NHA, Collection 74, folder 10.

208 **Margaret:** NHA, Collection 74, folder 10.

Hussey's death: Sanford notation in first edition of L&H in NHA. *Inquirer,* May 9, 1829.

209 **Gilbert Smith:** Banks, #228; *Vineyard Gazette* (June 5, 1966).

Percival: Long; forthcoming James Ellis biography; *Dictionary of American Biography.*

209 **Paulding:** Meade. *Dictionary of American Biography.*

Globe: William H. Macy, Letter to the Editor, *Inquirer*, September 27, 1890.

210 **On William and son Augustus:** Albert Johannsen, *The House of Beadle and Adams*, vol. 2 (Norman: University of Oklahoma Press, 1950–62). 62–64.

"Obscure writer"; attribution of Betsey Jane Ward: Don C. Seitz, *Artemus Ward: A Biography and Bibliography* (New York: Harper, 1919), 338.

William as a Melville source: F. DeWolfe Miller, "Another Chapter in the History of the Great White Whale," in Henry Murray and Howard Vincent, eds., *Melville and Hawthorne in the Berkshires* (Kent, Ohio: Kent State University Press, 1968), 109–17; Joel Myerson, "Comstock's White Whale and *Moby-Dick*," *American Transcendental Quarterly* 29 (1976), 8–27; Robert R. Craven, " 'Roger Starbuck' (Augustus Comstock) and *Moby-Dick*," *Melville Society Extracts* (November 1981), 1–5, and "Two New Sightings of the White Whale," *Melville Society Extracts* 63 (September 1985), 12–16.

William in *The Boston Pearl and Literary Gazette*: The series of eight articles ran weekly from July 18 to September 5, 1835; the first two were titled "The Art of Whaling," the others were titled "Whaling in the Pacific."

William Comstock's minor and attributed writing: William is certainly the author of *Mysteries of New York* (1845). Lyle Wright in *American Fiction 1851–75* names William as author of "The Village Slander," a short moralistic sketch in the collection *Tales and Takings* (New York: Carlton and Porter, 1856). A drama, *The Intolerants*, is attributed to William by Frank Pierce Hill in *American Plays*; the play was published in 1827, when William was twenty-three. Its sophisticated treatment of ecclesiastical history and the Fathers of the church is a bit hard but not impossible to reconcile with the youth of the supposed author. Two temperance pieces, *Rum* and *The Drunkard*, may also be by William Comstock.

211 **William on authorship of L&H:** In *In the Heart of the Sea*, Nathaniel

Philbrick treats a well-educated Nantucketer, William Coffin, Jr., as a likely collaborator in the writing of Owen Chase's *Narrative of the . . . Shipwreck of the Whale-ship Essex* and adds, "Years later, he would ghostwrite Obed Macy's much praised history of Nantucket; there is also evidence that he helped write an account of the notorious *Globe* mutiny" (203). It is notably curious that William Comstock in his preface to *The Terrible Whaleman*, attributes the poem "The Young Mutineer" to a "Captain Coffin"—even though Glover was widely recognized as the poem's author.